Beginning HTML with CSS and XHTML

Modern Guide and Reference

David Schultz and Craig Cook

Apress®

Beginning HTML with CSS and XHTML: Modern Guide and Reference

Copyright © 2007 by David Schultz, Craig Cook

ISBN-13 (pbk): 978-1-59059-747-7

ISBN-10 (pbk): 1-59059-747-8

Printed and bound in the United States of America 9 8 7 6 5 4 3 2 1

Lead Editor: Chris Mills
Technical Reviewer: Gez Lemon
Editorial Board: Steve Anglin, Ewan Buckingham, Gary Cornell, Jonathan Gennick, Jason Gilmore,
    Jonathan Hassell, Chris Mills, Matthew Moodie, Jeffrey Pepper, Ben Renow-Clarke, Dominic Shakeshaft,
    Matt Wade, Tom Welsh
Project Manager: Richard Dal Porto
Copy Edit Manager: Nicole Flores
Copy Editors: Nicole Abramowitz, Kim Wimpsett
Assistant Production Director: Kari Brooks-Copony
Production Editor: Laura Esterman
Compositor: Susan Glinert
Proofreader: Lisa Hamilton
Indexer: John Collin
Artist: April Milne
Cover Designer: Kurt Krames
Manufacturing Director: Tom Debolski

Distributed to the book trade worldwide by Springer-Verlag New York, Inc., 233 Spring Street, 6th Floor, New York, NY 10013. Phone 1-800-SPRINGER, fax 201-348-4505, e-mail orders-ny@springer-sbm.com, or visit http://www.springeronline.com.

For information on translations, please contact Apress directly at 2855 Telegraph Avenue, Suite 600, Berkeley, CA 94705. Phone 510-549-5930, fax 510-549-5939, e-mail info@apress.com, or visit http://www.apress.com.

The source code for this book is available to readers at http://www.apress.com in the Source Code/Download section.

Contents at a Glance

Contents

■CHAPTER 10 Client-Side Scripting Basics 251

■CHAPTER 11 Putting It All Together 281

Foreword

In 1999, I bought a book about the web. This brave and still relatively new world had caught my interest, and the pocket-sized *Rough Guide to the Internet* featured four or so pages of rudimentary HTML. After about three hours I had built a web page and linked to another one. This first web page looked awful, but I was excited. Later that day I somehow managed to upload it to a domain, and I realized I had created a website—an actual website.

So naïve was I back then that I assumed I'd need to leave my home computer on in order for other web users to see my pages! How amazed I was at work the next day when I successfully called my little website up in front of the boss.

So, I decided to buy another book, called *Learn HTML in a Weekend*. It was a very long weekend. This and other preliminary books taught me a lot, but much of it badly; my code was littered with font tags, frames, and tables for layout. CSS had not really taken hold back then.

In the beginning, we used HTML to do all the hard work because we didn't know any better. This difficult, limiting, and weighty approach to building websites was born out of HTML's generosity, it being a rich language with early specifications offering rather too much scope for abuse. I can accept that now, but I'm unsure why so many recent books still preoccupy the reader with ill-advised and outdated techniques that can be achieved much better and more easily with web standards.

I care about how people learn to build websites, and I know it can be impenetrable for beginners. Equally, I worry that many professionals are still ripping off clients with shoddy workmanship. This is why I'm so happy to introduce this book. David Schultz and Craig Cook understand that building websites is a craft, and with *Beginning HTML with CSS and XHTML: Modern Guide and Reference* they bring you years of experience condensed into an enjoyable, carefully structured reference focused on responsible, powerful HTML, CSS, XHTML and even JavaScript—the perfect introductory package.

You'll find a wealth of practical examples that you can actually use. As a stickler for top-notch code, I'm especially impressed that everything within validates as HTML Strict (which you'll learn more about soon) and that David and Craig have ensured all methods work cross-browser and will stand up to whatever twists and turns the Internet takes next.

You are embarking upon a great adventure, but you have in your hands the best possible map and two expert guides to hold your hand. Soon you'll reach your destination and will be waxing lyrical to anyone who'll listen about your grasp of web standards, wondering why the old boys still work with their outdated methods. Mighty explorers, this book will tell you all you need to know.

Simon Collison

Author of *Beginning CSS Web Development*, Apress 2006

About the Authors

 **DAVID SCHULTZ** is an IT team leader for a major national retailer. He has more than 15 years of IT experience in various positions using several different platforms and computer languages. He has a bachelor of science degree in management information systems from Oakland University located in Rochester, Michigan. His interest in computers started when he received his first computer, a Commodore 64, back in the 1980s. Today, his preference is to work with Microsoft's ASP.NET platform. David has been a technical reviewer on many books from several publishers. He is also an author, reviewer, and editor for the www. ASPToday.com website. In his spare time, he enjoys family time, video games, pinball, and movies.

 **CRAIG COOK** has been designing and building websites since 1998, though he still silently harbors the aspiration to draw comic books. His background is in traditional graphic design, and he has a degree in commercial graphics from Pittsburg State University (Kansas). Although he spent years learning how to make ink stick to paper, he soon fell in love with the web, and the affair continues to this day. In addition to his passions for design and technology, Craig has an affinity for science-fiction novels, zombie movies, and black T-shirts. He occasionally muses on these subjects and others at his personal website, www.focalcurve.com. Craig lives and works near San Francisco.

About the Technical Reviewer

GEZ LEMON works as an accessibility consultant for TPG. A keen accessibility advocate, Gez participates in the Web Content Accessibility Guidelines Working Group and is a member of the Web Standards Project's Accessibility Task Force. In his spare time, Gez talks about accessibility issues on his blog, Juicy Studio.

Acknowledgments

Writing a book is no small task. Although the authors' names go on the cover and they get most of the credit, tons of people behind the scenes at Apress really make it happen. In particular, I want to thank Chris Mills for approaching me and keeping me enthused about the project throughout the life cycle. A ton of thanks goes to the technical editor, Gez Lemon, for keeping me to the standards and providing really great feedback. Elizabeth Seymour and Richard Dal Porto did a great job of keeping me on track and getting me through the tedious process. Thanks to the Apress production team for making all those last-minute changes and doing the magic that brings a manuscript to print. I also want to thank my coauthor, Craig Cook, for the ideas and contributions he made to the book, which are all much appreciated.

Finally, I would have never been able to complete this long journey without the understanding and support of my family—my wife, Kim, and my children, Justin, Jessica, and Crystal.

David Schultz

I must first thank all of the authors, artists, designers, coders, bloggers, evangelists, and gurus on whose shoulders I stand. I've been inspired and guided by the work and teachings of John Allsopp, Douglas Bowman, Andy Budd, Dan Cederholm, Tantek Çelik, Joe Clark, Andy Clarke, Simon Collison, Derek Featherstone, Aaron Gustafson, Christian Heilmann, Jon Hicks, Molly Holzschlag, Shaun Inman, Roger Johansson, Jeremy Keith, Ian Lloyd, Scott McCloud, Eric Meyer, Cameron Moll, Keith Robinson, Richard Rutter, Dave Shea, Jeffrey Zeldman . . . and many others equally deserving of being name dropped, but I'm trying to keep this to one page.

I should also extend gratitude to all the daily-grinders and cubicle-dwellers who strive to build a better web—not for riches and adoration but simply because they love what they do and care about doing it right. To everyone who has embraced web standards and accessibility, furthering the cause in your own subtle ways and reclaiming the earth that was scorched by the dark Browser Wars: you're making the web a better place to live. Take a bow.

Many kind thanks to everyone who contributed to making this book an eventual reality: to Chris Mills, for sharing barbecued brisket and asking me to participate in this project; to Gez Lemon, for pointing out my mistakes and oversights with gently brutal honesty; to David Schultz, my coauthor, for doing so much of the hard work; to Elizabeth Seymour, Richard Dal Porto, Grace Wong, Nicole Abramowitz, Kim Wimpsett, Laura Esterman, and everyone else at Apress, for their patience with my often-sluggish pace throughout this entire process.

Special thanks must be given to my friends Jolene, Jannyce, and Bill. They were the readers I imagined I was writing for whenever I struggled to find the right words. I hope I succeeded.

I'm endlessly grateful of my parents, R.L. and Beverly, for instilling me with a desire to learn, a passion to create, and a compulsion to instruct.

Craig Cook

Introduction

The World Wide Web has come a long way in a relatively short period of time. Since its debut in the early 1990s, the web has quickly evolved from an esoteric collection of academic papers into a fully fledged and pervasive medium, an equal to print, radio, and television. The web is a vast repository of information on every subject imaginable, from astrophysics and ancient philosophy to the care and feeding of hermit crabs. It has become an integral part of many people's daily lives and is the platform for many aspects of modern business and commerce. But at its heart, the web is still just a way to share documents.

This book will show you how to create documents of your own so you can share them on the web. You'll become intimately familiar with the rules and constructs of HyperText Markup Language (HTML), the computer language the web is built on. It's a simple language, and the basic rules are easy to pick up and put to use. HTML is a tool, and once you know how to use it, you're limited only by your imagination.

Not very long ago, parts of HTML were frequently misused, and the rules were largely ignored—because we had no other choice or simply didn't know any better. But the web has matured a lot in the last few years, and we've since learned that sometimes following the rules really is the best approach. Unfortunately, many of the outdated methods that came about during the web's unruly, rebellious youth are still in common practice today. This book will help you avoid the mistakes of the past and build a better web for the future. You'll learn how to use HTML effectively and responsibly and to make your web documents clean, meaningful, and accessible to as many people and devices as possible.

If you've been around the web for a little while, you've likely heard about Cascading Style Sheets (CSS), and you may be curious about just what they are. In a nutshell, CSS is a language that describes how web documents should be visually presented. It's very powerful and flexible and is also pretty dang cool. However, CSS is a rich, complex language in its own right, and we can't possibly cover every facet of it in these pages. But as you'll soon see, CSS is directly connected to HTML, and you'll first need to understand markup before you can put CSS to good use. This book will introduce you to CSS and offer many practical examples of how you can use it. We'll give you the solid grounding in HTML you'll need as a starting point to delve deeper into the art and craft of designing web pages with CSS.

Who This Book Is For

This book is for anyone interested in learning how to build web pages from the ground up using modern best practices. We assume you're familiar with the Internet and the World

Wide Web, and you probably wouldn't pick up a book with "HTML" in the title unless you'd at least heard of it. Beyond that, we don't assume any prior knowledge of web design or computer programming. As you advance through this book, the topics get a little more advanced as well. But fear not: this is a book for beginners, and we'll walk you through the tough parts.

Even if you're not a beginner, this may be well worth a read. Only a few short years ago, the common approach to building web pages was very different from how things are done today. A lot has changed in recent times, so if you're a more experienced web developer looking to get back to basics and see what all this "semantic XHTML and CSS" mumbo-jumbo is about, this is the book for you.

How This Book Is Structured

Here we present a brief road map of where this book is going to take you. The first two chapters lead you through the bare essentials you'll need to start creating your own web documents. Throughout the bulk of this book, Chapters 3 through 10, you'll dig into different subject areas within HTML and XHTML, becoming familiar with all of the different elements at your disposal. Along the way, you'll also see examples of some of the many CSS techniques you might use to visually design your pages. We finish up with Chapter 11, where you'll see a case study that takes much of what you've learned throughout the previous chapters and puts it together into a functional website, built from scratch with XHTML and CSS.

- Chapter 1, "Getting Started," takes a high-level view of how the web works and what you'll need in order to create your own XHTML documents.

- Chapter 2, "XHTML and CSS Basics," presents the basic syntax and rules to follow when you assemble web documents and style sheets, laying the foundation for the rest of the book.

- Chapter 3, "Moving A<head>," introduces the document's head element, explaining why it's so important and showing you the different components you can place within it.

- Chapter 4, "Adding Content," explores how you'll add content to your documents and give your text a stable, meaningful structure.

- Chapter 5, "Using Images," describes how you can add pictures to your web pages for meaningful communication as well as decoration.

- Chapter 6, "Linking to the Web," looks at how you can include links in your documents that point to other documents, either within your own site or elsewhere on the Internet.

- Chapter 7, "Using Tables," shows you how to structure complex data in tables, organizing related information in sets of connected rows and columns.

- Chapter 8, "Building Forms," will show you how to create forms that allow your visitors to input their own information and interact with your website.

- Chapter 9, "Adding Style to Your Documents: CSS," dives deeper into the use of CSS, covering a few of the more advanced topics you'll need to understand when you visually style your web pages.

- Chapter 10, "Client-Side Scripting Basics," outlines the basics of the JavaScript language, which you can use to make your web pages more dynamic and interactive.

- Chapter 11, "Putting It All Together," puts the topics discussed throughout the book to use, taking you step-by-step through the creation of a functioning website.

At the back of the book, you'll find four appendixes for your reference. In order, they cover XHTML 1.0 Strict, color names and values, special characters, and CSS browser support.

Conventions Used in This Book

Throughout this book, we'll provide numerous examples of XHTML and CSS coding. Most of these examples appear in numbered listings, separated from the regular text. They look something like Listing 1.

Listing 1. *An Example Code Listing*

```
<!DOCTYPE html PUBLIC "-//W3C//DTD XHTML 1.0 Strict//EN"
  "http://www.w3.org/TR/xhtml1/DTD/xhtml1-strict.dtd">
<html xmlns="http://www.w3.org/1999/xhtml" xml:lang="en" lang="en">
  <head>
    <title>Just an Example</title>
  </head>
  <body>
    <p>Hello, world!</p>
  </body>
</html>
```

Sometimes a line of code is too long to fit within the limited width of a printed page, and we're forced to wrap it to a second line. When that happens, we'll use the symbol ➥ to let you know a line is wrapped only to fit the page layout; the real code would appear on a single line.

We'll occasionally add notes, tips, and cautions that relate to the section you've just read. They appear distinct from the main text, like so:

■**Tip** Don't overlook these extra tidbits. They're relevant to the current topic and deserve some special attention.

We may also sometimes wander off on a slight tangent that isn't really part of the topic at hand but is still important information you should know. To keep things flowing smoothly, we'll place such supplemental information in sidebars, which look like this:

SIDEBARS

Sidebars offer extra information, exploring a related topic in more depth without derailing the main topic. The term *sidebar* comes from magazine and newspaper publishing, where these sorts of accompanying stories are often printed in another column alongside the main article.

Downloading the Code

All the markup and CSS you'll see in this book is available for download in the Source Code/Download section of the Apress website (http://www.apress.com). Once you've downloaded and unzipped the file, you'll find each chapter's source code in a separate folder; you can pick it apart and refer to it at your leisure. You can also find the source code at this book's companion website, http://www.beginninghtmlbook.com.

Contacting the Authors

You can contact David Schultz through e-mail at david.schultz@apress.com.
You can reach Craig Cook through his website at http://www.focalcurve.com.

CHAPTER 1

Getting Started

We're going to ease you into the book with some general information about the Internet and World Wide Web; this will lay a foundation of useful knowledge to help you as you begin to create your own web pages with HTML and CSS. This chapter won't be a comprehensive overview by any means, but it will get you up to speed on some of the terminology and concepts you'll need to be familiar with throughout the rest of this book. If you feel you're already pretty web-savvy, having used and worked with websites for some time, you can probably skip ahead to Chapter 2 and start getting your hands dirty.

Introducing the Internet and the World Wide Web

"The Internet" is simply a catchall phrase referring to the vast, globe-spanning network of computers that are connected to each other and are able to transmit and receive data, shuttling information back and forth around the world at nearly the speed of light. It has been around in some form for almost half a century now, ever since a few very smart people figured out how to make one computer talk to another computer. The Internet has since become so ubiquitous and pervasive, impacting so many aspects of modern life, that it's hard to imagine a world without it.

The World Wide Web is just one facet of the Internet, like a bustling neighborhood in a much larger city. It's made up of millions of files and documents residing on different computers across the Internet, all cross-referenced and interconnected to weave a web of information around the world, which is how it gets its name. In its relatively short history, the web has grown and evolved far beyond the simple text documents it began with, carrying other types of information through the same channels: images, video, audio, and fully immersive interactive experiences. But at its core, the web is fundamentally a text-based medium, and that text is usually encoded in HTML (more on that in a minute).

Many different devices can access the web: desktop and laptop computers, personal digital assistants (PDAs), mobile phones, game consoles, and even some household appliances. Whatever the device, it in turn operates software that has been programmed to interpret HTML. These programs are technically known as *user-agents*, but the more

1

familiar term is *web browsers*. A web browser is specifically a program intended to visually render web documents, whereas some user-agents interpret HTML but don't display it.

Throughout this book we'll often use the word *browser* to mean any user-agent capable of handling and rendering HTML documents, and we'll use the term *graphical browser* when we're specifically referring to one that renders the document in a visually enhanced format, in full color, and with styled text and images. It's important to make this distinction because some web browsers are *not* graphical and render only plain, unstyled text without any images.

A browser or user-agent is also known as a *client*, because it is the thing requesting and receiving service. The computer that serves data to the client is, not surprisingly, known as a *server*. The Internet is riddled with servers, all storing and processing data and delivering it in response to client requests. The client and the server are two ends of the chain, connected to each other through the Internet.

What Is HTML?

If the web is to be woven from connected bits of digital text, there must be some technological means to establish that connection. This is the basis of *hypertext*, wherein a string of words in one document can be directly linked to another document somewhere else on the web. HyperText Markup Language (HTML) is the computer coding language used to convert ordinary text into active text for display and use on the web and also to give plain, unstructured text the sort of structure human beings rely on to read it. Without some kind of structure imposed on it, plain text would just run together with nothing to distinguish one string of words from another.

HTML consists of encoded markers called *tags* that surround and differentiate bits of text, indicating the function and purpose of the text those tags "mark up." Tags are embedded directly in a plain-text document where they can be interpreted by computer software. They're called *tags* because, well, that's what they are. Just as a price tag displays the cost of an item and a toe tag identifies a cadaver, so too does an HTML tag indicate the nature of a portion of content and provide vital information about it. The tags themselves are not displayed and are distinct from the actual content they envelop.

HTML has been carefully designed to be a simple and flexible language. It's a free, open standard, not owned or controlled by any company or individual. There is no license to purchase or specialized software required to author your own HTML documents. Anyone and everyone is free to create and publish web pages, and it's that very openness that makes the web the powerful, far-reaching medium it is. HTML exists so that we can all share information freely and easily.

However, you do have to follow certain rules when you author documents in HTML—there are certain ways they should be assembled to make certain they'll work properly. The rules are maintained by the World Wide Web Consortium (W3C), a nonprofit organization that defines many of the open technical standards the web is built on, collectively referred to as *web standards*. Standardizing web languages allows everyone—authors as well as people who make the software that interprets those languages—to adhere to the same set of agreed-upon rules, like the rules of grammar and punctuation that help you understand this sentence.

The Evolution of HTML

HTML first appeared in the early 1990s—based on the preexisting Standard Generalized Markup Language (SGML)—and was created specifically for marking up documents for use on the newly born World Wide Web. Since its inception, HTML has gone through many changes and enhancements. New features have been added, while other features have become outdated and removed from the specifications. The formal act of retiring a feature from standard specifications is known as *deprecation*; deprecated features should be phased out and avoided in new documents.

The technical specifications for all official versions of HTML are freely available from the W3C at its website (http://www.w3.org). These specifications can be difficult to read because they're extremely technical in nature, written primarily for computer scientists and software vendors who program web user-agents. But this kind of standardization is essential for the widespread adoption of the web, ensuring that websites operate consistently across different browsers and operating systems. The web is intended to be "platform independent" and "device independent," and adherence to web standards is what makes this possible.

In the early years of the web, the language specifications were not always followed as closely as they should have been. Competing browsers supported different features and introduced nonstandard features of their own. This made web development troublesome for authors in those days, often leading them to create multiple versions of their sites aimed at different browsers. Thankfully, this is no longer necessary. The web browsers of today follow the standards much more consistently than the previous generation did, advancing the web toward the ultimate goal of a truly universal medium.

One Language, Many Versions

As HTML has progressed and evolved over time, new versions of the language have been released to introduce the new features and deprecate the old. The very first version of HTML, 1.0, was published in 1993. It was further refined and extended with HTML 2.0 in 1995, followed closely by HTML 3.0 in 1996. Version 4.0 was published in 1997, and a few minor (but significant) changes were released in 1999 as HTML 4.01. This was to be the final, complete specification for the HTML language. A new kid called eXtensible HTML, or XHTML, joined the class in 2000, and it was praised as the wave of the future.

XHTML is a reformulation of HTML following the more stringent rules of eXtensible Markup Language (XML), which is a powerful language that allows web authors to create their own customized tags. XHTML, unlike XML, offers a finite set of predefined tags to choose from. XHTML is similar to HTML 4.01, with just a few more rules dictating how it must be written. XHTML 1.0 is the current version, and XHTML 1.1 and 2.0 are already under development but haven't yet been finalized as formal recommendations as of this writing.

Throughout the rest of this book, you'll be learning how to author your own web documents following the XHTML 1.0 specifications. Even so, HTML 4.01 is still very much alive and kicking, so most of what you'll learn from this book can be applied just as well to that earlier language.

▓Note Though HTML 4.01 was long held as "the final version" of the HTML language, a recent initiative within the W3C has started drafting a specification for HTML 5. The version is still in the early stages of development and hasn't yet been published as we write this book.

One Version, Three Flavors

As if all the different versions of HTML weren't confusing enough, there are multiple versions of those versions, each with slightly different rules and features. The three "flavors" of XHTML are Strict, Transitional, and Frameset:

- *XHTML 1.0 Strict* is the most stringent in its rules. Deprecated features are forbidden outright, and the rules must be followed to the letter if a document is to be well formed.

- *XHTML 1.0 Transitional* is a bit more relaxed than Strict, allowing some outdated features to still linger in a well-formed document. This variant is intended for authors making the transition from earlier versions of HTML to XHTML 1.0.

- *XHTML 1.0 Frameset* applies only to situations when frames are being used to lay out a web page. (*Frames* are a feature from earlier versions of HTML that allowed a page to be split into multiple panes, each displaying a different document. They've been deprecated in XHTML Strict and Transitional, which is why this special flavor exists.)

All of the markup examples you'll be seeing in this book follow the XHTML 1.0 Strict rules. You can learn much more about the different versions of HTML and XHTML, and the various flavors of each, at the W3C website (`http://www.w3.org`).

Validating Your Documents

Having a strict set of rules is all well and good, but how can you be sure you've followed them correctly? An XHTML document can be automatically *validated*, checking it against the chosen rule set to ensure that it's put together properly, something like a spell checker for markup. The W3C has created an online validation tool (available at `http://validator.w3.org/`, shown in Figure 1-1) for just this purpose. This web-based service allows you to validate your documents by either entering the location of a page on the web, uploading a file from your computer, or simply pasting your markup directly into a form on the website.

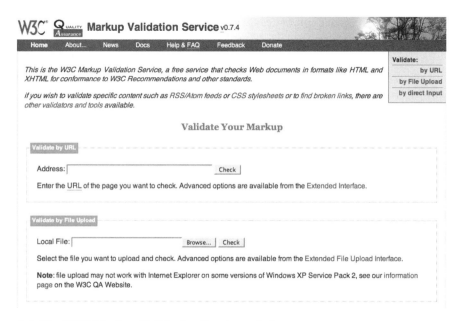

Figure 1-1. *The W3C Markup Validation Service website*

The W3C Markup Validation Service can automatically analyze your markup and display any errors it encounters so you can correct them. It will also display validation *warnings*, which are simply cautions about issues you might want to address but are not quite as severe as errors; warnings can be ignored if you have good reason to do so, but *errors* are flaws that really must be fixed. When no errors are found, you'll see a joyful banner declaring that your document is valid. A *well-formed* document is one that is valid and correctly assembled according to the rules of the language. Other validation tools are also available—both online and offline—that can help you check your documents.

Most web browsers are still able to interpret and render invalid documents, but only because they've been designed to compensate for minor errors. Valid, well-formed documents are much more stable, and you won't have to depend on a browser's built-in error handling to display them correctly.

Separating Content from Presentation

HTML is intended to bestow a meaningful structure upon unstructured text, designating that different blocks of words are in fact different types of content. A headline is not the same as a paragraph; those two types of content should be delineated with different tags, making their innate difference emphatically clear to another computer. But human beings are used to reading text that looks a certain way—we expect headlines to appear in a large, boldfaced font to let us know that it's a headline and not something else. Early browser developers knew this, and they programmed their software to display different types of content in different styles.

From its humble roots, the web quickly took off and soon was no longer the exclusive domain of computer scientists. Graphic designers discovered this exciting new medium and sought ways to make it more aesthetically appealing than ordinary, unadorned text. However, HTML lacked a proper means of influencing the display of content; it was strictly intended to provide structure. Designers were forced to repurpose many of the features in HTML, taking advantage of the way browsers displayed content in an effort to create something more visually compelling. Unfortunately, this resulted in many websites of the day being built with *presentational markup* that was messy, overcomplicated, hard to maintain, and had nothing to do with what the content *meant* but only how it should *look*.

In the late 1990s, when the web was still in its infancy, a new technology called Cascading Style Sheets (CSS) was introduced. It was an entirely different language; one specifically intended to describe how HTML documents should be visually presented while leaving the structural markup clean and meaningful. A style sheet written in CSS can be applied to an HTML or XHTML document, adding an attractive layer of visual design without negatively impacting the markup that serves as its foundation.

Separating content from presentation allows both aspects to become stronger and more adaptable. An XHTML document can be easily modified without completely reconstructing it to correct the design. An entire website can be redesigned by changing a single style sheet without rewriting one line of structural markup.

It took some time for the popular browsers to catch up and fully support CSS as it was intended, but today's browsers (a few lingering bugs notwithstanding) support CSS well enough that presentational markup can be a thing of the past.

Throughout this book, you'll be learning to write meaningful, structural markup to designate your content according to its inherent purpose. Along the way, you'll see many examples of how you can visually style your content with CSS, avoiding the trap of presentational markup. Like XHTML, CSS is an open standard that you can learn about at the W3C website (`http://www.w3.org/Style/CSS/`).

Working with XHTML and CSS

Though XHTML and CSS can seem overwhelming when you first dive in, creating your own web pages is actually quite easy once you get the hang of it. All you really need is a way to edit text files, a browser to view them in, and a place to store the files you create.

Choosing an HTML Editor

XHTML documents are plain text, devoid of any special formatting or style—all of the visual formatting takes place when a graphical web browser renders the document. To create and edit plain-text electronic documents, you'll need to use software that can do so without automatically imposing any formatting of its own. Fortunately, every operating system comes with some kind of simple text-editing program:

- Windows users can use Notepad, which can be found under Start ➤ All Programs ➤ Accessories ➤ Notepad. WordPad is another Windows alternative, but it will format documents by default. If you use WordPad, be sure to edit and save your documents as plain text, not "rich text."

- Linux users can choose from several different text editors, such as vi or emacs.

- Mac users can use TextEdit, which ships natively with OS X in the Applications folder. Like WordPad for Windows, TextEdit defaults to a rich-text format. You can change this by selecting Format ➤ Make Plain Text.

In addition to these basic text editors, numerous other, more advanced text editors are available for Windows, Linux, and Macintosh systems, many specially designed for editing web documents. Some of them can even be had free of charge. There are also so-called What You See Is What You Get (WYSIWYG, pronounced as "wizzy wig") editors on the market that offer a graphical interface wherein you can edit documents in their formatted, rendered state while the software automatically produces the markup behind it. However, this is no substitute for understanding how XHTML and CSS really work, and some WYSIWYG editors can generate convoluted, presentational markup. Handcrafting your documents in plain text is really the best way to maintain control over every aspect of your markup, and many professionals swear by it.

Choosing a Web Browser

As we mentioned earlier, a web browser is the software you use to view websites, and you almost certainly already have one. Every modern computer operating system comes with some sort of web browser installed, or you can choose one of the many others on the market:

- Microsoft Internet Explorer is the default browser on Windows operating systems.

- Apple Safari is the default browser for Mac OS X.

- Mozilla Firefox is a free browser available for Windows, Mac OS X, and Linux (`http://www.mozilla.com/firefox/`).

- Netscape Navigator is available for Windows, Mac OS X, and Linux and is based on the same software that powers Firefox (`http://browser.netscape.com`).

- Opera is another free browser available for a wide range of operating systems (`http://www.opera.com`).

- Konqueror is a free browser and file manager for Linux (`http://www.konqueror.org`).

- OmniWeb is a browser for Mac OS X that costs a small fee, though a free trial version is available (`http://www.omnigroup.com/applications/omniweb/`).

Ordinary XHTML documents don't require any other software to operate. All of your files can be stored locally on your computer's hard drive, and you can view pages in their rendered state by simply launching your browser of choice and opening the document you want to view (you can find the command to open a local file under the File menu in most graphical browsers).

Hosting Your Web Site

You can save all of your work locally on your own computer, but when it's time to make it available to the World Wide Web, you need to move those files to a web server. You have a few hosting options if you're building your own website:

- *Using web space provided by your ISP.* An Internet service provider (ISP) is a company that connects you to the Internet. Many service providers offer a limited amount of web space where you can host your own site. Ask your ISP whether web space is included with your service contract and how you can use it.

- *Using free web space*: Many companies provide free web hosting, though *free* is a relative term since free web hosts are often supplemented by advertising. If you're not bothered by such ads appearing on your website, free hosting may be a quick solution to getting your files online.

- *Paying for web hosting*: Perhaps the best option is to purchase service from a company that specializes in hosting websites. Many offer hosting packages for as little as $10 (US) per month and include more robust features than free hosting or ISP hosting provides (such as e-mail service, server-side scripting, and databases). Research your options, and choose a host that can meet your needs.

We won't go into all the particulars of getting your site online with a web host. After all, this is still the first chapter, and numerous resources online can provide more information. To learn more about hosting your websites when the time comes, just visit your favorite web search engine and have a look around for information about "web hosting basics" or some similar phrase. One good place to start is the Wikipedia entry about web hosting service (http://en.wikipedia.org/wiki/Web_hosting), which offers a fairly detailed introduction to set you on your way.

Introducing the URL

Every file or document available on the web resides at a unique address called a Uniform Resource Locator (URL). The term Uniform Resource Identifier (URI) is sometimes used interchangeably with URL, though URI is a more general term; a URL is a type of URI. We'll be using the term URL in this book to discuss addressed file locations. It's this address that allows a web-connected device to locate a specific file on a specific server in order to download and display it to the user (or employ it for some other purpose; not all files on the web are meant to be displayed).

The Components of a URL

A web URL follows a standard syntax that can be broken down into a few key parts, diagrammed in Figure 1-2. Each segment of the URL communicates specific information to both the client and the server.

The *protocol* indicates one of a few different sets of rules that dictate the movement of data over the Internet. The web uses HyperText Transfer Protocol (HTTP), the standard protocol used for transmitting hypertext-encoded data from one computer to another. The protocol is separated from the rest of the URL by a colon and two forward slashes (://).

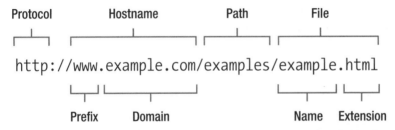

Figure 1-2. *The basic components of a URL*

A *hostname* is the name of the site from which the browser will retrieve the file. The web server's true address is a unique numeric Internet Protocol (IP) address, and every computer connected to the Internet has one. IP addresses look something like "65.19.150.101," which isn't very easy on the eyes and is certainly a challenge to remember. A *domain name* is a more memorable alias that can be used to direct Internet traffic to an IP address. Many web hostnames feature a *domain prefix*, further naming the particular server being accessed (especially when there are multiple servers within a single domain), though that prefix is frequently optional. A prefix can be almost any short text label, but "www" is traditional. It's possible for another entire website to exist separately within a domain under a different prefix, known as a *subdomain*. A hostname will also feature a *domain suffix* (sometimes called an *extension*) to indicate the category of domain the host resides in, such as ".com" for a U.S. commercial domain, ".edu" for a U.S. educational institution, or ".co.uk" for a commercial website in the United Kingdom.

The *path* specifies the directory on the web server that holds the requested document, just as you probably save files in different virtual folders on your own computer. Files on a web server may be stored in subdirectories—like folders within folders—and each directory in the path is separated by a forward slash (/). This path is the route a client will follow to reach the ultimate destination file. The top-level directory of a website (the one that contains all other files and directories) is called the *site root* directory and doesn't appear in the URL.

The specific file to retrieve is identified by its file name and *extension*. You can give your files just about any name you want, and a file extension indicates what type of file it is. An HTML (or XHTML) document will have an extension of .html or .htm (the shorter version is used on some servers that support only three-letter file extensions). CSS files use the .css extension, JavaScript files use .js, and so forth. A web server can be configured to recognize these extensions and handle the files appropriately, processing different types of files in different ways.

You won't see a file name and extension in every URL you encounter. Most web servers are configured to automatically locate a specially named file when a directory is requested without a specified file name. This could be the file called index.html, default.html, or some other name, depending on the way the server has been set up. Indeed, most of the various parts of the URL may be optional depending on the particular server configuration.

The URL is the instrument that allows you to build links to other parts of the web, including other parts of your own site. You'll use URLs extensively in the XHTML and CSS you author, which is why we've spent so much time exploring them in this first chapter.

Absolute and Relative URLs

A URL can take either of two forms when it points to a resource elsewhere within the same site. An *absolute URL* is one that includes the full string, including the protocol and hostname, leaving no question as to where that resource is found on the web. You'll use an absolute URL when you link to a site or file outside your own site's domain, though even internal URLs can be absolute.

A *relative URL* is one that points to a resource within the same site by referencing only the path and/or file, omitting the protocol and hostname since those can be safely assumed. It might look something like this:

```
examples/chapter1/example.html
```

If the destination file is held within the same directory as the file where the URL occurs, the path can be assumed as well so only the file name and extension are required, like so:

```
example.html
```

If the destination is in a directory above the source file, that relative path can be indicated by two dots and a slash (../), instructing the browser to go up one level to find the resource. Each occurrence of ../ indicates one up-level directive, so a URL pointing two directories upwards might look like this:

```
../../example.html
```

Almost all web servers are configured to interpret a leading slash in a relative URL as the site root directory, so URLs can be "site root relative," showing the full path from the site root down:

```
/examples/chapter1/example.html
```

Lastly, if the destination is a directory rather than a specific file, only the path is needed:

```
/examples/chapter1/
```

Relative URLs are a useful way to keep file references short and portable; an entire site can be moved to another domain, and all of its internal URLs will remain fully functional.

Summary

This chapter has provided a high-level overview of what the Internet and World Wide Web are and how they work. You've been introduced to HTML and CSS and are beginning to understand how you can make these languages work together to produce a rendered web page. We covered a few different text editors you can use to create your documents and some popular web browsers you can view them with. You've also learned a little about web hosting and lot about the components of a URL, information you'll find essential as you begin assembling your own websites. We haven't gone into all the gory details in this introduction—after all, we've got the rest of the book to cover them. In the next chapter, you'll finally get to sink your teeth into some real XHTML and CSS. Buckle up, this should be a fun ride!

CHAPTER 2

■■■

XHTML and CSS Basics

Chapter 1 briefly introduced you to XHTML and CSS, and in this chapter we'll show you how you can author markup and style sheets to create your own web pages. You'll become familiar with the essential components of XHTML documents and how they should be correctly assembled. As you know, you must adhere to some standards when authoring a document for the web, and we're going to be following the rules of XHTML 1.0 Strict throughout this book. XHTML is an updated reformulation of HTML, with just a few more stringent rules to obey, and we'll point out the differences between the two languages in this chapter.

Later in the chapter, we'll guide you through the essentials of CSS so you can use it to visually style your web pages. XHTML provides the structure that supports the content of your web pages, while CSS provides the polish to make your content more attractive and memorable. Designing websites with CSS isn't possible without some solid bedrock of markup underneath, so let's begin at the beginning.

The Parts of Markup: Tags, Elements, and Attributes

The linchpin of XHTML—as well as other markup languages—is the *tag*. Tags are the coded symbols that separate and distinguish one portion of content from another while also informing the browser of what type of content it's dealing with. A user-agent can interpret the tags embedded in an XHTML document and treat different types of content appropriately. Most of the tags available in XHTML have names that describe exactly what they do and what type of content they designate, such as headings, paragraphs, lists, images, quotations, and so on.

Tags in XHTML are surrounded by angle brackets (< and >) to clearly distinguish them from ordinary text. The first angle bracket (<) marks the beginning of the tag, immediately followed by the specific *tag name*, and the tag ends with an opposing angle bracket (>). For example, this is the XHTML tag that indicates the beginning of a paragraph:

```
<p>
```

Notice that the tag name is written in lowercase, which is a requirement of XHTML; tag names are not case-sensitive in HTML (and many web authors write them in uppercase to make their markup more readable), but they must be lowercase in XHTML (that's one of those more stringent rules that separates XHTML from HTML).

Most tags come in matched pairs: one *opening tag* (also called a *start tag*) to mark the beginning of a segment of content and one *closing tag* (also called an *end tag*) to mark its end. For example, the beginning of a paragraph is indicated by the opening tag, <p>, and the paragraph ends with a </p> closing tag; the slash after the opening bracket is what distinguishes it as a closing tag. A full paragraph would be marked up as follows:

```
<p>Hello, world!</p>
```

These twin tags and everything between them forms a complete *element*, and elements are the basic building blocks of an XHTML document. Some elements don't require a closing tag in older versions of HTML—the appearance of a new opening tag implies that the previous element has ended and a new one is beginning. But in XHTML, *all* elements must end with a closing tag . . . almost all, that is.

Some tags indicate *empty elements*, which are elements that do not, and in fact *cannot*, hold any contents. Empty elements don't require a closing tag but are instead "self-closed" in XHTML with a *trailing slash* at the end of a single tag that represents the entire element. For example, the following tag represents a line break, an empty element that forces the text that follows it to wrap to a new line when a browser renders the document (you'll learn more about this element in Chapter 4):

```
<br />
```

The space before the trailing slash isn't strictly required, but it will help older browsers interpret the tag correctly—without that space, some rare, old browsers fail to notice the tag's closing bracket. Some empty elements are also known as *replaced elements*; the element itself isn't actually rendered by a graphical browser but is instead replaced by some other content. Empty elements in HTML should not include a trailing slash.

An element's opening tag can carry *attributes* to provide more information about the element—specific properties that element should possess. An attribute consists of an *attribute name* followed by an *attribute value*, like so:

```
<p class="greeting">Hello, world!</p>
```

This paragraph includes a class attribute with a value of "greeting," making it distinct from other paragraphs that don't include that attribute (you'll learn more about the class attribute later). An attribute's name and its value are connected by an equal sign (=), and the value is enclosed in quotation marks. All attribute values must be quoted in XHTML, using either single quotes (' . . . ') or double quotes (" . . . ") so long as both of them match (quoting a value like " . . . ' wouldn't be valid). Quoting attribute values was optional in HTML but is required in XHTML Strict. Some attributes don't require a value in HTML (an attribute without a value is called a *minimized attribute*), but all attributes must have a value in XHTML—minimizing attributes isn't allowed. Like tag names, attribute names must be lowercase in XHTML but aren't case-sensitive in HTML. Attribute values are never case-sensitive, especially since some values might need to use capital letters. Even so, it's not a bad idea to use lowercase wherever practical, for consistency's sake.

An element's opening tag can include several attributes separated by spaces, and attributes must appear *only* in an opening tag (or an empty element's lone, self-closing tag). Some elements require specific attributes, while others are optional—it all depends on the individual element, and you'll be learning about all of them throughout the rest of this book, including which attributes each element may or must possess.

Figure 2-1 illustrates the components of an element.

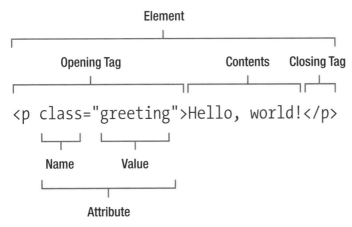

Figure 2-1. *The basic components of an XHTML element*

Block-Level and Inline Elements

The entire range of elements can be divided into two basic types: block-level and inline. A *block-level* element is one that contains a significant block of content that should be displayed on its own line, to break apart long passages of text into manageable portions such as paragraphs, headings, and lists. An *inline* element usually contains a shorter string of text and is rendered adjacent to other text on the same line, such as a few emphasized words within a sentence.

Many nonempty, block-level elements can contain other block-level elements, and all can contain text and inline elements. A nonempty, inline element, on the other hand, can contain only text or other inline elements. For example, the em element is inline and is used to add emphasis to the text within it, while the p element is block-level and designates a paragraph of text. Because em is inline, it cannot contain block-level elements, so the following example is wrong and invalid:

```
<em><p>Hello, world!</p></em>
```

You'll find out which elements are block-level and which are inline as you progress through this book, exploring each element in greater detail.

Nesting Elements

Elements can be *nested* like Russian nesting dolls, each one residing within its containing element. They must be nested correctly, with each closing tag appearing in the correct order to close an inner element before you close its container. The following markup is an example of an improperly nested set of elements:

```
<p><em>Hello, world!</p></em>
```

The opening `<em>` tag occurs after the opening `<p>` tag, but the closing `</p>` tag occurs *before* the closing `</em>` tag. To ensure correct nesting of elements, always close them in the reverse order in which they were opened:

```
<p><em>Hello, world!</em></p>
```

White Space

When you create your XHTML documents as plain text, you're free to format them however you want. Line breaks and indentions can help make your markup more readable as you work, as you'll see in most of the markup examples in this book. Indenting nested, block-level elements can make it easier to see where a particular element opens and closes, and thus you're less likely to run into nesting problems or forget to end an element with the correct closing tag.

Web browsers ignore any extra line breaks and carriage returns, collapsing multiple spaces into a single space. To illustrate, here's a bit of markup with a lot of extra space:

```
<p>

Wide       open
            spaces   !
     </p>
```

This is a rather extreme example—one you'd probably never commit yourself—but it serves to demonstrate how all of those spaces are collapsed when a browser renders the document. Although the spaces and returns are intact in the markup, your visitors would see something like this:

```
Wide open spaces!
```

Sometimes you may want to preserve extra spaces, tabs, and line breaks in your content—when you're formatting poetry or presenting computer code on your pages, for instance. The pre element can delineate passages of preformatted text in just such cases, and you'll learn more about that element in Chapter 4.

Standard Attributes

We'll be listing each element's required and optional attributes as they're covered individually throughout this book. But some common attributes can be assigned to practically any element (and are almost always optional). To spare you the repetition, we'll cover those attributes here, divided into a few categories.

Core Attributes

These attributes include general information about the element and can be validly included in the opening tag of almost any element:

- class: Indicates the class or classes to which a particular element belongs. Elements that belong to the same class may share aspects of their presentation, and classifying elements can also be useful in client-side scripting. A class name can be practically any text you like but can be made up only of letters, numbers, hyphens (-), and underscores (_); other punctuation or special characters aren't allowed in a class attribute. Any number of elements may belong to the same class. Furthermore, a single element may belong to more than one class, with multiple class names separated by spaces in the attribute value.

- id: Specifies a unique identifier for an element. An ID can be almost any short text label, but it must be unique within a single document; more than one element cannot share the same identifier. The id attribute cannot contain any punctuation or special characters besides hyphens (-) and underscores (_). The first character in an ID must be a letter; it cannot begin with a numeral or any other character.

- style: Specifies CSS properties for the element. This is known as *inline styling*, which you'll learn more about later in this chapter. Although the style attribute is valid with most elements, it should almost always be avoided because it mixes presentation with your content.

- title: Supplies a text title for the element. Many graphical browsers display the value of a title attribute in a "tooltip," a small, floating window displayed when the user's cursor lingers over the rendered element.

Internationalization Attributes

Internationalization attributes contain information about the natural language in which an element's contents are written (such as English, French, Latin, and so on). They can be included in almost any element, especially those that contain text in a language different from the rest of the document's content.

- `dir`: Sets the direction in which the text should be read, as specified by a value of `ltr` (left to right) or `rtl` (right to left). This attribute usually isn't needed, since a language's direction should be inferred from the `lang` and `xml:lang` attributes.

- `lang`: Specifies the language in which the enclosed content is written. Languages are indicated by an abbreviated language code such as `en` for English, `es` for Spanish (Español), `jp` for Japanese, and so on. You can find a listing of the most common language codes at `http://webpageworkshop.co.uk/main/language_codes`.

- `xml:lang`: Also specifies the language in which the enclosed content is written. This is the XML format for the `lang` attribute, as it should be used in XML documents. XHTML documents are both XML and HTML (depending on how the server delivers them), so both the `lang` and `xml:lang` attributes may be applied to an element, both with the same language code as their value.

Focus Attributes

When some elements—especially links and form controls—are in a preactive state, they are said to have *focus* because the browser's "attention" is concentrated on that element, ready to activate it. You can apply these focus attributes to some elements to enhance accessibility for people using a keyboard to navigate your web pages:

- `accesskey`: Assigns a keyboard shortcut to an element for easier and quicker access through keyboard navigation. The value of this attribute is the character corresponding to the access key. The exact keystroke combination needed to activate an access key varies between browsers and operating systems.

- `tabindex`: Specifies the element's position in the tabbing order when the Tab key is used to cycle through links and form controls.

Note Numerous *event attributes* are available for client-side scripting, including `onclick`, `ondblclick`, `onkeydown`, `onkeypress`, `onkeyup`, `onmousedown`, `onmousemove`, `onmouseout`, `onmouseover`, and `onmouseup`. Each of these events occurs when the user performs the indicated action upon the element. However, use of such *inline event handlers* is strongly discouraged, so we won't be covering these optional attributes in any detail. Scripted behavioral enhancements are best separated from the document's content and structure, just as presentation should be separated. Chapter 10 offers a general introduction to client-side scripting.

Adding Comments

It's often useful to embed comments in your documents. They're notes that won't be displayed in a browser but that you (or someone else) can read when viewing the original markup. Comments can include background on why a document is structured a particular way, instruction on how to update a document, or a recorded history of changes. Comments in XHTML use a specialized tag structure:

```
<!-- Use an h2 for subheadings -->
<h2>Adding Comments</h2>
```

A comment starts with `<!--`, a set of characters the browser recognizes as the opening of a comment, and ends with `-->`. Web browsers won't render any content or elements that occur between those markers, even if the comment spans multiple lines. Comments can also be useful to temporarily "hide" portions of markup when you're testing your web pages.

```
<!-- Hiding this for testing
<h2>Adding Comments</h2>
End hiding -->
```

Although a browser doesn't visibly render comments, the comments are still delivered along with the rest of the markup and can be seen in the page's source code if a visitor views it. Don't expect comments to remain completely secret, and don't rely on them to permanently remove or suppress any important content or markup.

The XHTML Document

So far, we've been using the words *document* and *page* repeatedly, and you might think those terms are interchangeable. But generally speaking, when we refer to a *document*, we're talking about the plain-text file that contains the XHTML source code, while a *page* is the visible result when a graphical web browser renders that document. A document is what you author, and a page is what you (and the visitors to your website) will see and use.

An XHTML document must conform to a rigid structure to be considered valid and well formed, with a few required components arranged in a precise configuration. Listing 2-1 shows the basic skeleton of a well-formed document, with all the required pieces in their proper places.

Listing 2-1. *A Basic XHTML Document*

```
<!DOCTYPE html PUBLIC "-//W3C//DTD XHTML 1.0 Strict//EN"
  "http://www.w3.org/TR/xhtml1/DTD/xhtml1-strict.dtd">
<html xmlns="http://www.w3.org/1999/xhtml" lang="en" xml:lang="en">
```

```
<head>
  <title>My first web page</title>
</head>
<body>
  <p>XHTML is easy!</p>
</body>
</html>
```

As simple as it seems, this is actually a complete, valid, well-formed document. Every web page you create will begin with a framework just like this. Next, we'll discuss a few of the components in a bit more detail.

The Doctype

An XHTML document begins with a *Document Type Declaration* (*doctype*, for short), a required component that—as the name suggests—declares what type of document this is and the set of standardized rules the document intends to follow. Each "flavor" of XHTML has its own corresponding doctype.

- *XHTML 1.0 Strict*:

```
<!DOCTYPE html PUBLIC "-//W3C//DTD XHTML 1.0 Strict//EN"
  "http://www.w3.org/TR/xhtml1/DTD/xhtml1-strict.dtd">
```

- *XHTML 1.0 Transitional*:

```
<!DOCTYPE html PUBLIC "-//W3C//DTD XHTML 1.0 Transitional//EN"
  "http://www.w3.org/TR/xhtml1/DTD/xhtml1-transitional.dtd">
```

- *XHTML 1.0 Frameset*:

```
<!DOCTYPE html PUBLIC "-//W3C//DTD XHTML 1.0 Frameset//EN"
  "http://www.w3.org/TR/xhtml1/DTD/xhtml1-frameset.dtd">
```

The doctype declaration is a sort of tag, but despite its enclosing angle brackets, it's not an element in XHTML, so it doesn't require a closing tag or trailing slash. In fact, it's not truly part of the document's markup at all; it merely relays information about the document to the user-agent so it can determine what kind of document it's dealing with and render the page according to the proper rules.

The doctype must appear in your XHTML documents exactly as we've shown here, complete with capitalization and quotes, though it doesn't have to be broken onto two lines. Other versions of HTML have their own doctypes, but we'll be using XHTML 1.0 Strict throughout this book. For a more exhaustive investigation into the parts of a doctype declaration, see Brian Wilson's informative explanation at `http://www.blooberry.com/indexdot/html/tagpages/d/doctype.htm`.

Doctype Switching: Compliance Mode vs. Quirks Mode

When a web browser downloads an HTML or XHTML document, it must make a number of programmed assumptions in order to parse the document's markup and apply the presentation suggested by the author's CSS. The earliest browsers that supported CSS did so largely according to their own rules, rather than following the standardized specifications. This was a major stumbling block in the adoption of CSS and web standards in general. A page might be rendered perfectly in one graphical browser and appear completely broken in another.

As browsers improved their support of CSS—that is, moved toward better compliance with web standards—they were faced with a dilemma. Many websites had already been designed with built-in dependencies on the inconsistent, inaccurate renderings of older browsers. Suddenly opting to follow the rules could cause millions of web pages to seem "broken" in the latest version of a web browser when they looked just fine the day before. The site didn't change overnight; only the browser's method of rendering it did.

This dilemma inspired the introduction of the *doctype switch*. When a document includes a full, correct doctype, a modern browser can assume the entire document is well formed and authored according to web standards. The browser can then render the page in a mode intended to comply with the established standards for markup and CSS, a mode known as *compliance mode* or *strict mode*. If the doctype is missing, incomplete, or malformed, the browser will assume it's dealing with an outdated document and revert to its loose and tolerant rendering mode, known as *quirks mode* because it's intended to adjust to the various quirks of nonstandard and improperly constructed markup (it's also sometimes called *compatibility mode*). Older browsers lack a built-in doctype switch and so are forever locked in their outdated quirks modes.

To correctly invoke compliance mode in modern web browsers, a complete doctype must be included as the very first line of text in a document; only white space is allowed to appear before it. Any markup, text, or even comments appearing before the doctype declaration will throw most modern browsers into quirks mode, with often-unpredictable results. Designing websites with CSS is considerably easier and the results are more consistent when the document is rendered in compliance mode. Hence, including a complete and correct doctype is essential. And because a doctype is already a required part of a valid web document, modern browsers will always render your pages in compliance mode if you build your documents correctly.

Peter-Paul Koch offers additional information and opinions on quirks mode at his aptly named website, Quirks Mode (`http://www.quirksmode.org/css/quirksmode.html`). To find out just how documents are rendered differently in quirks mode, see Jukka Korpela's article "What Happens in Quirks Mode?" (`http://www.cs.tut.fi/~jkorpela/quirks-mode.html`).

The html Element

The actual markup begins after the doctype with the html element, which acts as a container for the entire document. This is known as the *root element*, the one from which all other elements sprout and grow. The html element has no other properties of its own; it's strictly a container that defines where the document begins and ends. Any elements or content that appear outside this element (apart from the doctype, which isn't an element) will make the entire document invalid.

Required Attributes

- xmlns: A URL specifying an XML namespace, which is http://www.w3.org/1999/xhtml for XHTML documents

Optional Attributes

There are no optional attributes for the html element.

Standard Attributes

- dir

- id

- lang

- xml:lang

A *namespace* is where element and attribute names are specified for XML languages. XML is an extensible markup language, allowing authors to define their own customized elements and attributes. For example, an animal element with a species attribute could be useful for documents about animals, and such customized names could be defined in a special namespace. XHTML 1.0, on the other hand, has a *predefined* set of element and attribute names, and the correct URL of its namespace is http://www.w3.org/1999/xhtml (XHTML 1.1 and 2 can be extended with a custom namespace, but those versions of XHTML haven't yet been released as official standards). The namespace is declared in an XHTML document via the xmlns attribute of the root html element.

The standard lang and xml:lang attributes are optional for the html element (as they are for most other elements). Because this is the root element from which all other elements descend, the language declared here will be passed on to every other element in the document, so it's recommended to include them.

CONTENT TYPES

Web servers and clients rely on standardized *content types* to differentiate one type of content from another, in order to determine how the data should be processed. Plain, unformatted text is delivered with a content type of text/plain, a JPEG image is delivered with a content type of image/jpeg, an MPEG video uses video/mpeg, and so on. Most of this goes on automatically, behind the scenes between the server and the client, and a web author usually doesn't need to be concerned with content types. Content types are also known as *Internet media types* or *MIME types* (MIME stands for Multipurpose Internet Mail Extensions, but the standard is used on the web as well).

HTML documents use a content type of text/html, so both the server and the client know exactly what that document is and how it should be handled. However, we've said before that XHTML is a reformulation of HTML following the stringent rules of XML. But the truth is that XHTML *is* XML, and should most correctly be served as such with a content type of application/xml+xhtml. Unfortunately, many popular web browsers (most notably Internet Explorer for Windows, the most dominant browser in the world) don't correctly interpret XHTML documents served with the correct content type. Those browsers, unable to cope with XHTML delivered as XML, will fail to render the document. This is simply unacceptable for most web authors since the overwhelming majority of the browsing public would be unable to see and use their sites.

Furthermore, devices that parse XML are required to stop processing the document on the first error they encounter. A single validation error would make the entire web page fail if it was being treated as true XML. As much as we might want to keep our documents strictly valid, it's simply not always possible, especially when third-party software and content management systems are involved. Alas, delivering XHTML documents with the correct content type is rarely practical at this time.

Luckily, XHTML documents can optionally be served with a content type of text/html, just as other versions of HTML are. This effectively means XHTML is treated as if it were HTML 4.01, sacrificing some of the power of XML for the sake of wider compatibility with web browsers. You still gain some benefits from using XHTML, ensuring your documents are well formed and forward compatible, but for all intents and purposes you're simply writing HTML 4.01 with a few tighter constraints.

And the Rest . . .

The rest of the document consists of the head and body elements; the head element contains information about the document itself (including the required title element), while the body element contains all the content that will ultimately be rendered by a browser, to be seen and used by your visitors. These elements are covered in detail in the next two chapters (in fact, Chapter 3 is devoted entirely to the head element).

All in all, the basic structure of an XHTML document is quite simple, requiring only a doctype, a root element, a head with a title, and a body.

The Document Tree

It's helpful to visualize the structure of an XHTML document as an inverted tree, with all the elements represented as connected branches. The tree begins with the root element at the top and all other elements descending downward, making it more like a family tree than the leafy, wooden sort. Because of this, genealogy terms are often used to refer to the relationships between elements. Figure 2-2 shows the family tree of a simple document.

In the diagram, the tree begins with the root element, which has two *child* elements: the head and the body. That body element has two children of its own: a level-one heading (the h1 element, covered in Chapter 4) and a p element for a single paragraph (also covered in Chapter 4). Those two elements are *siblings* of each other, sharing the body element as their common *parent*. They're also *descendants* of the html element, which is their *ancestor*. The paragraph contains an em element and an a element, sibling children of their parent paragraph, descended from the ancestral body and html elements.

We'll use these terms—children, siblings, parents, descendants, and ancestors—often throughout this book.

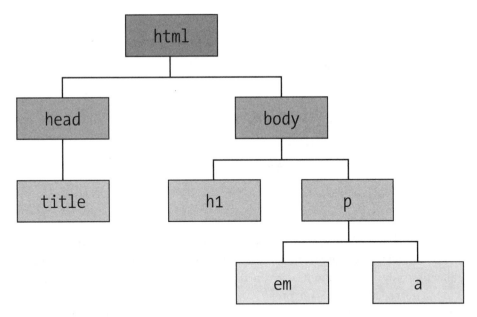

Figure 2-2. *A simple document tree*

CSS Fundamentals

CSS can add style to your pages, enhancing and improving the presentation of your content. The structure is supplied by XHTML—each element designates a different portion of content, and attributes pass along more information about those elements. CSS acts as another layer to influence the presentation of those XHTML elements when they're rendered. Colors, fonts, text sizes, backgrounds, and the arrangement of elements on the page are all presentational aspects of your content, and all can be controlled through artful application of CSS.

Anatomy of a CSS Rule

If elements are the building blocks of markup, the building block of CSS is the *rule*. It's a set of instructions that a browser can follow to alter the appearance of XHTML elements based on the presentational values you supply. A CSS rule consists of a few component parts, diagrammed in Figure 2-3.

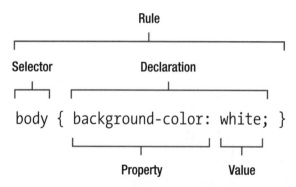

Figure 2-3. *The components of a rule in CSS*

The *selector* is the part of the rule that targets an element that will be styled. Its scope can be very broad, affecting every instance of a particular element or very narrow and specific, affecting only a few elements or even just one. We'll cover the different kinds of selectors in the next section of this chapter.

A *declaration* comprises two more parts: a *property* and a *value*. The property is that aspect of an element's presentation that is being modified, such as its color, its width, or its placement on the page. Dozens of properties are available in the CSS language, and you'll become familiar with many of them in the pages of this book.

The property value delivers the specific style that should be applied to the selected element. The values accepted depend on the particular property, and some properties accept multiple values, separated by spaces.

Declarations reside in a set of curly braces ({ and }), and multiple declarations can apply to the same selector, thus modifying several aspects of an element's presentation in the course of a single rule. A property and its value are separated by a colon (:) and the declaration ends with a semicolon (;). That semicolon is important to separate multiple declarations, but if there's only one declaration in the rule or if it's the last declaration in a series, the terminating semicolon is optional. It's not a bad idea to get in the habit of including a semicolon at the end of every declaration, even when there's only one, just to play it safe.

If your CSS doesn't conform to this basic structure and syntax—if you forget the closing brace or the colon separating a property from its value, for example—the entire rule or even the entire style sheet might fail. Just like XHTML, a style sheet should be well formed and properly constructed. The W3C provides a CSS validation service (http://jigsaw. w3.org/css-validator/) that can help you catch goofs and glitches in your style sheets.

CSS Selectors

A selector, as its name implies, selects an element in your XHTML document. A few different types of selectors are available, with varying levels of specificity to target a large number of elements or just a few. *Specificity* is a means of measuring a given selector's scope, in other words how many or few elements it selects. CSS is designed so that more specific selectors override and supersede less specific selectors. Specificity is one of the more nebulous and hard-to-grasp concepts in CSS but is also one of the most powerful features of the language. We'll cover the rules of specificity in more detail later, but let's first introduce the selectors.

Universal Selector

The universal selector is merely an asterisk (*) acting as a "wild card" to select any and all elements in the document. For example, this rule:

```
* { color: blue; }
```

would apply a blue foreground (text) color to *all* elements. Headings, paragraphs, lists, cells in tables, and even links—all would be rendered in blue because the universal selector selects the entire universe. This is the least specific selector available, since it's not specific at all.

Element Selector

An element selector selects all instances of an element, specified by its tag name. This selector is more specific than the universal selector, but it's still not very specific since it targets every occurrence of an element, no matter how many of them there may be. For example, the rule:

```
em { color: red; }
```

gives every em element the same red foreground color, even if there are thousands of them in a document. Element selectors are also known as *type selectors*.

Class Selector

A class selector targets any element that bears the given class name in its class attribute. Because a class attribute can be assigned to practically any element in XHTML, and any number of elements can belong to the same class, this selector is not extremely specific but is still more specific than an element selector. In CSS, class selectors are preceded by a dot (.) to identify them. For example, this rule will style any elements belonging to the "info" class, whatever those elements happen to be:

```
.info { color: purple; }
```

ID Selector

An ID selector will select only the element carrying the specified identifier. Practically any element can have an id attribute, but that attribute's value may be used only once within a single document. The ID selector targets just one element per page, making it much more specific than a class selector that might target many. ID selectors are preceded by an octothorpe (#). (This is often called a *hash, number sign,* or *pound,* but *octothorpe* is the character's proper name. It also sounds cool and will impress people at dinner parties.) The following rule would give the element with the ID "introduction" a green foreground color:

```
#introduction { color: green; }
```

Pseudo Class Selector

A pseudo class is somewhat akin to a class selector (and is equal to classes in specificity), but it selects an element in a particular state. It's preceded by a colon (:), and only a few pseudo classes are available:

```
:link { color: blue; }
:visited { color: purple; }
:active { color: red; }
:hover { color: green; }
:focus { color: orange; }
```

The :link pseudo class selects all elements that are hyperlinks (which you'll learn much more about in Chapter 6). The :visited pseudo class selects hyperlinks whose destination has been previously visited (recorded in a web browser's built-in history). The :active pseudo class selects links in an active state, during that interval while they're being activated (while clicking a mouse or pressing the Enter or Return key). The :hover pseudo class selects any element that is being "hovered" over by a user's pointing device. Although any element can be in a hover state, this most commonly applies to links (though some older browsers supported this pseudo class only for links and no other elements). The :focus pseudo class selects any element in a focused state. Some browsers don't support :focus, most notably Internet Explorer 6 for Windows. However, Internet Explorer does (incorrectly) treat the :active pseudo class as if it were :focus, but only for links and not any other elements.

Descendant Selector

One of the most useful and powerful selectors in the CSS arsenal, a descendant selector can be assembled from two or more of the basic selector types (universal, element, class, pseudo class, and ID), separated by spaces, to select elements matching that position in the document tree. These are also called *contextual selectors* because they target elements based on their context in the document. For example:

```
#introduction em { color: yellow; }
```

That rule will color any em element within the element with the id value introduction yellow. Descendant selectors allow for very precise selection of just the elements you want to target, based on the structure of your XHTML document. This more elaborate example:

```
#introduction .info p * { color: pink; }
```

would select all elements that are descendants of a p element that is a descendant of an element with the class info that is a descendant of the element with the ID introduction. You can see how the scope of a descendent selector can be very narrow indeed, targeting only a few elements that meet the selector's criteria.

Combining Selectors

You can combine two or more selector types, such as an element and an ID or an ID and a class. These combinations can also narrow down the specificity of your selectors, seeking out only the elements you want to style and leaving others alone. This rule:

```
p.info { color: blue; }
```

selects only paragraphs (p elements) belonging to the info class. Another element in that class would be overlooked, and other paragraphs *not* belonging to the info class are also left untouched.

Combining selectors within a descendant selector can target elements with surgical precision:

```
p#introduction a.info:hover { color: silver; }
```

This rule would apply only to hovered links (a elements) belonging to the info class that are descendants of the paragraph with the ID introduction.

Grouping Selectors

You can group several selectors together as part of a single rule so the same set of declarations can apply to numerous elements without redundantly repeating them. A comma separates each selector in the rule:

```
p, h1, h2 { color: blue; }
```

The previous rule applies the same color value to every instance of the p, h1, and h2 elements. The more complex set of selectors in this rule:

```
p#introduction em, a.info:hover, h2.info { color: gold; }
```

will target all em elements descended from the paragraph with the ID introduction and all hovered links with the class info as well as h2 elements (a second-level heading) in the info class (remember that different types of elements can belong to the same class).

Grouping and combining selectors is a great way to keep your style sheets compact and manageable.

Advanced Selectors

The selectors you've seen so far are all part of CSS 1, the first standardized version of CSS introduced way back in 1996. This version of CSS is very well supported in today's generation of graphical web browsers, so you can use all of these selectors with fair confidence that most of your visitors will see their intended effect.

Since CSS 1, newer versions have come about, including CSS 2.1 and CSS 3. These updates to the CSS specifications have introduced a number of new and exciting selectors:

- *Attribute selectors* target an element bearing a particular attribute and even an attribute with a specified value.

- *Pseudo element selectors* target elements that don't specifically exist in the markup but are implied by its structure, such as the first line of a paragraph or the element immediately before another element.

- *Child selectors* select an element that is an immediate child of another element and not its other descendants.

- *Adjacent sibling selectors* target elements that are immediate siblings of another element, sharing the same parent in the document.

Unfortunately, CSS 2.1 and CSS 3 haven't yet been released by the W3C as official recommendations, though you can see them in their draft status at the W3C website to learn about these selectors and how they work (http://www.w3.org/Style/CSS/). These advanced selectors are already supported by many of the latest graphical browsers, but not all of them (and even some modern browsers don't support all of these selectors). Such advanced CSS features should be used with care combined with intensive cross-browser testing. For the purposes of this book, we'll stick with the CSS 1 selectors we've covered here, and they're all you'll need for most of what you may want to accomplish.

Specificity and the Cascade

As we mentioned earlier, each type of selector is assigned a certain level of specificity, measuring how many possible XHTML elements that selector might influence. Examine these two CSS rules, one with an element selector and the other with a class selector:

```
h2 { color: red; }
.title { color: blue; }
```

and this snippet of XHTML, an h2 element classified as a title:

```
<h2 class="title">Specificity and the Cascade</h2>
```

The first rule selects all h2 elements, and the second rule selects all elements belonging to the title class. But the element shown fits *both* criteria, causing a conflict between the two CSS rules. A graphical browser must choose one of the two rules to follow to determine the heading's final color. In CSS, a more specific selector trumps a less specific selector. Because a class selector is more specific than an element selector, the second rule has greater specificity, and the heading is rendered in blue.

Modern web browsers follow a complex formula to calculate a selector's specificity, which can be rather confusing to noncomputers like us. Thankfully, you'll rarely need to calculate a selector's numeric specificity value if you just remember these few rules:

- A universal selector isn't specific at all.

- An element selector is more specific than a universal selector.

- A class or pseudo class selector is more specific than an element selector.

- An ID selector is more specific than a class or pseudo class.

- Properties in an inline style attribute are most specific of all.

Specificity is also cumulative in combined and descendant selectors. Each of the base selector types carries a different weight in terms of specificity—a selector with two classes is more specific than a selector with one class, a selector with one ID is more specific than a selector with two classes, and so on. The specificity algorithm is carefully designed so that a large number of less specific selectors can never outweigh a more specific selector. No number of element selectors can ever be more specific than a single class, and no number of classes can ever be more specific than a single ID. Even if you assembled a complex selector made up of hundreds of element selectors, another rule with just one ID selector would still override it.

Understanding specificity will allow you to construct CSS rules that target elements with pinpoint accuracy. For a more in-depth explanation of how specificity is calculated by web browsers, see the W3C specification for CSS 2.1 (http://www.w3.org/TR/CSS21/cascade.html#specificity) along with Molly Holzschlag's more approachable clarification at http://www.molly.com/2005/10/06/css2-and-css21-specificity-clarified/.

At this point you might be wondering what happens when two selectors target the same element and also have the same specificity. For example:

```
.info h2 { color: purple; }
h2.title { color: orange; }
```

If an h2 element belonging to the title class is a descendant of another element in the info class, both of these rules should apply to that h2. How can the browser decide which rule to obey? Enter the cascade, the *C* in CSS.

Assuming selectors of equal specificity, style declarations are applied in the order in which they are received, so later declarations override prior ones. This is true whether the declarations occur within the same rule, in a separate rule later in the same style sheet, or in a separate style sheet that is downloaded after a prior one. It's this aspect of CSS that gives the language its name: multiple style sheets that *cascade* over each other, adding up to the final presentation in the browser. In the earlier example, the h2 element would be rendered in orange because the second rule overrides the first.

For another example, the following rule:

```
p { color: black; color: green; }
```

contains two declarations, but paragraphs will be rendered in green because that declaration comes later in the cascade order.

The sometimes-complex interplay between specificity and the cascade can make CSS challenging to work with in the beginning, but once you understand the basic rules, it all becomes second nature. You'll learn more about the cascade order later in this chapter, but first we'll explain how you can attach style sheets to your XHTML documents.

Attaching Style Sheets to Your Documents

To style your pages with CSS, you'll also need to connect your style sheets to your documents. When a graphical browser downloads the XHTML document and parses it for rendering, it will automatically seek out CSS rules to instruct it on how the various elements should be presented. You can include style sheets with your documents in a few ways, each with its own benefits and some drawbacks.

Inline Styles

You can include CSS declarations within the optional style attribute of each element in your markup. Inline styles aren't constructed as rules, and there is no selector because the properties and values are attached directly to the element at hand, as in Listing 2-2. An inline style is the most specific of all because it applies to exactly *one* element and no others.

Listing 2-2. *An Example of Inline Styles*

```
<h2 style="color: red;">Good eats for hungry geeks</h2>

<p style="color: gray;">Our fresh pizzas, hearty pasta dishes, and
succulent desserts are sure to please. And don't forget about our
daily chalkboard specials!</p>
```

However, you should avoid using inline styles. They mix presentation with your structural markup, thus negating one of the primary advantages of using CSS. They're also highly redundant, forcing you to declare the same style properties again and again to maintain consistent presentation. Should you ever want to update the site in the future—changing all your headings from red to blue, for example—you would need to track down every single heading in every single document to implement that change, a daunting task on a large and complex website.

Still, an inline style might be an efficient approach on a few rare occasions, but those occasions are very few and far between, and another solution is always preferable; inline styles should be a last resort only when no other options are available.

Embedded Style Sheets

You can embed style rules within the head element of your document, and those rules will be honored only for the document in which they reside. An embedded style sheet (sometimes called an *internal style sheet*) is contained within the style element, shown in Listing 2-3 and covered in greater detail in Chapter 3.

Listing 2-3. *An Example of an Embedded Style Sheet*

```
<!DOCTYPE html PUBLIC "-//W3C//DTD XHTML 1.0 Strict//EN"
  "http://www.w3.org/TR/xhtml1/DTD/xhtml1-strict.dtd">
<html xmlns="http://www.w3.org/1999/xhtml" lang="en" xml:lang="en">
  <head>
    <title>Spaghetti and Cruft : Our Menu</title>
    <style type="text/css">
      h2 { color: red; }
      p { color: gray; }
    </style>
  </head>
  <body>
    <h2>Good eats for hungry geeks</h2>

    <p>Our fresh pizzas, hearty pasta dishes, and succulent
    desserts are sure to please. And don't forget about our
    daily chalkboard specials!</p>
  </body>
</html>
```

Embedding a style sheet in the head of your document does further separate presentation from your structured content, and those rules will be applied throughout that document, but it isn't an efficient approach if you're styling more than one page at a time. Other documents within the same website would require embedded style sheets of their own, so making any future modifications to your site's presentation would require updating every single document in the site.

External Style Sheets

The third and best option is to place all your CSS rules in a separate, external style sheet, directly connected to your documents. An external style sheet is a plain-text file that you can edit using the same text editing software you use to create your XHTML documents, saved with the file extension .css. This approach completely separates presentation from content and structure—they're not even stored in the same file. A single external style sheet can be linked from and associated with any number of XHTML documents, allowing your entire website's visual design to be controlled from one central file. Changes to that file will propagate globally to every page that connects to it. It's by far the most flexible and maintainable way to design your sites, exercising the true power of CSS.

An XHTML document links to an external style sheet via a link element in the document's head, and you'll learn more about that in the next chapter. For now, Listing 2-4 shows a simple example.

Listing 2-4. *Linking to an External Style Sheet*

```
<!DOCTYPE html PUBLIC "-//W3C//DTD XHTML 1.0 Strict//EN"
  "http://www.w3.org/TR/xhtml1/DTD/xhtml1-strict.dtd">
<html xmlns="http://www.w3.org/1999/xhtml" lang="en" xml:lang="en">
  <head>
    <title>Spaghetti and Cruft : Our Menu</title>
    <link rel="stylesheet" type="text/css" href="styles.css" />
</head>
  <body>
    <h2>Good eats for hungry geeks</h2>

    <p>Our fresh pizzas, hearty pasta dishes, and succulent
    desserts are sure to please. And don't forget about our
    daily chalkboard specials!</p>
  </body>
</html>
```

When a graphical browser downloads and begins processing the document, it will follow that link to retrieve the external style sheet and process it as well, automatically following its rules to render the page. An external style sheet is downloaded only once and then *cached* in the browser's memory for use on subsequent pages, keeping your documents lighter and improving the speed of your entire website.

The Cascade Order

You're not limited to a single style sheet; several different CSS files can be linked to from one document, with each style sheet having its own link element in the document's head. Depending on the complexity of your site, you might have one style sheet containing general rules for the entire site while pages within a certain section can link to a second style sheet to define specific styles for that subset of pages. You might also prefer to break your styles apart based on their purpose: for example, one style sheet defining colors and backgrounds and another style sheet defining your page layout.

You can also combine all three methods—inline, embedded, and external—to style your web pages, although it's rarely advisable. If just one page on your site needs some additional rules, you might choose to include an embedded style sheet within that document alone. You may even, very rarely, want to call out one element for special treatment and use an inline style for just that element. In almost every case, external style sheets are the best approach: they eliminate presentational markup, improve a site's performance, and are much easier to maintain.

With so many CSS rules being dictated from so many different sources, some overlap is to be expected. You already have specificity on your side, with more specific selectors overruling general selectors. But specificity alone isn't enough to resolve all the potential style conflicts a graphical browser might run into when trying to render a web page. Where specificity fails, the *cascade order* steps in to sort things out.

CSS rules are applied to content in the order in which they are received; later rules override previous rules. Separate style sheets are downloaded in a particular order as well. In the case of external style sheets, their order is indicated by the order in which the link elements appear in the document; rules in later linked style sheets override rules in previously linked style sheets. Rules embedded in a document's style element are processed after all external style sheets. If more than one style sheet is embedded in a document— each in its own style element—later embedded style sheets override previous ones. Inline declarations in an element's style attribute are applied even after embedded style sheets.

In addition to *author style sheets*, every modern graphical web browser has its own built-in style sheet to define the default presentation of various elements. When you view a web page without any of the author's CSS applied, you're simply seeing it rendered with the *browser style sheet*, which comes first in the cascade order so all the author's styles override those defaults. To complicate matters just a bit further, most web browsers allow the end user to attach their own customized style sheets—known as a *user style sheet*— which comes second in the cascade order, thus overriding the browser's default styles but not the author's.

To break it down, the cascade order for multiple style sources is as follows:

1. Browser style sheet

2. User style sheet

3. External author style sheets (in the order in which they're linked)

4. Embedded author style sheets (in the order in which they occur)

5. Inline author styles

And don't forget, the cascade works within each style sheet as well. To remember how the cascade works, follow this rule of thumb: *the style closest to the content wins.* Whichever value is declared last will be the one applied when the content is rendered.

!important

In some extremely rare cases where both specificity and the cascade may not be sufficient to apply your desired value, the special keyword !important (complete with preceding exclamation point) can force a browser to honor that value above all others. This is a powerful and dangerous tool and should be used only as a last resort to resolve conflicting styles beyond your control (for example, if you're forced to work with third-party markup that uses inline styles that you're unable to modify directly).

The !important directive must appear at the end of the value, before the semicolon, like so:

```
h1 { color: red !important; }
```

A value declared as !important is applied to the rendered content regardless of where that value occurs in the cascade or the specificity of its selector. That is unless another competing value is also declared to be !important; specificity and the cascade once again take over in those cases. There's one notable exception to be aware of: !important values in a user style sheet always take precedence, even overriding !important values in author style sheets. This gives the ultimate power to the user, which is only right; after all, it's their computer.

Formatting CSS

Like XHTML documents, external style sheet files are plain text. You're free to format your CSS however you like, just as long as the basic syntax is followed. Extra spaces and carriage returns are ignored in CSS; the browser doesn't care what the plain text looks like, just that it's technically well formed. When it comes to formatting CSS, the most important factors are your own preferences. Individual rules can be written in two general formats: *extended* or *compacted.*

Extended rules break the selector and declarations onto separate lines, which many authors find more readable and easier to work with. It allows you to see at a glance where each new property begins and ends, at the expense of a lot of scrolling when you're working with long and complex style sheets. Listing 2-5 shows a few simple rules in an extended format.

Listing 2-5. *CSS Rules in Extended Format*

```css
h1, h2, h3 {
  color: red;
  margin-bottom: .5em;
}

h1 {
  font-size: 150%;
}

h2 {
  font-size: 130%;
}

h3 {
  font-size: 120%;
  border-bottom: 1px solid gray;
}
```

Compact formatting condenses each rule to a single line, thus shortening the needed vertical scrolling, but it can demand horizontal scrolling in your text editor when a rule includes many declarations in a row. Listing 2-6 demonstrates the same set of rules compacted to single lines and with unnecessary spaces removed.

Listing 2-6. *CSS Rules in Compacted Format*

```css
h1,h2,h3{color:red;margin-bottom:.5em;}
h1{font-size:150%;}
h2{font-size:130%;}
h3{font-size:120%;border-bottom:1px solid gray;}
```

Another advantage of compacted rules is a slight reduction in file size. Spaces, tabs, and carriage returns are stored as characters in the electronic file, and each additional character adds another byte to the overall file size that must be downloaded by a client. A long style sheet might be a considerably larger file in an extended format because of all the extra space characters. In fact, you could choose to remove *all* excess spaces and place your entire style sheet on a single line for optimal compression, but that might be overkill and make your CSS much harder to work with. To reconcile maximum readability with minimal file size, some authors work with style sheets in an extended format and then automatically compress the entire thing to a single line when moving it to a live web server.

A few extra spaces in a compacted rule can at least make it easier to scan, spreading a one-line rule out a bit by including spaces between declarations and values. For lack of a better term, we'll call this format *semicompacted*, as shown in Listing 2-7.

Listing 2-7. *CSS Rules in Semicompacted Format*

```
h1, h2, h3 { color: red; margin-bottom: .5em; }
h1 { font-size: 150%; }
h2 { font-size: 130%; }
h3 { font-size: 120%; border-bottom: 1px solid gray; }
```

In the end, the choice is entirely yours, and you should author your style sheets in a way that makes sense to you.

CSS Comments

You can add comments to your style sheets for the same reasons you might use comments in XHTML: to make notes, to pass along instructions to other web developers, or to temporarily hide or disable parts of the style sheet during testing. A comment in CSS begins with /* and ends with */, and anything between those markers won't be interpreted by the browser. Just like comments in XHTML, CSS comments can span multiple lines.

```
/* These base styles apply to all heading levels. */
h1, h2, h3, h4, h5, h6 { color: red; margin-bottom: .5em; }
/* Adjust the size of each. */
h1 { font-size: 150%; }
h2 { font-size: 130%; }
h3 { font-size: 120%; }
/* Temporarily hiding these rules
h4 { font-size: 100%; }
h5 { font-size: 90%; }
h6 { font-size: 80%; }
End hiding */
```

Summary

This chapter has covered a lot of ground to get you up to speed on the inner workings of XHTML and CSS. You've seen how you can author XHTML documents, using tags to define elements and adding attributes to relay more information about them. Throughout the rest of this book, you'll become intimately familiar with most of the elements you'll use when you create your own web pages.

HTML was first introduced in the early 1990s, but the language has already undergone many changes in its short and bright career. XHTML is a stricter reformulation of earlier versions of HTML, with just a few rules that differentiate the two, as shown in Table 2-1.

Table 2-1. *HTML 4.01 Strict vs. XHTML 1.0 Strict*

HTML 4.01 Strict	XHTML 1.0 Strict
Tag and attribute names are not case-sensitive.	Tag and attribute names must be written in lowercase.
Some attributes can be minimized, and attribute values don't require quotes.	All attributes must have a specified value, and the value must be quoted.
Some elements don't require closing tags, and empty elements should not be closed with a trailing slash.	All elements must be closed, either with a closing tag for nonempty elements or with a trailing slash for empty elements.

The second part of this chapter gave you a crash course in CSS, unveiling the mechanics of this rich and powerful language. You learned about CSS selectors and how specificity and the cascade work together to give you great control over how your content is presented. You'll use XHTML to build the structure of your documents and then use CSS to apply a separate layer of polished presentation. In the following chapters, you'll see glimpses of how you can use CSS in different ways to create different visual effects. Chapter 9 will delve a bit deeper to show you a few ways to use CSS to lay out your pages by placing elements where you want them to appear on-screen, all without damaging their underlying structure.

From here on, we'll assume you've reached an understanding of the basic rules of syntax for authoring your own XHTML and CSS, and the rest of this book will dig into the real meat of markup. To get things rolling, Chapter 3 is a detailed examination of the head element, where you'll include vital information about the documents you create.

Moving A<head>

The title of this chapter says it all; we're moving ahead and starting to get into creating XHTML documents. This chapter explains the head element, which contains information about the document. While the head element and its contents aren't displayed in the browser, they can play a critical role in defining special features in your document, such as JavaScript code, the name of your document, and any styling that your document should have.

The head Section

Many people consider the head a section as well as an element. The head can contain several other elements, which this chapter focuses on. One of the more interesting things about the head element is that is doesn't contain any elements that are actually displayed in your document. The first thing you need to learn is how to create the head element itself.

Chapter 1 presented the basic structure of an XHTML document. Based on the sample presented in Chapter 1 and the rules presented in Chapter 2, you should realize that the head section is contained in the html section. The head section must contain the head element, and it may contain any of the following elements as well: base, link, meta, script, style, and title. I describe each of these elements in detail throughout the remainder of this chapter. Let's start with the head element.

<head>

For each tag, I present a summary of the available attributes. I break the attributes down into three sections: required, optional, and standard. A required attribute must be present if you use the tag. An optional attribute is just that: it's optional and may or may not be present. If you need more detail on the standard attributes, refer back to Chapter 2.

The <head> tag contains information about the XHTML document, including key words that describe the site, links to other files that the document is making use of such as CSS files, and more. Nothing in the head section is displayed to users in the browser, except the contents of the <title> element, in the browser's title bar.

Required Attributes

No attributes are required for the head element.

Optional Attributes

- Profile: A space-separated list of URLs that contains metadata information about the document

Standard Attributes

- dir

- lang

- xml:lang

Usage

Listing 3-1 illustrates an empty head element that should help remind you where it lives.

Listing 3-1. *An Empty head Element*

```
<!DOCTYPE html
PUBLIC "-//W3C//DTD XHTML 1.0 Strict//EN"
"http://www.w3.org/TR/xhtml1/DTD/xhtml1-strict.dtd">
<html>
    <head>
    </head>
    <body>
    </body>
</html>
```

The Supporting Elements

The remainder of this chapter goes through each of the tags you can use within the head element. Adding or removing any of these elements may or may not affect the visual presentation of your document.

<base>

The <base> tag helps make links (discussed in Chapter 6) shorter and maintenance easier. You use the <base> tag to specify a base URL for all the links in a document.

Required Attributes

- `href`: Specifies a URL to be used as the base URL for links in the document

Optional Attributes

The `base` element doesn't offer any optional attributes.

Standard Attributes

No standard attributes are available for the `base` element.

Usage

As you'll learn in Chapter 5, when you wish to include an image in your XHTML document, you need to specify where the image can be found. Using the `<base>` tag can make life easier when several images reside in the same directory. For example, if your document includes several images all from the same directory, you could use the `<base>` tag to shorten the URL link. Also, if you decide to move the images to a new location, updating the links would be a snap. All you would need to do is change the `href` attribute in the `<base>` tag.

For example, let's say you want to display an image that resides at the following URL address:

`http://www.apress.com/images/logo.gif`

Listing 3-2 shows you how to make use of the `<base>` tag.

Listing 3-2. *Using the <base> Tag with an Image*

```
<!DOCTYPE html
PUBLIC "-//W3C//DTD XHTML 1.0 Strict//EN"
"http://www.w3.org/TR/xhtml1/DTD/xhtml1-strict.dtd">
<html>
    <head>
        <base href=" http://www.apress.com/images/" />
    </head>
    <body>
        <img src="logo.gif" alt="The Apress logo" />
    </body>
</html>
```

When the browser goes to retrieve the image, it takes the base URL specified in the `<base>` tag and combines it with the requested file. Using the `<base>` tag to retrieve images is most effective when you have several images, because it saves on your typing and reduces the overall size of your document.

<link>

The link element defines defines the relationship between two linked documents. It is most often used to link external style sheets into the current document.

Required Attributes

The link element does not require any attributes.

Optional Attributes

- charset: Sets the character set used by the document being linked to. You can find a listing of available character sets at http://www.iana.org/assignments/character-sets.

- href: The URL pointing to the document that is being linked.

- media: Refers to the type of media intended for the document that is being linked to. Common values include all, braille, print, projection, screen, and speech. The media attribute allows you to specify a different style sheet for different media types. For example, you may want the screen to be colorful and bright, but some of your users may have a monochrome printer. This attribute allows you to use a different style sheet for each media type.

- rel: Defines the relationship between the document being linked to and the current document. Common values include alternate, appendix, bookmark, chapter, contents, copyright, glossary, help, home, index, next, prev, section, start, stylesheet, and subsection.

- rev: The opposite of rel, this attribute defines the relationship between the current document and the document being linked to.

- type: Specifies the Multipurpose Internet Mail Extensions (MIME) type of the target URL. The most common values are text/css for external style sheets, text/javascript for JavaScript files, and image/gif for .gif image files. The MIME type tells the browser what type of file is being downloaded and how to handle it. You can find a listing of common MIME types at http://www.webmaster-toolkit.com/mime-types.shtml.

Standard Attributes

- class

- dir

- id

- lang

- style

- title

Usage

The following code shows you how to link to an external style sheet—a common use of the link element:

```
<head>
    <link rel="stylesheet" type="text/css" href="main.css" />
</head>
```

<meta>

The <meta> tag provides information about your document. Search engines often use this information to catalog pages on the Internet. You use the <meta> tag to provide keywords and descriptions that search engines can use to catalog your document. Another common use is to allow for automated refreshes of your document within a browser using the http-equiv attribute. The term *meta* refers to metadata, which is a term often described as data about data. The <meta> tag provides data about the data in the document.

Required Attributes

- content: The value to be associated with a name or http-equiv

Optional Attributes

- http-equiv: Connects the content attribute value to a specific HTTP response header. You can use this attribute to request the browser to do something or to reference information about the document from an external source.

- name: Assigns extra information to a document. The value of this attribute comes from the content attribute. Some common names include author, keywords, description, and summary.

- scheme: Defines a format used to interpret the value set in the content attribute.

Standard Attributes

- `dir`

- `lang`

- `xml:lang`

Usage

The best way to explain this tag is by simply showing a few short samples. Oftentimes, you may want your document to be associated with specific keywords on a search site. By adding the `keywords` name and a comma-separated list, you're providing clues for a search engine. For example, you could use the following XHTML for this book:

```
<meta name="keywords" content="HTML, XHTML, CSS, Javascript" />
```

You could also use the `description` name value to provide a short description to search engines about your document:

```
<meta name="description" content="This is an introduction to HTML/XHTML." />
```

Tip It's a good idea to always be concise in what you make available to search engines. People who use a search engine are looking for specific information. The site `http://www.webmarketingnow.com/tips/meta-tags-uncovered.html#google` has some really good examples and explanations of using different meta elements.

The `http-equiv` attribute provides the ability to do some pretty neat things. First, you can use it along with the `refresh` value to specify that you want your document to be refreshed at a specific interval. This sample refreshes the document every 15 seconds (bear in mind that you should use this with caution; otherwise, you may end up really annoying your web site visitors!):

```
<meta http-equiv="refresh" content="15" />
```

You can find a listing of other `http-equiv` tags at `http://vancouver-webpages.com/META/metatags.detail.html`.

<script>

The `<script>` tag plays a key role in making your site more dynamic and feature-rich. It allows you to add scripting languages to your XHTML documents that respond to user actions. Chapter 10 covers the basics of JavaScript.

Required Attributes

- `type`: Defines the MIME type of the script included. You must set this attribute as `text/javascript` when using JavaScript.

Optional Attributes

- `charset`: Defines the character encoding used in the script

- `defer`: Tells the browser that the script won't generate any document content, so the browser can continue parsing and drawing the page

- `src`: Uses a URL to point to a document that contains the JavaScript

Standard Attributes

- `xml:space`

Usage

The use of scripting can really bring life to your documents. In Chapter 10, you'll dive into the details of adding scripting to your documents.

<style>

The last chapter briefly introduced the `<style>` tag when discussing internal style sheets. The sole purpose of the `<style>` tag is to create internal style sheets for your document.

Required Attributes

- `type`: Defines the style type and is pretty much always set to `text/css`, unless you are using some kind of proprietary style language, which you shouldn't really be doing anyhow.

Optional Attributes

- `media`: Defines what media the style should affect. Some of the possible values include `screen`, `print`, `tty`, `tv`, `projection`, `handheld`, `braille`, `aural`, and `all`. `all` is the default media value, assumed when a media attribute is not specified. Visit `http://www.w3schools.com/css/css_mediatypes.asp` for the specifics on the media types.

Standard Attributes

- `dir`

- `lang`

- `title`

- `xml:space`

Usage

The `media` attribute lets you have different styles for different output devices. For example, you may produce some online reports that users may want to print on their printer. Most likely, you'd want to make the text on the screen larger and possibly in a different font than that on a printed page. Listing 3-3 shows an example of a style sheet that makes the screen font size 16 pixels, while making the text on the printed page 12 pixels. Both the screen and printed media have normal font weight (as opposed to bold). Note the use of the `@media` rule, which allows for the use of multiple media types within a single style sheet.

Listing 3-3. *The style Element Using Several Different Media Types*

```
<style type="text/css">
    @media screen
    {
        ptext {font-size:16px}
    }
    @media print
    {
        ptext {font-size:12px}
    }
    @media screen,print
    {
        ptext {font-weight:normal}
    }
</style>
```

■Tip CSS has an @import statement that instructs the browser to retrieve and use the styles from an external style sheet. Typically, you use the @import statement in the <style> tag (it has to appear prior to any other rules), as shown here, although it can also be used in external style sheets to import other stylesheets:

```
<style type="text/css">
    @import "http://www.mysite.com/css/style.css"
</style>
```

Any rule that is in the external style sheet takes precedence over rules that precede the actual @import statement. You can also use multiple @import statements to bring in several different style sheets. In addition, the order of the @import statements is important. The rules are applied top down, so those at the top of the list take precedence over those at the bottom of the @import list. For more information on using the @import statement, refer to Chapter 9.

<title>

The <title> tag allows you to provide a title to your document. Browsers typically display this value in their title bar, and they use it as the default name in a bookmark.

Required Attributes

No attributes are required for the title element.

Optional Attributes

There are no optional attributes for the title element.

Standard Attributes

- class

- dir

- id

- lang

- style

- xml:lang

Usage

To add a title to your document, you simply need to put the text you wish to use between the opening and closing tags of the title element, as Listing 3-4 shows.

Listing 3-4. *Sample to Illustrate the title Element*

```
<!DOCTYPE html
PUBLIC "-//W3C//DTD XHTML 1.0 Strict//EN"
"http://www.w3.org/TR/xhtml1/DTD/xhtml1-strict.dtd">
<html>
    <head>
        <title>This text will be displayed within the titlebar</title>
    </head>
    <body>
    </body>
</html>
```

Figure 3-1 shows the results of Listing 3-4.

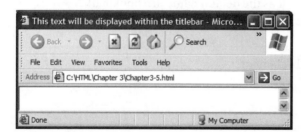

Figure 3-1. *The title element displayed within a browser*

■**Tip** It's a good idea to always set a title, because it's displayed in the title bar of the browser. This allows users to know what document they're viewing, even if they don't have the full browser window displayed. If you don't specify a <title>, the document will display an empty title.

Summary

This chapter has explained the head section in detail, including each element and its attributes. Several samples helped to enforce the point as needed. In Chapter 4, you'll learn how to add content to your document through the use of many new tags.

CHAPTER 4

■ ■ ■

Adding Content

Now that you've got a handle on the basics, the real fun can begin: it's time to start adding content to your web pages. In this chapter, you'll learn about most of the XHTML elements you'll need to organize your content and give it a meaningful structure. Along the way, you'll see examples of how the different elements are rendered by a web browser with its default styling. Then we'll show you a few simple ways you can use CSS to enhance the presentation of your text.

Content and Structure

The content of your web page consists of everything your visitors will see, read, and use. However, content is more than simply words and images; it's also the message, the thing your words and images are actually about. Your content is the information that you're trying to communicate to your audience, and the web is a conduit for moving that information from one place (you) to another (them).

The World Wide Web originated as a purely textual medium, built upon the written word. Pictures were soon added to the mix, and eventually sound, animation, and video made the web the rich multimedia tapestry it is today. But the vast bulk of online content still takes the form of written text, and that is unlikely to change any time soon. Most of the time you spend surfing the web is probably spent reading.

Human beings rely on some structure to make text readable and understandable. As you read this book, you're looking for visual cues to help you organize the words into concise pieces that you can process and comprehend. You recognize the significance of such things as punctuation, capitalization, spacing, and font size. You know just by looking at it that this paragraph ends after this sentence.

Computers don't read the same way humans do—they can't interpret a string of words and grasp the concept behind them, they don't see the visual cues we use to separate one string of words from another, and they can't automatically group related sentences into useful blocks. Instead of visual cues, a computer requires a structure composed of clear markers indicating the nature of each portion of text. That is the essence of a markup language: embedded instructions that a computer can follow in order to make content readable and usable by humans.

In Figure 4-1, the "before" image shows a sample of text as it would appear in a web browser without any XHTML structure. It's nothing but a large mass of words, all mashed together and difficult to read (even if you're fluent in pseudo-Latin filler text). You can break down that blob of words into discernable, readable portions by adding a few bits of structural markup. The "after" image is much more readable (the words are still nonsense, but we're making a point).

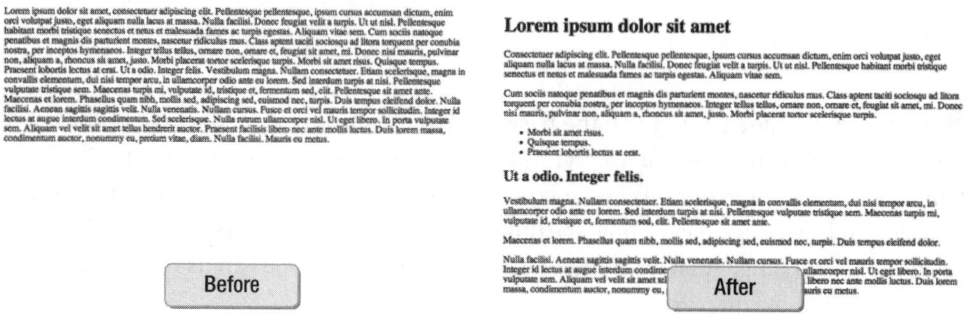

Figure 4-1. *Some example text, with and without structure*

Providing a solid structure for your content will make it stronger and more flexible. By using XHTML to insert encoded statements to the browser that tell it "this is a heading" and "this is a paragraph" and "this word is emphasized," you'll make your content work better, for both machines and people alike. And by organizing your content logically with the proper elements, you'll also be building in the framework you'll need to style your pages with CSS.

A beautiful <body>

Before you can add content to your document, you'll need a place to put it. The head element contains information about the document itself, none of which (apart from the title) is displayed on-screen. All of your content resides in the body element.

body

The body element comes after the head element and must be closed before the closing </html> tag, as seen in Listing 4-1—the head and body are both contained by the html element. Any content appearing outside the body element will make the document invalid, and that content might not be displayed.

Listing 4-1. *An XHTML Document with an Empty body Element*

```
<!DOCTYPE html PUBLIC "-//W3C//DTD XHTML 1.0 Strict//EN"
  "http://www.w3.org/TR/xhtml1/DTD/xhtml1-strict.dtd">
<html xmlns="http://www.w3.org/1999/xhtml">
  <head>
    <title>Spaghetti and Cruft : Geek Pizzeria</title>
  </head>
  <body>
    ...
  </body>
</html>
```

The body element is block-level and can only contain block-level children; any text or inline elements must be nested in another block-level parent, not directly within the body element. If you move to a new house, you'll put all your small items into boxes before loading them onto the truck; otherwise, they would rattle around loose and probably arrive broken. Think of the body element like that big moving truck, and all your smaller bits of content need to be packed safely in their own containers. In the next section, you'll learn some of the major structural elements you'll need to properly package your content.

Required Attributes

No attributes are required for the body element.

Optional Attributes

The body element doesn't offer any optional attributes.

Standard Attributes

- class

- dir

- id

- lang

- style

- title

- xml:lang

■**Caution** Older versions of HTML allowed several presentational attributes to appear in the `<body>` tag: `background` to define a background image, `bgcolor` to apply a background color, `text` to set the main text color, `link` to set the color of unvisited links, `vlink` to color visited links, and `alink` to color active links. These attributes have all been deprecated and are not valid in XHTML 1.0 Strict. Their effects are now achieved with CSS.

You may also encounter the attributes `topmargin`, `leftmargin`, `marginheight`, and `marginwidth` in the `<body>` tag of some older web documents. These were proprietary attributes introduced by browser manufacturers and have never been part of any official standardized specification. They too are presentational, nonstandard, and invalid, and you shouldn't use them.

Meaningful Portions

Semantics is the study of meaning in language. Web designers have borrowed the term from the field of linguistics and use it to refer to the *inherent meaning* of an XHTML element or attribute, as opposed to the way it would be *visually rendered* by a web browser. As you work to keep your content and presentation separate, you should always be considerate of an element's semantic value, choosing the most meaningful element to fit the meaning of the content inside it.

p

As you probably learned in grammar school, a paragraph is one or more sentences expressing a single thought or idea, or about one aspect of a topic. It's the standard unit of written prose. You can tell a web browser how to separate groups of sentences into easily digestible portions by marking each paragraph's boundaries with a p element. Listing 4-2 shows two paragraphs in XHTML, where the beginning of one paragraph is indicated by an opening `<p>` tag, and a closing `</p>` tag marks its end. Blank lines between elements aren't necessary, but they can help make your markup more readable as you work. Paragraphs are block-level elements that are only allowed to contain text and inline elements.

Listing 4-2. *Two Example Paragraphs*

```
<p>Spaghetti and Cruft opened our doors in 1999, bringing great pizza and
pasta to the heart of the city's trendy Riverbend district. We handcraft
our pizzas on the spot using only the best ingredients, and then we bake them to
perfection in our rustic wood-fired brick oven. We sell pizza by the slice
or by the pie and even offer catering for any occasion all around the
neighborhood.</p>
```

```
<p>Our broad menu of pasta dishes puts a modern twist on Old Italia, served
in heaping bowlfuls sure to satisfy any appetite (though we bet you'll want
seconds anyway). But it's not all noodles and crust at Spaghetti and Cruft;
we also have fresh veggie sides, an all-you-can-eat salad bar, and the best
cannolis in town!</p>
```

Figure 4-2 shows what these paragraphs will look like in a browser. Because p is a block-level element, each paragraph begins on a new line and is followed by a blank line of white space. In the past, many web designers would inject empty paragraphs (<p></p>) into their documents to add more vertical space on the page. This is presentational markup and should be avoided—an empty paragraph has no meaning. If you need to add vertical white space to your page layout, use CSS.

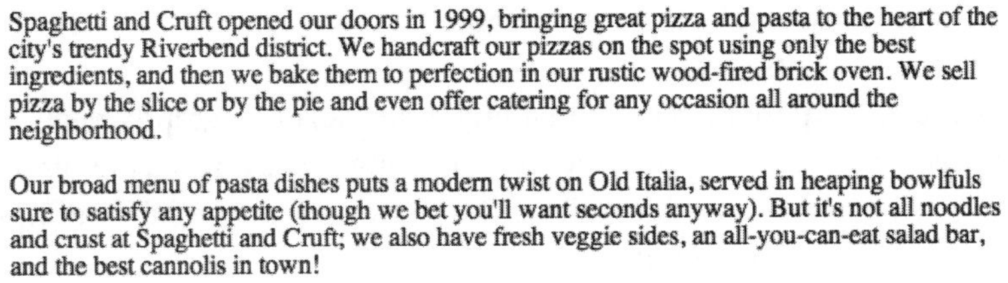

Spaghetti and Cruft opened our doors in 1999, bringing great pizza and pasta to the heart of the city's trendy Riverbend district. We handcraft our pizzas on the spot using only the best ingredients, and then we bake them to perfection in our rustic wood-fired brick oven. We sell pizza by the slice or by the pie and even offer catering for any occasion all around the neighborhood.

Our broad menu of pasta dishes puts a modern twist on Old Italia, served in heaping bowlfuls sure to satisfy any appetite (though we bet you'll want seconds anyway). But it's not all noodles and crust at Spaghetti and Cruft; we also have fresh veggie sides, an all-you-can-eat salad bar, and the best cannolis in town!

Figure 4-2. *The browser renders the two paragraphs as separate blocks.*

Required Attributes

The p element doesn't have any required attributes.

Optional Attributes

There are no optional attributes for the p element.

Standard Attributes

- class

- dir

- id

- lang

- style

- title

- xml:lang

■**Caution** Previous versions of HTML included an `align` attribute for paragraphs (and most other block-level elements), allowing the designer to specify whether the contents should be aligned to the left or right, centered, or justified (meaning the column is evenly aligned on both the left and right sides). The `align` attribute is deprecated and should not be used in XHTML 1.0 Strict; its modern CSS equivalent is the `text-align` property.

Headings: h1, h2, h3, h4, h5, and h6

Headings act as titles to introduce a new section of content. XHTML offers a range of six heading elements to indicate the relative importance of a heading or its rank in the document's hierarchy (and, by association, the importance or rank of the content that follows the heading). You can organize your document as a simple outline, separated into specific topics or areas of interest, sorted from the top down in order of importance, and with each section containing subsections of its own.

Listing 4-3 shows some content marked up as headings and short paragraphs; each heading introduces the content that follows it. Different heading levels imply a hierarchy of importance; the top-level heading introduces the entire section, while the subheadings beneath it introduce lesser sections within that.

Listing 4-3. *A Mixture of Headings and Paragraphs*

```
<h1>Praise for Spaghetti and Cruft: Geek Pizzeria</h1>
<p>See what people are saying about us!</p>

<h2>Customer feedback</h2>
<p>Our loyal customers love us (and we love them).</p>

<h2>Reviews</h2>
<p>Even those stuffy restaurant critics can't resist our charms.</p>
```

The h1 element designates the top-level heading—the most important one on the page. Since there can logically be only one "most important" heading, it's customary for only one h1 to occur within a single document, often used for the name of the website or the title of the page you're viewing. This isn't a requirement of XHTML, but rather just a good semantic rule of thumb. You should also try to keep your headings in the proper sequence—an h5 shouldn't come before an h2 unless it makes good sense to change their natural order, which it rarely does.

Figure 4-3 shows the previous markup as rendered by a browser. Most graphical web browsers will automatically display headings in a boldfaced font and at different sizes for each level, h1 being the largest and h6 being the smallest. Because of this default styling, headings have often been abused in the past for their presentational effects. Avoid committing this error, and use headings in a meaningful way. An h2 is "the second-most important heading," not "the second largest font." You can use CSS to alter the default appearance of headings, including their font size.

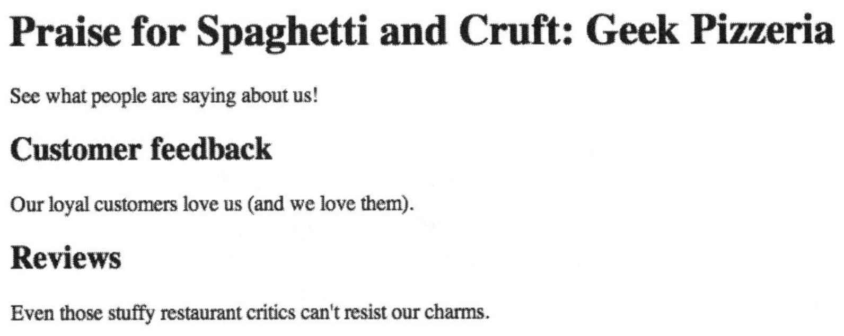

Praise for Spaghetti and Cruft: Geek Pizzeria

See what people are saying about us!

Customer feedback

Our loyal customers love us (and we love them).

Reviews

Even those stuffy restaurant critics can't resist our charms.

Figure 4-3. *Different heading levels appear in different sizes by default.*

Headings are block-level elements and may only contain text or inline elements.

Required Attributes

There are no required attributes for heading elements.

Optional Attributes

Heading elements don't offer any optional attributes.

Standard Attributes

- class

- dir

- id

- lang

- style

- title

- xml:lang

■**Caution** As with paragraphs, previous versions of HTML allowed the presentational `align` attribute in heading elements. This has since been deprecated and isn't valid in XHTML 1.0 Strict. To change the alignment of text in block-level elements, use the CSS `text-align` property.

---

blockquote

The `blockquote` element designates a long quotation, such as a passage from a book or a blurb from a review. It's a block-level element and can only contain block-level children. Almost any other structural markup can reside in a `blockquote` (paragraphs, headings, lists, and even other `blockquote`s), but all of its contents should be part of the original quotation.

If you're quoting an online source, even if the quotation comes from elsewhere on your own website, you can include the URL of the original source in the optional `cite` attribute of the opening `<blockquote>` tag. The `cite` attribute's value should be a URL rather than a name or title. To cite a source by name, use the `cite` element, which you'll learn about later in this chapter.

Listing 4-4 shows a block quotation, including a source URL in the `cite` attribute. The quoted text resides in a nested paragraph, not directly within the `blockquote` element.

Listing 4-4. *Example Markup for a Block Quotation*

```
<h2>Reviews</h2>
<p>Even those stuffy restaurant critics can't resist our charms.</p>

<blockquote cite="http://example.com/food/reviews/SpaghettiCruft/">
  <p>Spaghetti and Cruft offers tasty wood-fired pizzas at affordable
  prices, served in a hip, relaxed atmosphere. Comfortable seats, free
  WiFi and abundant power outlets make this a popular spot for the
  neighborhood technophiles to linger with their laptops.</p>
</blockquote>
```

Most graphical browsers will display the `blockquote` element as an indented block of text, as you can see in Figure 4-4. In the past, some web designers misused this element to create wider margins around their text, whether it was a quotation or not. Once again, that's presentational markup that confuses the content's meaning. You should only use a `blockquote` for actual quotations, and you should use CSS to control margins.

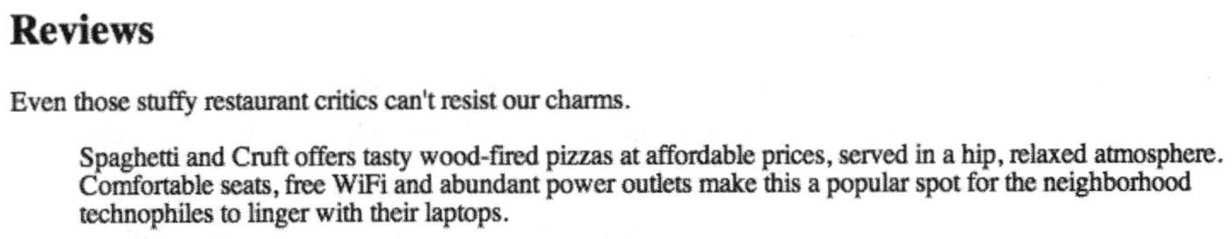

Reviews

Even those stuffy restaurant critics can't resist our charms.

> Spaghetti and Cruft offers tasty wood-fired pizzas at affordable prices, served in a hip, relaxed atmosphere. Comfortable seats, free WiFi and abundant power outlets make this a popular spot for the neighborhood technophiles to linger with their laptops.

Figure 4-4. *The default rendering of a block quotation as an indented portion of text*

Required Attributes

The blockquote element doesn't have any required attributes.

Optional Attributes

- cite: The URL of the quotation's original source

Standard Attributes

- class

- dir

- id

- lang

- style

- title

- xml:lang

address

Contrary to this element's name, address isn't intended for just any postal address; its purpose is to provide contact information for the person or organization responsible for the particular document you're reading. The address element harkens back to the early days when primarily academics and programmers used the web. A researcher at a university might publish her findings on the Internet and include her name, position, and e-mail address to stake her claim. In that sense, think of the address element more like a byline or attribution than a physical location on a street in a town somewhere (though it can include a physical address as well). The address element says, "This is who is responsible for this document, and here's how to reach them."

The address element is block-level and can only contain text or inline elements. With nested block-level elements forbidden, you're somewhat limited in the elements you can use to format the contents of an address. Listing 4-5 shows some contact information wrapped in an address element, with line breaks inserted to provide some formatting (you'll learn more about the br element later in this chapter).

Listing 4-5. *Contact Info Marked Up with the address Element*

```
<address>
Andy Clarke<br />
MODern Web Designer<br />
1000 Stiff Upper Lip Street, Manchester, UK<br />
http://stuffandnonsense.co.uk
</address>
```

This example would be semantically appropriate in a document authored by Andy Clarke, but if you simply wish to name-drop Andy in a document that *you're* responsible for, some other element would be called for (probably a paragraph).

The contents of an address element are usually displayed in an italicized font, as you can see in Figure 4-5. Of course, if you don't like the looks of it, you can always change its presentation with CSS.

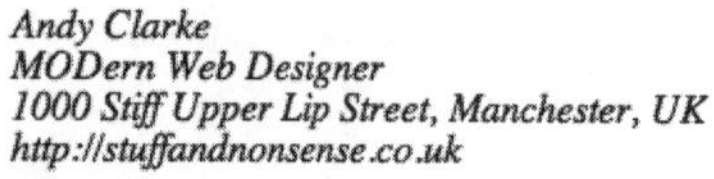

Andy Clarke
MODern Web Designer
1000 Stiff Upper Lip Street, Manchester, UK
http://stuffandnonsense.co.uk

Figure 4-5. *Most visual browsers display the address element in italics by default.*

Required Attributes

The address element doesn't have any required attributes.

Optional Attributes

There are no optional attributes for the address element.

Standard Attributes

- class

- dir

- id

- lang

- style

- title

- xml:lang

pre

As you learned in Chapter 2, white space in XHTML is "collapsed" when the document is rendered by a browser; multiple spaces are reduced to a single space, and carriage returns are ignored. However, you can use the pre element to define a block of preformatted text in which white space and line breaks should be preserved exactly as they appear in the markup. This element is especially useful for displaying computer code or poetry where line breaks and indention are important, such as in the haiku in Listing 4-6.

Listing 4-6. *Poetry Contained by a pre Element to Preserve Its Formatting*

```
<pre>
Dough spins in the air
  Tomato, cheese, in oven
    Pizza nirvana
</pre>
```

The pre element is block-level and can only contain inline elements. Its contents are typically rendered in a monospace typeface by default, as shown by Figure 4-6.

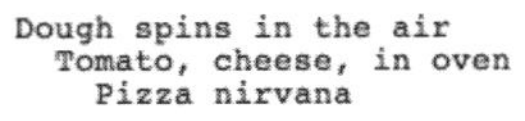

```
Dough spins in the air
   Tomato, cheese, in oven
      Pizza nirvana
```

Figure 4-6. *The spaces and returns remain intact when the content is rendered.*

Required Attributes

There are no required attributes for the pre element.

Optional Attributes

The pre element doesn't offer any optional attributes.

Standard Attributes

- class

- dir

- id

- lang

- style

- title

- xml:lang

■Caution In previous versions of HTML, the width attribute allowed web designers to indicate the width of a pre element, specified in the number of characters allowed on one line. This attribute has been deprecated and should not be used in XHTML 1.0 Strict.

Lists

A list is simply a collection of two or more related items. A list consisting of a single item is perfectly valid and may even be semantically correct in same cases, but normally a list groups several items together. There are three types of lists in XHTML: unordered lists, ordered lists, and definition lists.

ul

An unordered list is designated by the ul element and is used for lists wherein the sequence of the items isn't especially significant, such as a list of ingredients—the order in which you fetch them from the pantry doesn't matter so long as you get everything on the list. Each list item is in turn defined by its own li element, all contained by the surrounding <ul> and </ul> tags. The ul element is block-level and only li elements are allowed as its children; no text or elements can appear in an unordered list unless an li contains them.

Listing 4-7 shows the ingredients for making pizza dough in an unordered list, with each item living in its own li element (more on that one in a moment).

Listing 4-7. *An Unordered Listing of Ingredients*

```
<ul>
  <li>1 cup warm water</li>
  <li>1 packet active dry yeast</li>
  <li>2 1/2 to 3 cups all-purpose flour</li>
  <li>2 tablespoons olive oil</li>
  <li>1/2 teaspoon salt</li>
</ul>
```

By default, unordered lists are displayed in graphical browsers slightly indented and with a bullet marking each list item, as seen in Figure 4-7. Later in this chapter, you'll see how you can change the default bullet using CSS, replacing it with a different character or even an image.

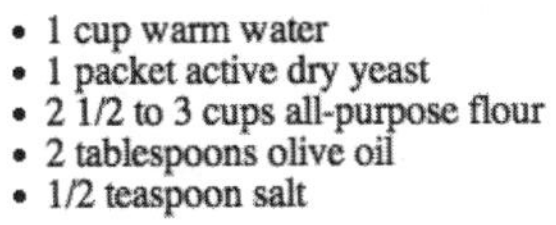

- 1 cup warm water
- 1 packet active dry yeast
- 2 1/2 to 3 cups all-purpose flour
- 2 tablespoons olive oil
- 1/2 teaspoon salt

Figure 4-7. *The bullets are rendered automatically when this list of ingredients is displayed in a web browser.*

Required Attributes

The ul element doesn't have any required attributes.

Optional Attributes

The ul element doesn't feature any optional attributes.

Standard Attributes

- class

- dir

- id

- lang

- style

- title

- xml:lang

ol

The ol element defines an ordered list, one in which the items are meant to be read or followed in a specific sequence, such as the steps in a recipe. Listing 4-8 shows an example. Note that the items are not numbered in the XHTML markup.

Listing 4-8. *A Deliberate Sequence of Steps, Marked Up As an Ordered List*

```
<ol>
  <li>Combine the water, yeast, oil, salt and two thirds of the
  flour in a large bowl and mix thoroughly.</li>
  <li>Gradually add the remaining flour until the dough holds
  its shape, being careful not to let it become too dry. You may
  not need all the flour.</li>
  <li>Place the dough on a lightly floured surface and knead
  for five minutes until it becomes smooth and elastic.</li>
  <li>Transfer the dough to a lightly oiled bowl, cover with
  plastic wrap and let it rise until it has doubled in size.</li>
  <li>When the dough has risen, place it on a floured surface,
  divide it into two equal portions rolled into balls. Allow the
  dough to rest for 15 minutes before forming your pizzas.</li>
</ol>
```

As you can see in Figure 4-8, each item in an ordered list is displayed with a number beside it in a visual browser, with those numbers created automatically.

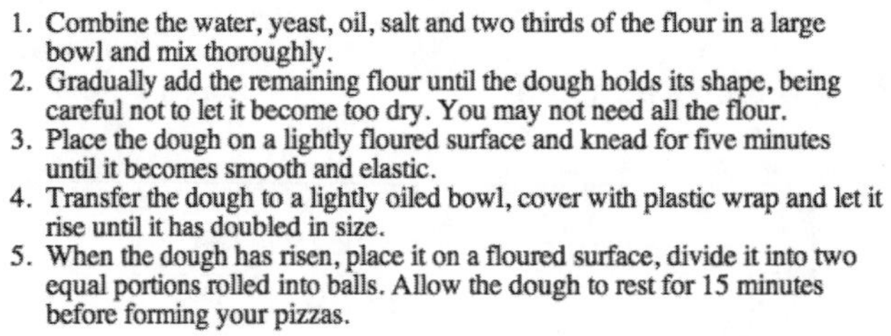

1. Combine the water, yeast, oil, salt and two thirds of the flour in a large bowl and mix thoroughly.
2. Gradually add the remaining flour until the dough holds its shape, being careful not to let it become too dry. You may not need all the flour.
3. Place the dough on a lightly floured surface and knead for five minutes until it becomes smooth and elastic.
4. Transfer the dough to a lightly oiled bowl, cover with plastic wrap and let it rise until it has doubled in size.
5. When the dough has risen, place it on a floured surface, divide it into two equal portions rolled into balls. Allow the dough to rest for 15 minutes before forming your pizzas.

Figure 4-8. *The web browser numbers the list items automatically.*

Like unordered lists, the ol element is block-level and can only have lis as children.

Required Attributes

No attributes are required for the ol element.

Optional Attributes

There are no optional attributes for the ol element.

Standard Attributes

- class

- dir

- id

- lang

- style

- title

- xml:lang

li

In both ordered and unordered lists, individual items are defined by the block-level li element. A list item can contain text or other elements—even more lists. Listing 4-9 shows an elaborate list, including more lists nested inside it. The containing list has only a single item in this example, but you could include several different specialty pizzas within that list, each following the same pattern in its own li.

Listing 4-9. *Example of a Complex, Unordered List*

```
<h2>Specialty Pizzas</h2>
<ul>
  <li>
    <h3>Barbecue Chicken Pizza</h3>
    <p>This hearty American departure from Italian
    tradition is one of our most popular pizzas.</p>
    <ul>
      <li>Spicy barbecue sauce.</li>
      <li>Chunks of mesquite grilled chicken.</li>
      <li>Blend of three cheeses:
```

```
        <ul>
        <li>Mozzarella</li>
        <li>Monterey Jack</li>
        <li>Smoked Gouda</li>
        </ul>
      </li>
      <li>Thin-sliced red onion.</li>
      <li>Roasted red peppers.</li>
    </ul>
  </li>
</ul>
```

When one list is nested within another, the inner list will, by default, be styled differently according to its level of nesting. Figure 4-9 shows how this list is rendered, and you can see that each nested list is indented a bit further and displayed with a different style of marker.

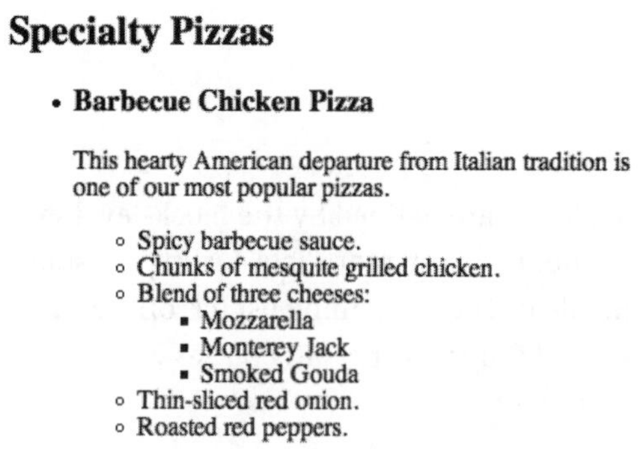

Specialty Pizzas

- **Barbecue Chicken Pizza**

  This hearty American departure from Italian tradition is one of our most popular pizzas.

  - Spicy barbecue sauce.
  - Chunks of mesquite grilled chicken.
  - Blend of three cheeses:
    - Mozzarella
    - Monterey Jack
    - Smoked Gouda
  - Thin-sliced red onion.
  - Roasted red peppers.

Figure 4-9. *The list as it appears in a browser with default styling*

Required Attributes

There are no required attributes for the li element.

Optional Attributes

The li element doesn't have any optional attributes.

Standard Attributes

- class

- dir

- id

- lang

- style

- title

- xml:lang

Definition Lists

A definition list is not merely a collection of items, but rather a collection of items and descriptions of each. Unlike ordered and unordered lists, a definition list doesn't contain list item (li) elements. Rather, items in a definition list may consist of definition terms (dt) and definition descriptions (dd). A single term may have several associated descriptions, or a single description may apply to several terms grouped before it. The list is segmented wherever a dt immediately follows a dd, thus marking the beginning of a new sequence of terms and descriptions.

There is an implied semantic connection between a term and its descriptions. The dt and dd elements are bound to each other, paired together to form the structure of the list. Because of this semantic symbiosis, definition lists are sometimes used to mark up content that isn't technically a list of terms and definitions. A series of questions and their answers, a set of images and their captions, or a sequence of dialog showing the names of the speakers and their speeches are all potential uses of a definition list.

dl

The dl element creates a definition list. It's a block-level element, which in turn must contain at least one term (dt) or at least one description (dd)—only the dt and dd elements are allowed as children of a dl.

Required Attributes

The dl element doesn't have any required attributes.

Optional Attributes

The dl element doesn't have any optional attributes.

Standard Attributes

- `class`

- `dir`

- `id`

- `lang`

- `style`

- `title`

- `xml:lang`

dt

The `dt` element, which is block-level and can only contain text and/or inline elements, designates a term or item being described. A definition term is related to every description that follows it until a new `dt` element appears to begin a new sequence (or until the list ends with a closing `</dl>` tag).

Required Attributes

There are no required attributes for the `dt` element.

Optional Attributes

The `dt` element doesn't have any optional attributes.

Standard Attributes

- `class`

- `dir`

- `id`

- `lang`

- `style`

- `title`

- `xml:lang`

dd

The dd element contains a description of the dt elements that immediately precede it. In the case of multiple descriptions for a single term, each one should be wrapped in its own dd element. The element is block-level and may contain text, inline elements, and other block-level elements. If your description spans several paragraphs, mark them up as paragraphs (p) in a single dd rather than as separate dds—the entire contents of one dd element should comprise one description.

Required Attributes

The dd element doesn't require any attributes.

Optional Attributes

The dd element doesn't offer any optional attributes.

Standard Attributes

- class

- dir

- id

- lang

- style

- title

- xml:lang

Listing 4-10 shows the markup for a brief definition list. In the example, the first term's description consists of two paragraphs, while the second term has two distinct descriptions.

Listing 4-10. *A Definition List Featuring Two Terms*

```
<dl>
  <dt>Pizza</dt>
  <dd>
    <p>A flat, open-faced baked pie of Italian origin, consisting of
    a layer of bread dough covered with tomato sauce, cheese and a
    wide variety of optional toppings.</p>
    <p>Also called <em>pizza pie</em>.</p>
  </dd>
```

```
<dt>Pasta</dt>
<dd>Unleavened dough that is molded into any of a variety of shapes
and boiled.</dd>
<dd>A prepared dish containing pasta as its main ingredient.</dd>
</dl>
```

Most browsers will display dd elements slightly indented from their corresponding dt. When a dd contains other structural markup (such as paragraphs), the default margins of that nested element will apply. As you can see in Figure 4-10, the paragraphs in the first term's description have white space above and below them, while the second term's two descriptions have no top and bottom margins at all. You can modify all of this, of course, with CSS.

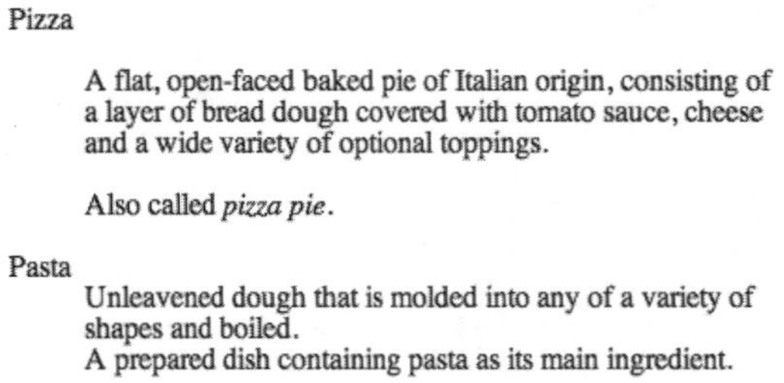

Pizza

> A flat, open-faced baked pie of Italian origin, consisting of a layer of bread dough covered with tomato sauce, cheese and a wide variety of optional toppings.
>
> Also called *pizza pie*.

Pasta

> Unleavened dough that is molded into any of a variety of shapes and boiled.
> A prepared dish containing pasta as its main ingredient.

Figure 4-10. *The definition list rendered with default browser styling*

Phrase Elements

We've covered most of the major structural elements you'll use to organize your content into meaningful, readable portions. Headings, paragraphs, and lists are the basic building blocks of structured text. In the next few sections, we'll be moving inside the blocks to pick out smaller morsels of content for special attention.

These inline elements are called *phrase elements* because they're intended to wrap around a short string of a few words, or even a single word, to give it added meaning and formatting that sets it apart from the other words that surround it. As you learned in Chapter 2, inline elements are only allowed to contain text and other inline elements.

em

The em element adds emphasis to a word or phrase. Its contents are displayed in an italicized font in most visual web browsers, but other devices may apply emphasis differently. For example, screen-reading software used by the visually impaired may read the contents of an em aloud with a different vocal inflection.

Required Attributes

There are no required attributes for the em element.

Optional Attributes

The em element doesn't have any optional attributes.

Standard Attributes

- class

- dir

- id

- lang

- style

- title

- xml:lang

strong

The strong element adds strong emphasis to text for those words or phrases that demand more importance than an em element can provide. Text in a strong element is displayed in a boldfaced font in graphical browsers, but may be emphasized differently by other devices.

Required Attributes

The strong element has no required attributes.

Optional Attributes

The strong element has no optional attributes.

Standard Attributes

- class

- dir

- id

- lang

- style

- title

- xml:lang

Listing 4-11 shows a passage of text with some emphasized phrases. For yet another level of emphasis, you can combine the strong and em elements (properly nested, of course), effectively declaring that the text within has extra-strong emphasis, which most browsers will display in a font that is both italicized and boldfaced.

Listing 4-11. *A Paragraph Containing Some Emphasized Phrases*

```
<p>A traditional pizza is round. Not only <em>should</em> a pizza be round,
but a proper pizza <strong>must</strong> be round. To reiterate,
<strong><em>real pizzas are round</em></strong>. Except when they're not.</p>
```

Figure 4-11 shows the rendered result of Listing 4-11.

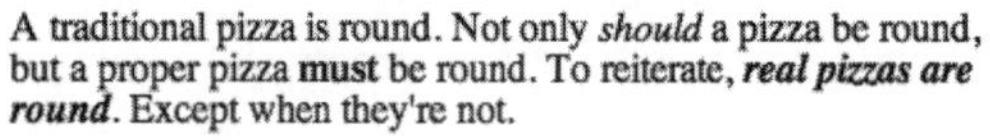

A traditional pizza is round. Not only *should* a pizza be round,
but a proper pizza **must** be round. To reiterate, ***real pizzas are
round***. Except when they're not.

Figure 4-11. *The contents of em are italicized, the contents of strong are boldfaced, and the combined elements show a combined style.*

cite

The cite element designates a citation or reference to some resource: a person; the title of a book, poem, song, or movie; or the name of a magazine, newspaper, or website. It's especially useful when attributing quotations, as in Listing 4-12, which shows two applications of the cite element: one to highlight the name of a source, and one to give attribution of a block quotation.

Listing 4-12. *Two Different Applications of the cite Element*

```
<p>Restaurant critic <cite>Norm Deplume</cite> had this to say
about our eatery:</p>
```

```
<blockquote cite="http://example.com/food/reviews/SpaghettiCruft/">
  <p>Spaghetti and Cruft offers tasty wood-fired pizzas at affordable
  prices, served in a hip, relaxed atmosphere. Comfortable seats, free
  WiFi and abundant power outlets make this a popular spot for the
  neighborhood technophiles to linger with their laptops.</p>
  <p><cite>Gotham Examiner, November 22, 2006</cite></p>
</blockquote>
```

Graphical browsers usually render the contents of a cite element in an italicized font, as shown in Figure 4-12, but—wait for it—you can change that with CSS.

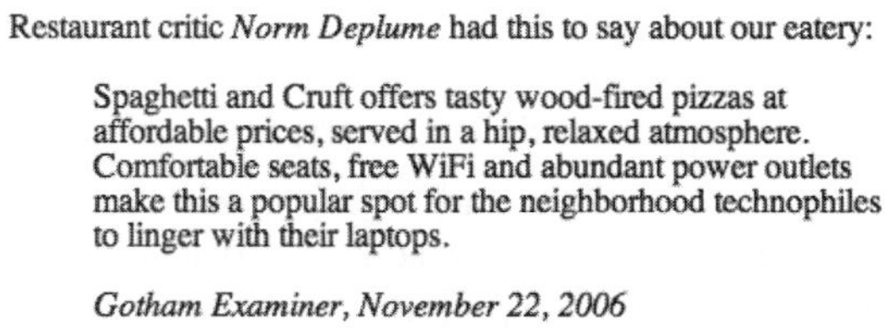

Restaurant critic *Norm Deplume* had this to say about our eatery:

> Spaghetti and Cruft offers tasty wood-fired pizzas at affordable prices, served in a hip, relaxed atmosphere. Comfortable seats, free WiFi and abundant power outlets make this a popular spot for the neighborhood technophiles to linger with their laptops.
>
> *Gotham Examiner, November 22, 2006*

Figure 4-12. *The cite element is italicized by default in most graphical browsers.*

Required Attributes

No attributes are required for the cite element.

Optional Attributes

There are no optional attributes for the cite element.

Standard Attributes

- class

- dir

- id

- lang

- style

- title

- xml:lang

q

The q element is intended to mark up short, inline quotations (as opposed to blockquote, which you should use for longer quotations of more than a sentence or two). Like the blockquote element, a q element may carry a cite attribute to include the URL of the quotation source, as you see in Listing 4-13.

Listing 4-13. *The q Element, Complete with a URL in a cite Attribute*

```
<p>Norm Deplume, food critic for <cite>The Gotham Examiner</cite>, recently
commended our geek-friendly attitude, even saying that we're
<q cite="http://example.com/food/reviews/SpaghettiCruft/">a popular
spot for the neighborhood technophiles to linger with their laptops.</q></p>
```

According to the W3C specifications, a web browser should automatically render the opening and closing quotation marks at the beginning and ending of a q element. However, not all currently popular browsers support the element correctly, so it's unfortunately impractical to use it. If you do make use of the q element, you shouldn't include quotation marks of your own—you'll end up with duplicate punctuation in the browsers that render the element correctly.

Figure 4-13 shows the q element as rendered by two popular browsers on two common operating systems. Mozilla Firefox 2.0 for Mac OS X generates quotation marks automatically, but Internet Explorer 6 for Windows XP doesn't.

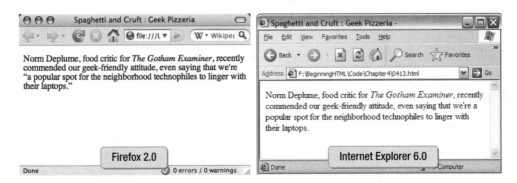

Figure 4-13. *A view of the same markup from two different browsers: Firefox draws the punctuation, but Internet Explorer doesn't.*

Required Attributes

The q element doesn't have any required attributes.

Optional Attributes

- `cite`: The URL of the quotation's original source

Standard Attributes

- `class`

- `dir`

- `id`

- `lang`

- `style`

- `title`

- `xml:lang`

dfn

The `dfn` element is used to signify the defining instance of a term, especially one that may reoccur throughout the rest of the page. If the term is defined in context, the `dfn` element alone is enough to communicate that a new word is being introduced. If the term's meaning isn't made clear by the adjacent text, you should include a brief definition in a `title` attribute. A `dfn` is usually displayed (by graphical browsers) in an italicized font to set it off from the surrounding text.

Required Attributes

There are no required attributes for the `dfn` element.

Optional Attributes

The `dfn` element doesn't have any optional attributes.

Standard Attributes

- `class`

- `dir`

- `id`

- lang

- style

- title

- xml:lang

Listing 4-14 shows an example of a dfn element that includes a short definition in its title attribute.

Listing 4-14. *A dfn Element with a Definition in Its title Attribute*

```
<p>Spaghetti and Cruft offers free wireless broadband internet access so
laptop-toting patrons can check their e-mail, publish updates to their
<dfn title="short for weblog, a kind of online journal">blogs</dfn>, or
even do some honest work.</p>
```

Abbreviations: abbr and acronym

An abbreviation is a shortened form of a lengthy term. For example, *etc.* is an abbreviation of *et cetera* (the Latin phrase meaning "and so forth"), and *Inc.* is an abbreviation of *Incorporated*. Abbreviations can also be formed from the initial letters of a multiword phrase such as *ATM* for *Automatic Teller Machine* or *CSS* for *Cascading Style Sheets*, or from initials extracted from the syllables of a long word, such as *DNA* for *deoxyribonucleic acid* (these are also called *initialisms*). You can indicate an abbreviation in XHTML with the abbr element.

An acronym is a specific type of abbreviation, being a pronounceable word formed from the first letters of a multiword phrase—*laser* from *light amplification by simulated emission of radiation* and *PIN* from *personal identification number*—or the first portion of each word, as in *defcon* from *defense condition* and *sysadmin* from *system administrator*. You can mark up acronyms with the acronym element.

To know the difference between abbreviations and acronyms, just remember that an acronym is a word that can be spoken; if you can't pronounce it, it's probably not an acronym. Because acronyms are themselves abbreviations, there is considerable semantic overlap between these two elements. It's important to distinguish the two on the web because screen-reading software can be designed to read the initials in an abbr element, but attempt to pronounce an acronym. Even so, many unpronounceable abbreviations (such as *ATM* or *CSS*) are still thought of as acronyms. If in doubt, use abbr, the more general of the two elements.

The abbr and acronym elements may be used similarly to dfn to point out the defining instance of a term; thereafter, the term can be used normally. Of course, not every abbreviation needs to be specifically called out; common ones such as *etc.* and *Inc.* probably don't require explanation. Use your best judgment based on your understanding of the content and your audience.

Both abbr and acronym should include the expanded form of the term in a title attribute, as seen in Listing 4-15.

Listing 4-15. *A Bit of Content Featuring an Abbreviation and an Acronym*

```
<p>We accept all major credit cards, as well as
<abbr title="Automatic Teller Machine">ATM</abbr> cards
(you'll need to provide your
<acronym title="Personal Identification Number">PIN</acronym>).</p>
```

Most modern browsers display these elements with a dotted underline, as Firefox does in Figure 4-14. Many browsers display the value of the title attribute in a "tooltip" when the user's pointer lingers over the element, so even sighted readers can read the extended form of an abbreviation.

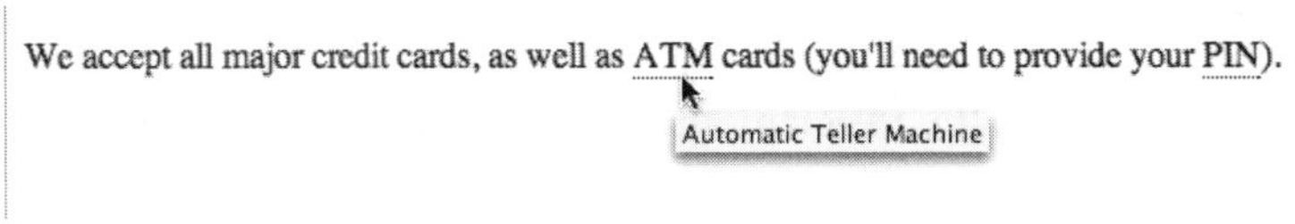

We accept all major credit cards, as well as ATM cards (you'll need to provide your PIN).

Automatic Teller Machine

Figure 4-14. *The content from Listing 4-15 as it appears in Firefox 2.0 for Mac OS X*

Required Attributes

The abbr and acronym elements don't have any required attributes.

Optional Attributes

There are no optional attributes for the abbr and acronym elements.

Standard Attributes

- class

- dir

- id

- lang

- style

- title

- xml:lang

Revising Documents: del and ins

There may be times when you need to update a phrase in your document but would like to clearly indicate what was updated. This is the purpose of the inline del and ins elements: del indicates deleted text, and ins indicates inserted text. Both del and ins may optionally include a cite attribute containing the URL of a page with details about the change and a datetime attribute to mark the date and time the revision was made. You can also include a short note about the change in a title attribute, as Listing 4-16 shows.

Listing 4-16. *Revisions Noted with the del and ins Elements*

```
<p>Beginning <del datetime="2007-01-04T06:49:15-08:00">January 5th</del>
<ins datetime="2007-01-04T06:49:35-08:00" title="Delayed one week ➥
while we hire more wait staff">January 12th</ins>, we'll be open until
2AM on Fridays and Saturdays.</p>
```

In most graphical browsers, the contents of del are displayed as a strikethrough (a horizontal line drawn through the text), and the ins element is displayed as underlined text, as shown in Figure 4-15. It's conventional for inserted text to follow the deleted text.

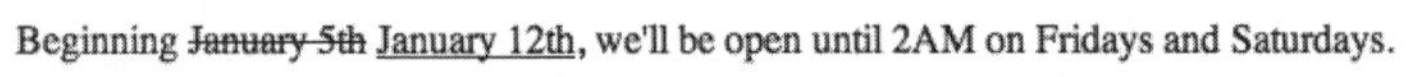

Beginning ~~January 5th~~ <u>January 12th</u>, we'll be open until 2AM on Fridays and Saturdays.

Figure 4-15. *Deleted text is displayed with a strikethrough, and inserted text is underlined.*

Required Attributes

No attributes are required for the del and ins elements.

Optional Attributes

- cite: The URL of a document featuring information on why the change was made

- datetime: The date and/or time the change to the document was made

Standard Attributes

- class

- dir

- id

- lang

- style

- title

- xml:lang

Note There are very specific requirements for formatting the value of the datetime attribute. See the W3C specs for details (http://www.w3.org/TR/NOTE-datetime).

---

bdo

The bdo element (bidirectional override) defines a segment of text where the direction should be reversed from the natural direction of the text surrounding it. The direction is indicated by the required dir attribute, which can have a value of either ltr for "left to right" or rtl for "right to left."

It's a very rare element, only useful in multilingual documents where one passage appears in a language that should be read in the opposite direction from the language used throughout the rest of the document. The language any content is written in should be indicated by the lang and xml:lang attributes, and in most cases, those attributes are sufficient; a browser should understand that different languages are read in different directions and render the text correctly. However, some language combinations cause the direction to be miscalculated, and the bdo element can counteract that error.

Listing 4-17 shows the bdo element used as if the emphasized word were written in a language different from the rest of the document. This example uses English text *for demonstration purposes only*—you would never do this in reality.

Listing 4-17. *The bdo Element in Action*

```
<p>A passage of text containing one <em lang="en" xml:lang="en">➡
<bdo dir="rtl">reversed</bdo></em> word.</p>
```

Figure 4-16 shows that the web browser reverses the text automatically.

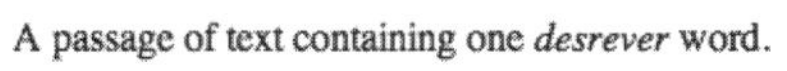

A passage of text containing one *desrever* word.

Figure 4-16. *When a browser renders the text, the contents of the bdo element are automatically written in the direction specified by the dir attribute.*

Required Attributes

- dir: The direction in which the enclosed text should be read: either ltr or rtl

Optional Attributes

The bdo element doesn't have any optional attributes.

Standard Attributes

- class

- id

- lang

- style

- title

- xml:lang

Programming: code, kbd, samp, and var

Several elements available in XHTML are specially intended for marking up computer code, allowing computer scientists, programmers, and web developers to publish and share their work. These are inline elements, and the same standard attributes apply to all.

The code element can be used to designate a portion of code. It's not specific to any programming language, so its contents could be CSS, JavaScript, PHP, Perl, C#, or any computer language that needs to be distinguished from surrounding human-language content. To aid readability, most graphical browsers display the contents of a code element in a monospace typeface—one in which every character is the same width, such as Courier.

The kbd element defines text or commands that the user should enter, while the samp element illustrates sample output of a program or script. Both of these are also typically displayed in a monospace typeface.

The var element is used to designate a programming variable or argument, and is usually displayed as italicized text.

The code, kbd, and samp elements are frequently combined with the pre element to preserve the formatting of their contents, as you can see in Listing 4-18.

Listing 4-18. *A JavaScript Function Marked Up with a code Element*

```
<pre><code>
function helloWorld() {
  var button = document.getElementById("button");
  if (button) {
    button.onclick = function(){
      alert("Hello world!");
    }
  }
}
</code></pre>
```

Figure 4-17 shows the markup as a web browser renders it. The computer code is rendered in a monospace typeface (Courier, in this case).

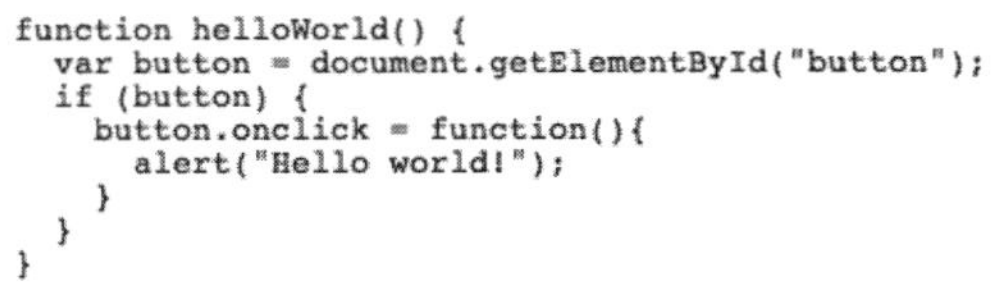

```
function helloWorld() {
  var button = document.getElementById("button");
  if (button) {
    button.onclick = function(){
      alert("Hello world!");
    }
  }
}
```

Figure 4-17. *Nesting the code element within a pre element preserves the formatting just as it appears in the markup.*

Required Attributes

There are no required attributes for these programming-related elements.

Optional Attributes

These programming-related elements don't feature any optional attributes.

Standard Attributes

- class

- dir

- id

- lang

- style

- title

- xml:lang

br

Long lines of text on a web page wrap naturally to a new line when they reach the edge of their container, with the break occurring in the space between two words. However, there may be times when you'll want to force text to wrap to a new line at a specific point. The br element creates a line break for just such occasions. It's an empty element, so it has no text content and consists of a single tag, self-closed with a trailing slash (/>).

You saw some line breaks when you read about the address element earlier in this chapter. Listing 4-19 shows another address, but this time its contents are all on a single line with brs inserted at strategic points.

Listing 4-19. *An address Element with Inserted Line Breaks*

```
<address>
Jon Hicks <br />Illustrator and cheese lover <br />http://hicksdesign.co.uk
</address>
```

Figure 4-18 shows the rendered content. Browsers ignore carriage returns in markup, but will forcefully break a line of text where directed.

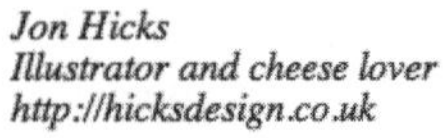

Jon Hicks
Illustrator and cheese lover
http://hicksdesign.co.uk

Figure 4-18. *The markup from Listing 4-19 as it appears in a browser, with the text wrapping at the specified points*

In the past, line breaks were often misused to affect the layout of pages by stacking several in a row to increase white space, to create lists by breaking between items, and to simulate the appearance of paragraphs by forcing line breaks between blocks of text. These are presentational hacks that shouldn't be committed. Use CSS margins, padding, and positioning to add space, and mark up lists and paragraphs as lists and paragraphs. You should use the br element sparingly and only when the text requires it.

Required Attributes

The br element doesn't have any required attributes.

Optional Attributes

There are no optional attributes for the br element.

Standard Attributes

- class

- id

- style

- title

■**Caution** Older versions of HTML featured a clear attribute for the br element, giving visual web browsers instruction on how text and other elements should flow around the line break. This presentational attribute has been deprecated in XHTML 1.0 Strict and replaced by the equivalent clear property in CSS.

---

hr

The block-level hr element creates a horizontal rule, a dividing line between sections of content. It's largely presentational, but the real semantic intent of an hr is to declare that the previous section has ended and a new section is beginning. It's an empty element and must be closed with a trailing slash (/>), as shown in Listing 4-20.

Listing 4-20. *A Horizontal Rule Separates Two Sections of Content*

```
<h2>Customer feedback</h2>
<p>Our loyal customers love us (and we love them).</p>
<hr />
<h2>Reviews</h2>
<p>Even those stuffy restaurant critics can't resist our charms.</p>
```

The hr element is block-level, so it will appear on its own line, but the amount of space above and below it will vary slightly in different browsers. Figure 4-19 shows the hr element rendered in Firefox 2.0 for Mac OS X. You can use CSS to specify the top and bottom margins of an hr for some improved consistency across browsers.

Customer feedback

Our loyal customers love us (and we love them).

Reviews

Even those stuffy restaurant critics can't resist our charms.

Figure 4-19. *A horizontal rule rendered by a web browser*

Required Attributes

The hr element doesn't have any required attributes.

Optional Attributes

No optional attributes exist for the hr element.

Standard Attributes

- class

- dir

- id

- lang

- style

- title

- xml:lang

■**Caution**   Older versions of HTML included a number of presentational attributes for horizontal rules: align to specify the alignment of the rule to the left, right, or center; size to specify the thickness of the rule; width to define its width in pixels; and noshade to override the 3-D shading effect some browsers use when rendering an hr. These are all deprecated and invalid in XHTML 1.0 Strict, and most of their effects can now be achieved with CSS.

Multipurpose Elements

Each of the elements we've covered so far has an inherent meaning and is meant to be used for specific types of content and to serve specific purposes. There are also two generic elements available in XHTML, to use when no other element quite meets your needs: div and span. They are semantically neutral—they don't really hold a specific meaning other than to group and distinguish portions of content—so they are among the most versatile elements in your markup tool kit.

div

The div element creates a logical division in your document, grouping related content and elements together. It's semantically neutral but not entirely meaningless; a div essentially states, "Everything in here belongs together and is separate from everything else."

   The div is extremely handy for organizing content into large blocks that you can then style with CSS or manipulate with JavaScript. For example, you may want your company logo, the name of your website, a set of navigation links, and a site search form to appear at the top of your page, separated from the main content. These components should each be marked up with their own meaningful elements, but they're all related because they form the overall branding and navigation of your site, so they could be collected in a single div element. You can easily apply CSS styles to the contents of that div by giving it a unique identifier via the id attribute. In Listing 4-21, a div identified as "main-content" wraps around and contains all the important content on the page, separating it from other major blocks such as site branding and navigation.

Listing 4-21. *A Block of Content Wrapped in a div Element*

```
<div id="main-content">
  <h1>About Us</h1>

  <p>Spaghetti and Cruft opened our doors in 1999, bringing great pizza and
  pasta to the heart of the city's trendy Riverbend district. We handcraft
  our pizzas on the spot using only the best ingredients, and then we bake them to
  perfection in our rustic wood-fired brick oven. We sell pizza by the slice
  or by the pie and even offer catering for any occasion all around the
  neighborhood.</p>

  <p>Our broad menu of pasta dishes puts a modern twist on Old Italia, served
  in heaping bowlfuls sure to satisfy any appetite (though we bet you'll want
  seconds anyway). But it's not all noodles and crust at Spaghetti and Cruft;
  we also have fresh veggie sides, an all-you-can-eat salad bar, and the best
  cannolis in town!</p>
</div>
```

A div is block-level and can contain text and any other elements, both block-level and inline. A div element's only default styling is to behave like any other block-level element; its contents begin on a new line and occupy the full available width. Because a div alone imparts no deeper semantic meaning to its contents, any text within it should ideally be nested in a more meaningful element.

Because divs are so versatile and act as useful boxes to be styled with CSS, there is a tendency for some web designers to overuse them, crowding their markup with an excessive number of divs for presentational purposes. This practice has come to be known as "divitis," and you should try to avoid it. Use divs wisely to support your content. Remember that the div element is a content-organization device, not a page-layout device.

Required Attributes

The div element doesn't have any required attributes.

Optional Attributes

There are no optional attributes for the div element.

Standard Attributes

- class

- dir

- id

- lang

- style

- title

- xml:lang

■**Caution** Older versions of HTML allowed the align attribute in div elements as well. It is now deprecated and invalid in XHTML 1.0 Strict.

---

span

The div's inline cousin is the span, which you can use to set apart an arbitrary segment of text to act as a "hook" for CSS styling, or to carry additional information about its contents through attributes in the opening `<span>` tag. As with `div`s, you should use `span`s only when a more semantically valuable element doesn't fit the bill.

Required Attributes

No attributes are required for the `span` element.

Optional Attributes

The `span` element has no optional attributes.

Standard Attributes

- `class`

- `dir`

- `id`

- `lang`

- `style`

- `title`

- `xml:lang`

Listing 4-22 shows a `span` nested within a top-level heading to distinguish the "last updated" date from the other heading text. You could then style the contents of this `span` with CSS to appear different from the rest of the heading. An `em` element could serve the same purpose, but would add unwanted emphasis to the date.

Listing 4-22. *A span Nested in a Heading*

```
<h1>Latest News from Spaghetti and Cruft
<span>Last updated on 11/22/2006</span></h1>
```

Embedding External Content

Most of the contents of your page will be part of the XHTML document, but there will often be times when you need to embed external content such as images, Java applets, Flash animations, or QuickTime videos. Such files must exist separately from the document, but you can reference them in your XHTML markup so the browser will display them on your page. You probably won't need to make use of these elements until you're quite comfortable with the other parts of XHTML first. This is a pretty advanced topic for a beginning-level book, so we'll keep it short.

object

The inline object element embeds a file or type of media that exists external to the XHTML document. Many objects occur in data formats that web browsers may not be equipped to handle, requiring a plug-in application to render them. You can use an object to place an image on your page, but it's more common to use the inline img element, covered in Chapter 5.

Required Attributes

There are no required attributes for the object element.

Optional Attributes

- archive: A space-separated list of URLs pointing to archives relating to the object

- classid: URL specifying the location of the object's implementation

- codebase: Specifies the base path of relative URLs

- codetype: The content type of the data expected when downloading the object

- data: The URL where the object's data can be found

- declare: When present, this attribute makes the current object a declaration only

- height: The height of the object in pixels or a percentage of the parent element

- standby: Text that will be displayed as the object is downloaded

- tabindex: Specifies the object's position in the document's tabbing order

- type: The object's content type

- usemap: Identifies a client-side image map to be used

- width: The width of the object in pixels or a percentage of the parent element

Standard Attributes

- class

- dir

- id

- lang

- name

- style

- title

- xml:lang

■**Caution** Previous versions of HTML included some presentational attributes for the object element: align, border, hspace, and vspace. These have all been deprecated in favor of CSS. The width and height attributes are also presentational but are still valid in XHTML.

---

param

A param element can be nested within an object element to define various object parameters and pass along additional information for the object to use. It's an empty element, so you should close it with a trailing slash (/>). A single object can contain several nested param elements.

Required Attributes

- name: The specific parameter being declared

Optional Attributes

- type: The parameter's content type

- value: The value of the parameter specified by the name attribute

- valuetype: The type of the value attribute: either data, ref, or object

Standard Attributes

- id

Listing 4-23 shows an example of the `object` element being used to embed an MPEG video onto a page. Within the `object` are some nested `param` elements declaring the source of the video and a command to the plug-in application to begin playing the video automatically.

Listing 4-23. *An Example of an MPEG Video Embedded with the object Element*

```
<p>Here's a short video of Jeremy making pizza.</p>
<div><object data="makingpizza.mpg" type="video/mpeg" width="368" height="272">
  <param name="src" value="makingpizza.mpg" />
  <param name="autoplay" value="true" />
</object></div>
```

Figure 4-20 shows the result of the markup in Listing 4-23.

Figure 4-20. *The video is displayed directly on the page, assuming the browser has the necessary plug-in.*

Presentational Elements

Throughout this book, we strongly discourage the use of presentational markup—those elements and attributes that only affect the display of content and contribute nothing to its function or meaning. Having said that, a few presentational elements remain valid even in XHTML 1.0 Strict, so we're including them here in the interest of completeness. You should be familiar with these elements, even if only to recognize them in order to avoid them. Standard attributes apply to all of these.

i and b

The i element designates text to be displayed in an italic font, and the b element designates boldfaced text. In nearly every case, when you need to italicize or embolden text, you'll be doing so to add emphasis. To emphasize text, you should use the preferred em and strong elements to deliver that message, to proudly declare that "this text means something important, so pay attention" rather than simply "this text looks different but doesn't have much else to say."

big and small

The text contained in a big element will be slightly larger than the text surrounding it, while the text contained in a small element will be slightly shrunken. These elements have little semantic value otherwise, and their presentational effects are usually best achieved by using a more meaningful element styled with CSS.

tt

The tt element stands for "teletype" and specifies that its text contents should be displayed in a monospace typeface. It's a presentational element that has no real meaning apart from text styling, so it's preferable to achieve the same result with the CSS equivalent, font-family: monospace.

sup and sub

You may occasionally need to include superscript or subscript characters in your text, especially of you're writing about mathematics or chemistry, or in certain languages that require it (French, for example). In these cases, you can use the sup and sub elements, for superscript and subscript, respectively. Superscript text is raised slightly higher than surrounding text, while subscripts are slightly lower. Listing 4-24 shows an example of these elements: sup is used in the Pythagorean Theorem for calculating right triangles, and sub used in the chemical formula for sulfuric acid.

Listing 4-24. *Examples of the sup and sub Elements*

```
<p>a<sup>2</sup> + b<sup>2</sup> = c<sup>2</sup></p>
```

```
<p>H<sub>2</sub>SO<sub>4</sub></p>
```

Figure 4-21 shows how a browser renders these elements. The contents of both elements appear slightly smaller than the ordinary text surrounding them.

$$a^2 + b^2 = c^2$$

$$H_2SO_4$$

Figure 4-21. *The example markup from Listing 4-24 when viewed in a web browser*

While the sup and sub elements are essentially presentational, there may be cases where they communicate more meaning than a span would. A superscript numeral in a mathematical formula can signify an exponent, so wrapping that numeral in a sup element may be semantically preferable to styling it strictly with CSS; the sup element itself carries that stylistic meaning. You should exercise your own judgment and use these elements only when the content warrants it.

THE FONT ELEMENT

In the early days of the World Wide Web, authors and designers lacked a means to alter the typography of their pages—that is, to choose different typefaces, colors, and sizes from whatever default settings were built into the web browsers of the day. The font element was soon introduced to HTML, giving web designers some influence over the presentation of text by simply wrapping it in a bit of additional markup:

```
<font face="Arial" size="3">Typography in action (sort of)</font>
```

However, peppering a document with dozens of presentational font elements added a lot of extra data to the file that did nothing to improve the real quality or utility of the content. And in the event of a redesign, every one of those <font> tags in every document over an entire site had to be located and modified. It wasn't pretty.

The advent of CSS a few years later finally gave designers the means to influence typography without extra markup, and to update the design of even the largest sprawling website by editing a single file. The font element was officially made obsolete. This element is strictly presentational, has no semantic value whatsoever, and has been deprecated for a decade. It should never be used. Ever.

Special Characters

You know by now that an XHTML document is simply plain text. There's nothing special at all about the file format; it's just written in a language that web devices are programmed to understand. Tags within that plain-text document are enclosed by angle brackets (< and >) to distinguish them from ordinary text. When a browser encounters those symbols, it can assume it's dealing with markup and behave accordingly. This raises one issue, of course: what if you need to use angle brackets in your text? If the browser treats them as part of a tag, the entire document falls apart.

XHTML includes a large number of *character references*, which offer a way to encode special characters that aren't part of the regular English alphanumeric set of characters (A–Z, a–z, 0–9, and most common punctuation). A character reference begins with an ampersand (&) and ends with a semicolon (;). Between those symbols there are two different ways to invoke the special character you desire: with a *character entity name* or a *numeric character reference*.

A character entity name is simply a predefined name referring to a particular symbol, like a nickname. The entity for the "less than" symbol (<) is < and its counterpart, the "greater than" symbol (>), is >. You can use these entities to render the symbols in your content and prevent them from being treated as tags.

Your other option, the numeric character reference, refers to a character by its assigned Unicode number, and is specified by an octothorpe (#) after the ampersand. The numeric character reference for the "less than" symbol is < and "greater than" is >. Most of the time, the much-easier-to-remember entity names are sufficient, but to ensure maximum compatibility with devices that parse XML but may not support the full range of entity names, numeric character references are usually recommended for XHTML documents.

Encoding special characters in this manner is known as *escaping*, because these embedded codes are excluded from the parsing of regular XHTML markup. One character you must be careful to escape is the ampersand itself; a non-escaped ampersand in your markup will be treated as the beginning of a character reference. In order to display an ampersand in your content, encode it with the entity & or the numeric reference &. This also goes for ampersands in URLs within an attribute (such as cite, src, or href).

Table 4-1 lists some of the most common (and useful) characters you may need, and you'll find the complete list in Appendix C of this book.

Table 4-1. *Common Character References*

Character	Description	Entity	Numeric Reference
&	ampersand	&amp;	&#38;
<	less than	&lt;	&#60;
>	greater than	&gt;	&#62;
'	left single quotation mark	&lsquo;	&#8216;
'	right single quotation mark	&rsquo;	&#8217;
"	left double quotation mark	&ldquo;	&#8220;
"	right double quotation mark	&rdquo;	&#8221;
	non-breaking space		
–	en dash	&ndash;	&#8211;

Table 4-1. *Common Character References (Continued)*

Character	Description	Entity	Numeric Reference
—	em dash	`&mdash;`	`&#8212;`
©	copyright	`&copy;`	`&#169;`
™	trademark	`&trade;`	`&#8482;`
®	registered trademark	`&reg;`	`&#174;`

■**Caution** A non-breaking space is a single character of white space that a browser will not treat as a break between words when text is wrapped. Many web designers use non-breaking spaces to force extra white space that won't be collapsed to a single space (such as indenting the first line of a paragraph), or as a placeholder in nonempty elements that have no content, to prevent them from being treated as empty (for example, `<p> </p>`). Using non-breaking spaces to force white space where it doesn't ordinarily belong should usually be avoided as presentational markup.

Styling Content with CSS

All of the examples you've seen so far show content rendered in a browser's default style, with its default fonts, colors, and spacing. CSS allows you to modify the presentation of almost every element on the page. Chapter 2 offers a general introduction to the basic concepts of CSS, but it's a broad and powerful language in its own right. Explaining every facet of its depths is well beyond the scope of this book. For more detailed instruction in the ways of CSS, we recommend Simon Collison's *Beginning CSS Web Development* (Berkeley, CA: Apress, 2006) as an excellent follow-up to the book you're reading right now.

But until then, we'll whet your appetite for CSS by showing you just a few ways you can use style sheets to make your text more distinctive and attractive.

Declaring Base Font Styles

A graphical web browser draws text on-screen using font files installed on your visitor's computer. Unfortunately, this limits your options to the few typefaces that are very common in most operating systems—ones with familiar names such as Times New Roman, Helvetica, Arial, Verdana, Georgia, Trebuchet, and Courier. However, you can achieve great things even with such a limited palette. Good typography is about more than just choosing a nice typeface; it's also about how you arrange text on the page.

Font Family

A font family is, well, a family of fonts. Also called a *typeface*, a font family consists of a set of variations on a single type design. The typeface known as Times New Roman, for example, includes normal, italic, bold, and bold italic versions in a few different sizes. Each of these variants is actually a distinct font—"12 point Times New Roman bold" is one font within the Times New Roman font family. These days, the terms "font," "typeface," and "font family" are often used interchangeably.

In CSS, a font family is declared using the font-family property, followed by a comma-separated list of your desired typefaces, in order of preference. When the browser renders the page, it looks on the user's computer system for the first font family listed. If it doesn't find that one, it will continue to the next, and so on. If it doesn't find any, the browser will simply fall back on its default typeface.

Listing 4-25 shows an example of a CSS style rule declaring a sequence of font families for the body element.

Listing 4-25. *A CSS Rule Setting the Font Family for an Element*

```
body {
    font-family: Georgia, "Times New Roman", Times, serif;
}
```

■**Note** The typeface Times New Roman has a name that includes spaces, so its name appears in quotation marks to group those words together. Font families with single-word names don't require quotes.

One very important aspect of CSS is the concept of *inheritance*. The values of some properties in CSS can be passed down from an ancestor element to its descendent elements, including most font-related properties. Since every element on the page is descended from the body element, they will all inherit their font styles from that common ancestor, without the need to redeclare the same styles over and over. You can then override or alter this base font family for different elements elsewhere in the style sheet.

Revisiting the style rule for the body element, let's say you've decided you'd prefer a sans serif typeface such as Trebuchet, whose full name is Trebuchet MS, so it will need to appear in quotes. If the browser doesn't find that one, you'll settle for Helvetica, and if the reader doesn't have Helvetica installed, you'll accept Arial. If it has none of these, then you'd at least like the text to be drawn in some kind of sans serif typeface, so you should end with the generic family name, sans-serif (the phrase "sans serif" must be hyphenated in CSS). You can see the revised rule in Listing 4-26.

Listing 4-26. *The Updated font-family Declaration, Listing a Variety of Sans Serif Typefaces*

```
body {
  font-family: "Trebuchet MS", Helvetica, Arial, sans-serif;
}
```

Figure 4-22 shows a "before and after" view of a sample web page. The left side shows the text in the default browser font (Times, in this case), and the right shows the same text after the new CSS has been applied.

Figure 4-22. *Some example text rendered in the browser's default typeface, and then in Trebuchet through the power of CSS*

GENERIC FONT FAMILIES

There are five generic font family names built into the CSS language. Using any of these in a `font-family` declaration will instruct the browser to render text in whatever default typeface it's configured to use for that generic family.

- *Serif*: A typeface featuring serifs, which are ornamental crosslines at the ends of a character's main strokes. Times New Roman and Georgia are serif typefaces.

- *Sans serif*: Literally, "without serif"; a typeface that lacks those ornamental flourishes. Helvetica and Arial are sans serif typefaces.

- *Monospace*: A typeface in which every character, including punctuation, occupies the same width. Courier and Monaco are monospace typefaces.

- *Cursive*: A fancy typeface modeled after handwriting. Brush Script MT and Apple Chancery are common cursive typefaces.

- *Fantasy*: A decorative or highly stylized typeface. Impact and Copperplate are fairly common fantasy typefaces.

Serif typefaces are best for print, as they remain readable at small sizes. On screen, however, the fine points of the serifs tend to be lost or blocky when rendered in pixels, so sans serif typefaces are generally easier to read on the web (though serifs can be quite lovely at larger sizes). Monospace typefaces are best for displaying computer code, where it's important to accurately make out each and every character. Cursive and fantasy typefaces are more decorative and can be difficult to read, so they should only be used for large headings or avoided entirely; never use a cursive or fantasy typeface for body text.

Font Size

You've changed the font family, but what about the size? Most browsers today render body text at a default size of 16 pixels, which might be a bit too large for your tastes. You can change this with the font-size property, and by applying the declaration to the body element, every other element on the page will inherit the same value. Listing 4-27 shows the style rule with a font-size declaration added, setting the base size to 12 pixels.

Listing 4-27. *A font-size Declaration Has Been Added to the body Style Rule*

```
body {
  font-family: "Trebuchet MS", Helvetica, Arial, sans-serif;
  font-size: 12px;
}
```

Figure 4-23 shows the change in text size.

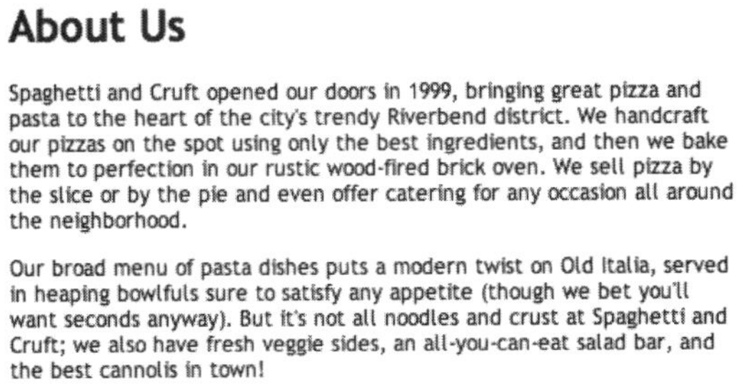

About Us

Spaghetti and Cruft opened our doors in 1999, bringing great pizza and pasta to the heart of the city's trendy Riverbend district. We handcraft our pizzas on the spot using only the best ingredients, and then we bake them to perfection in our rustic wood-fired brick oven. We sell pizza by the slice or by the pie and even offer catering for any occasion all around the neighborhood.

Our broad menu of pasta dishes puts a modern twist on Old Italia, served in heaping bowlfuls sure to satisfy any appetite (though we bet you'll want seconds anyway). But it's not all noodles and crust at Spaghetti and Cruft; we also have fresh veggie sides, an all-you-can-eat salad bar, and the best cannolis in town!

Figure 4-23. *The browser renders the text at the specified size, rather than its default size.*

The heading, an h1, has also become a bit smaller than it was previously. The default font size of headings is relative to the base size for normal text. When the font size is changed for the body element, the headings are resized in proportion to that value. But if you're not happy with the heading at its default size, you can modify it with a new style rule—this time for the h1 element, as you see in Listing 4-28. Thanks to inheritance, there's no need to restate the desired font family—only the font-size property with the new size to use for h1 elements.

Listing 4-28. *Adding a New Rule to Declare the Font Size of the h1 Element*

```
body {
  font-family: "Trebuchet MS", Helvetica, Arial, sans-serif;
  font-size: 12px;
}


h1 {
  font-size: 160%;
}
```

Figure 4-24 shows the result of the new declaration added in Listing 4-28.

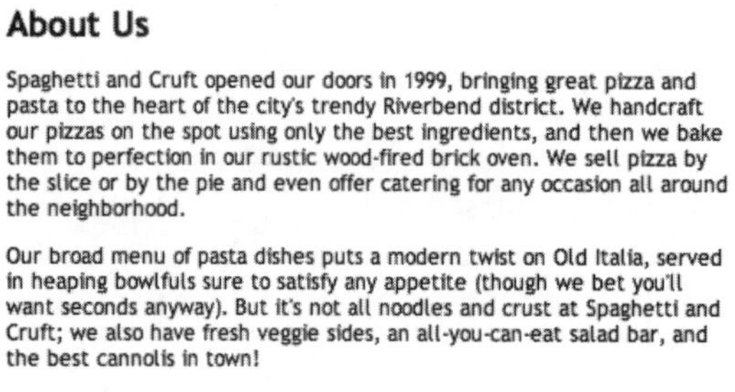

About Us

Spaghetti and Cruft opened our doors in 1999, bringing great pizza and pasta to the heart of the city's trendy Riverbend district. We handcraft our pizzas on the spot using only the best ingredients, and then we bake them to perfection in our rustic wood-fired brick oven. We sell pizza by the slice or by the pie and even offer catering for any occasion all around the neighborhood.

Our broad menu of pasta dishes puts a modern twist on Old Italia, served in heaping bowlfuls sure to satisfy any appetite (though we bet you'll want seconds anyway). But it's not all noodles and crust at Spaghetti and Cruft; we also have fresh veggie sides, an all-you-can-eat salad bar, and the best cannolis in town!

Figure 4-24. *The heading has been resized.*

The new rule specifies the font size as a percentage of whatever size was inherited from the element's ancestor—160% of 12 pixels in this case, which turns out to be around 19 pixels. You can declare font sizes using any of several units of measure: pixels, millimeters, centimeters, inches, points, picas, ems (one em is the height of a capital letter from top to baseline), exes (one ex is the height of a lowercase letter from top to baseline), or a percentage. You can also declare font sizes using a predefined set of *keywords*: xx-small, x-small, small, medium, large, x-large, and xx-large.

A keyword, em, ex, or percentage is a *relative* unit, calculated as a proportion of a size declared elsewhere. The others are all *absolute* units: a pixel is a pixel, and an inch is an inch. Some of these units are less practical than others; you'll probably never need to specify a font size in inches, millimeters, or centimeters, while points and picas are units used in printing that aren't really appropriate for screen display (though are perfect for an alternative printable style sheet). Most of the time, you'll want to use ems, percentages, keywords, and sometimes pixels for font sizes.

Most modern web browsers are able to resize text to suit the user's preference, so any size you specify in your CSS is more like a suggestion than a command. Always be aware that your visitors may see text larger or smaller than you originally intended.

Line Height

Line height is the height of a line of text measured from its baseline to the baseline of the preceding line (the *baseline* is the invisible line the text rests on; letters such as g and q have *descenders* that drop below the baseline). Line height shouldn't be confused with *leading*, which is the typographic term for added space between two lines, measured from the bottom of one line to the top of the following line. CSS doesn't offer a means to specify true leading, but you can achieve the same effect by increasing the line height of the text.

In the example you've been working with, let's say that you think the default line height is a little too close. Spreading those lines further apart will help the eye move through the text a bit more easily, so add a line-height declaration to your CSS rule for the body element, as you see in Listing 4-29. Every other element on the page will also inherit this value.

Listing 4-29. *Adding a line-height Declaration to the body Rule*

```
body {
    font-family: "Trebuchet MS", Helvetica, Arial, sans-serif;
    font-size: 12px;
    line-height: 1.5em;
}
```

You should specify line height with a relative unit—an em, in this case—which is calculated relative to the text size. A value of 1.5em means the line height will be one and a half times an element's font size, whatever that size happens to be. You could achieve the same effect with the value 150%; it's really just a matter of personal preference. You can see the result in Figure 4-25—each line of text has a bit more breathing room.

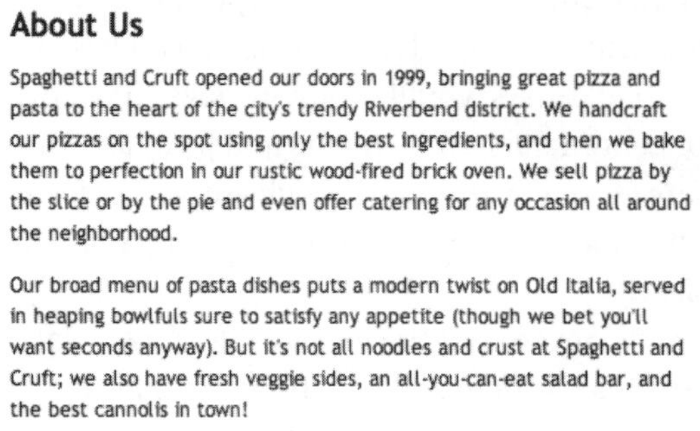

About Us

Spaghetti and Cruft opened our doors in 1999, bringing great pizza and pasta to the heart of the city's trendy Riverbend district. We handcraft our pizzas on the spot using only the best ingredients, and then we bake them to perfection in our rustic wood-fired brick oven. We sell pizza by the slice or by the pie and even offer catering for any occasion all around the neighborhood.

Our broad menu of pasta dishes puts a modern twist on Old Italia, served in heaping bowlfuls sure to satisfy any appetite (though we bet you'll want seconds anyway). But it's not all noodles and crust at Spaghetti and Cruft; we also have fresh veggie sides, an all-you-can-eat salad bar, and the best cannolis in town!

Figure 4-25. *Each line of text is separated by a little more white space by increasing the line height.*

Styling Lists

Lists are useful elements in XHTML. They're the right tool to reach for any time you need to arrange connected portions of content into a sequence of memorable chunks. Unfortunately, lists are rather unattractive by default, but you have the power of CSS on your side to compensate for their aesthetic shortcomings.

Changing Unordered List Markers

A special character marks each item in an unordered list to help the reader distinguish one item from the next. The list marker you're probably most familiar with is the bullet: a solid dot that's the same color as the list's text. CSS includes a few predefined alternative list markers, declared using the `list-style-type` property: `disc` (this is the default bullet), `circle` (an empty circle), or `square` (a solid square). The size of the marker is proportional to the text size. Listing 4-30 demonstrates the `list-style-type` property, replacing the standard round bullet with a small square.

Listing 4-30. *Using the list-style-type Property*

```
ul {
  list-style-type: square;
}
```

Figure 4-26 shows the results of the rule in Listing 4-30.

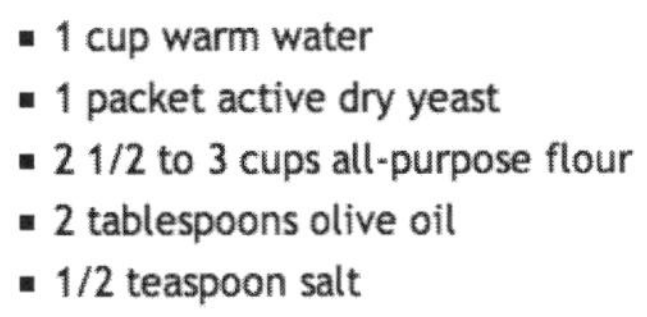

- 1 cup warm water
- 1 packet active dry yeast
- 2 1/2 to 3 cups all-purpose flour
- 2 tablespoons olive oil
- 1/2 teaspoon salt

Figure 4-26. *Unordered lists are now presented with a small square marking each item.*

If you like, the declaration list-style-type: none; will disable the item markers entirely without affecting the format of the list.

Using an Image As a List Marker

If none of the three standard list markers quite satisfies your creative desires, you can provide your own graphic to use via the list-style-image property, as shown in Listing 4-31.

Listing 4-31. *Using the list-style-image Property*

```
ul {
  list-style-image: url("/images/mybullet.gif");
}
```

The property's value is the file's URL, denoted by the url keyword with the URL itself contained in parentheses—the quotation marks are optional. The URL can be either absolute or relative (you learned about absolute and relative URLs in Chapter 1). As you see in Figure 4-27, a browser will load that image file in place of its standard bullet.

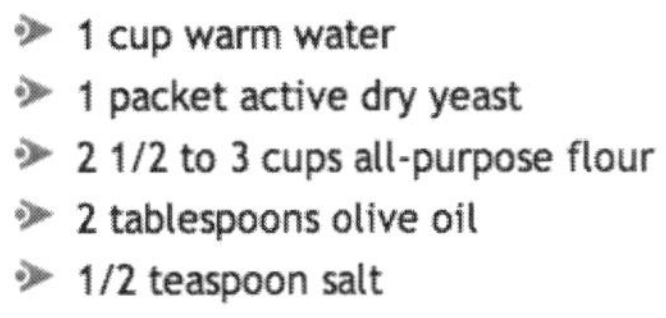

- 1 cup warm water
- 1 packet active dry yeast
- 2 1/2 to 3 cups all-purpose flour
- 2 tablespoons olive oil
- 1/2 teaspoon salt

Figure 4-27. *The image now appears next to each list item.*

Images used for list markers should be small and certainly no taller than the text size. Large images might push your list items apart to make room, as Figure 4-28 demonstrates.

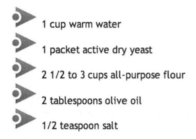

1 cup warm water

1 packet active dry yeast

2 1/2 to 3 cups all-purpose flour

2 tablespoons olive oil

1/2 teaspoon salt

Figure 4-28. *The list is unpleasantly reformatted, forced apart by the large image.*

Changing the Style of Ordered Lists

By default, items in an ordered list are numbered with Arabic numerals (1, 2, 3, etc.). You can change this with CSS, once again using the list-style-type property, and this time choosing from another set of accepted values:

- upper-roman: Uppercase Roman numerals (I, II, III, IV, etc.)

- lower-roman: Lowercase Roman numerals (i, ii, iii, iv, etc.)

- upper-alpha: Uppercase English letters (A, B, C, D, etc.)

- lower-alpha: Lowercase English letters (a, b, c, d, etc.)

- decimal: Arabic numerals (this is the default)

You can see this in action in Listing 4-32.

Listing 4-32. *Declaring Ordered Lists to be Rendered with Uppercase Roman Numerals*

```
ol {
  list-style-type: upper-roman;
}
```

Figure 4-29 shows the on-screen results of Listing 4-32.

I. Combine the water, yeast, oil, salt and two thirds of the flour in a large bowl and mix thoroughly.

II. Gradually add the remaining flour until the dough holds its shape, being careful not to let it become too dry. You may not need all the flour.

III. Place the dough on a lightly floured surface and knead for five minutes until it becomes smooth and elastic.

IV. Transfer the dough to a lightly oiled bowl, cover with plastic wrap and let it rise until it has doubled in size.

V. When the dough has risen, place it on a floured surface, divide it into two equal portions rolled into balls. Allow the dough to rest for 15 minutes before forming your pizzas.

Figure 4-29. *The browser generates the Roman numerals automatically.*

As with unordered lists, the declaration `list-style-type: none;` will prevent the display of any list item markers while the list remains intact.

Summary

Whew! We've covered a lot of ground in this chapter—in fact, a majority of the elements in the entire XHTML language. You learned how to organize your content into bite-sized pieces using meaningful elements that will communicate the true intent of your words, how to insert some useful special characters, and just a few ways you can use CSS to affect the presentation of text. You've also learned a few things you should *not* do when marking up your content. Be semantically responsible and choose elements for what they mean, not how they look.

Most of this chapter has been about adding text content to your documents, but not all content is text. In the next chapter, you'll learn how to add images to your web pages to communicate ideas that text alone just can't get across (at least not with less than a thousand words).

■■■

CHAPTER 5

Using Images

Chapter 4 was all about adding text content to your web pages, but now it's time to put the *multi* in *multimedia* and punch up your pages with pictures. Imagery of some sort is an important part of most websites to make them visually stimulating and memorable. The graphical elements of a design can form the basis of your site's branding and visual identity and can set your site apart from the millions of others on the World Wide Web.

Images can decorate, but they can also communicate; pictures are content too, and some ideas are much better communicated visually. Photos, illustrations, logos, icons, maps, charts, and graphs can get your ideas across in ways that text alone might not accomplish. Even so, it's important to remember that not everyone who visits your website will be able to see the images, and it's your responsibility as a web author to help everyone access the same vital information. This chapter shows you how to improve your site's accessibility by providing text alternatives when your images aren't available.

Images that you're using as content can be referenced from your XHTML document with the img element and will be rendered in the web browser right alongside your text. You can also use the object element, covered in Chapter 4, to embed images in your pages. However, current browser support of the object element is sketchy and inconsistent, so the img element remains the preferred, tried-and-true method. You should attach images that are strictly decorative (rather than informative) to your page with CSS, keeping your presentation separated from your content.

In this chapter, you'll learn how to use images in your web pages. You'll learn a few basics about digital image files, explore the inline img element to embed a graphic into the meat of your content, and see just a few ways you can use CSS to style inline images and integrate them into your page's layout. You'll also discover CSS background images, allowing you to improve the look of your page without changing its semantic structure.

How Digital Images Work

Like anything else that lives in a computer's electronic memory, a digital image is nothing more than data in the form of ones and zeros, collected into a virtual file. A computer reads that array of digits (each digit is a *bit*) and translates each set of bits into a signal that can be sent to a display device where the bits are converted into tiny dots of colored light that human beings can see—bright red, dark blue, pale gray, and so on. The file also includes encoded instructions about how these dots of light (called *pixels*, short for "picture elements") should be arranged, like a mosaic of tiles, to make up a discernable image. You can see the individual pixels if you look closely at a computer or television screen, or you can check out the extreme close-up in Figure 5-1.

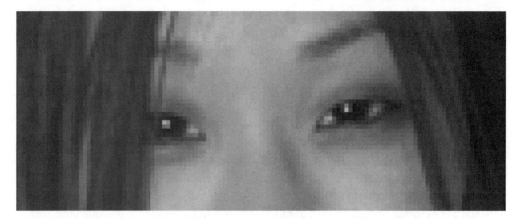

Figure 5-1. *Zooming in on a digital image reveals the tiny pixels that comprise it.*

Because these images are assembled from a "map of bits," they're called *bitmapped images*, and bitmaps are what we use to display images on the web. Storing the color and location of every single pixel adds up to a lot of data, especially when there are hundreds of thousands of pixels in the typical picture and millions of possible colors (up to 16,777,216 unique colors in a 24-bit image to be exact).

Images for the web are usually *compressed* to decrease the file size so that downloading a web page is tolerable, even on slower Internet connections. By either reducing the number of colors stored or reducing the number of pixels memorized, you can greatly reduce the overall file size as well. If you've ever downloaded a large file over a slow Internet connection, you know how grueling it can be. The goal of compressing an image is to achieve the smallest possible file without sacrificing too much of the original picture quality.

VECTOR GRAPHICS

In addition to bitmaps, there are also digital images whose data is stored as a set of mathematical instructions that a computer can follow to draw shapes on the screen or on paper. These are called *vector graphics*, and they can be rendered at any size without changing the original image's appearance or quality. Unfortunately, interpreting and rendering vector images requires specialized software that isn't included in most web browsers, so nearly all images used on the web are bitmaps.

There is an ongoing initiative to develop a vector graphic format specifically for use on the web. Based on XML, the *Scalable Vector Graphics* (SVG) language is not yet widely supported by web browsers, so its practical applications are limited for the time being. You can learn more about SVG at the W3C website (`http://www.w3.org/Graphics/SVG/`).

Web-Friendly Image Formats

You can compress digital images for the web using three formats: JPEG, GIF, and PNG. These formats each use a different means of compression, and each has its own particular benefits and drawbacks. Most web browsers (those that can display images, that is) have built-in software that will interpret and render files in these formats. Web browsers may not be able to render other formats, so you should stick to JPEG, GIF, and PNG. Almost any program you might use for creating or editing digital images will be able to export files in all of these formats.

JPEG

JPEG (pronounced "jay-peg") stands for Joint Photographic Experts Group, the organization that invented the format. The compression scheme reduces the size of the file by sampling the average color values of the pixels and then removing excess redundant pixels from the image. When the image is later decompressed and rendered, those deleted pixels are re-created based on the stored samples.

Because JPEG compression loses some information, the compression is said to be *lossy*, and decompressed JPEGs will never be quite the same quality as the originals. JPEG is in fact a *variable-loss* format and can be compressed at different levels—more compression means more pixels are discarded to create a smaller file, but the price is paid in quality. Highly compressed JPEGs will tend to appear blurry or with blocky smudges, called *artifacts*, where the pixels have been regenerated. In Figure 5-2 you see three pictures of Jolene, each the same JPEG image saved at a different level of compression (shown here at twice the original size for clarity). The file gets smaller as the image is more compressed, but the quality also declines.

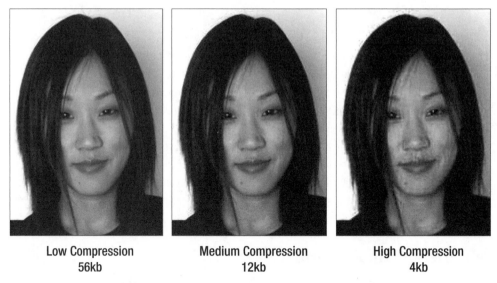

Low Compression
56kb

Medium Compression
12kb

High Compression
4kb

Figure 5-2. *The same JPEG image at three different levels of compression. The version on the far right is the smallest file, but the image quality has suffered greatly.*

Furthermore, every time you edit and save a JPEG image, you're essentially recompressing an image that has already been compressed, losing a bit more data in the process. Every generation of JPEG compression will degrade the image quality a little more, like making a photocopy of a photocopy. You should keep original, uncompressed versions of your images to work from, compressing to a JPEG file only when you're ready to put your images on the web.

The JPEG format saves disk space by sacrificing pixels but will store a lot of color information in a relatively small file, making it ideal for photographs and other images with many different colors or images where one color blends smoothly into another (called *continuous tone*). JPEG files use the file extension .jpeg or .jpg—the shorter version became customary because some computer operating systems don't allow four-letter (or more) file extensions.

GIF

GIF stands for Graphic Interchange Format; it compresses images by reducing the overall number of colors saved in the file, but it preserves the location of every pixel. Because GIF is considered to be a *lossless* format, it's a good choice for logos, icons, or graphics that feature text and need to maintain sharp outlines for readability. A GIF image can contain a maximum of 256 different colors but may contain fewer than that; storing fewer colors makes for a smaller file. Graphs, maps, line drawings, and any images with large areas of solid color, or few colors overall, are ideal candidates for GIF.

GIF images may also have some areas that are transparent, allowing whatever is behind the image to show through. Any given pixel is either completely transparent or completely opaque, so there will be a jagged edge where the transparent and opaque areas border each other. Most graphic editing programs enable you to specify a *matte color* for transparent GIFs, which can be the same as your page's background color to minimize "the jaggies." Figure 5-3 shows a transparent GIF against a checkerboard background. You can see the white matte surrounding the image, which would blend seamlessly with a solid white background color.

Figure 5-3. *A transparent GIF with a white matte. The checkerboard background is just for demonstration.*

Another special trait of GIF is support for rudimentary animation. The image can consist of a number of frames to be displayed in sequence, allowing for some very cool (and also some very annoying) effects. Of course, each frame in an animated GIF is additional information to store and will naturally increase the size of the file.

GIF files use the .gif extension.

■**Note** There's some debate about just how to pronounce the acronym GIF. Some people (including the people who invented the format) pronounce it like "jif," with a soft *g* sound. But in common usage it's often pronounced with a hard *g*, as in "gift." The truth is that both ways are equally correct, so say it whichever way sounds most natural to you.

PNG

Portable Network Graphic (PNG) is a format invented to be a free successor to the patented GIF, and it improves on its predecessor in several ways. Like a GIF, a PNG image can also contain a maximum of 256 colors (known as *8-bit color,* since 256 different values are the most that can be described using only 8 bits of data per pixel), and it supports transparency the same as GIFs do. Thanks to a different compression scheme, an 8-bit PNG file can sometimes be smaller than its GIF counterpart.

However, another variant of the PNG format can support 24-bit color to produce millions of unique colors; it's similar to JPEG in that respect, though it frequently results in larger files than JPEGs. Arguably the best feature of 24-bit PNG images is their capacity to include a transparent *alpha channel*, like an extra invisible layer embedded in the image to define areas of partial transparency. While the transparent pixels in a GIF or 8-bit PNG are completely transparent, the pixels in a 24-bit PNG can be only partially transparent, allowing some of the background to show through the image like a translucent overlay. You can see alpha transparency in action in Figure 5-4. The checkerboard background shows through the translucent parts of the image, allowing this logo to blend smoothly and seamlessly with any background.

Figure 5-4. *A 24-bit PNG with a transparent alpha channel. The checkerboard background shows through the translucent parts of the image.*

Unfortunately, many older browsers don't fully support PNGs with alpha transparency, including Internet Explorer for Windows prior to version 7. Until those older browsers become less prevalent, you'll need to be careful if and when you use alpha-transparent PNGs.

PNG files use the extension .png, delightfully pronounced as "ping."

A BIT ABOUT BITS

All data in the world of computers consists of ones and zeros, the "digits" that give us the term *digital*. Those ones and zeros represent two positions of a switch—1 for on, 0 for off—and form the basis of *binary code*, the root language of computers. Each digit is called a *bit*, and they are collected into groups of 8 bits called a *byte*. When dealing with larger collections of bytes, they're measured in multiples of 1,024; 1,024 bytes is a *kilobyte*, 1,024 kilobytes is a *megabyte*, 1,024 megabytes is a *gigabyte*, and so on. This is how we measure amounts of digital data.

The color value of every pixel in a bitmapped digital image is described with simple ones and zeros. More colors can be produced as more digits are devoted to describing the color of each pixel. The simplest images use only a single bit of data (1 or 0) per pixel to describe two possible colors—each pixel is either on or off, black or white. Since each bit has two possible values, the total number of possible colors is always 2 to the power of the number of bits. As the number of bits per pixel increases, so does the number of possible colors that can be described. Using 2 bits per pixel provides a total of four possible permutations (00, 01, 10, and 11), thus producing four possible colors (2^2). Four bits expands the number of colors to 16 (2^4). At 8 bits per pixel, the total possible colors number 256 (2^8).

GIF images store color information at the rate of 8 bits per pixel and hence can contain only a maximum of 256 different colors. JPEGs use 24 bits per pixel and can thus produce 16,777,216 possible colors, approaching the very limits of human vision. The PNG format supports either 8-bit color or 24-bit color.

In an 8-bit GIF or PNG, only a single digit is devoted to describing each pixel's transparency, so any given pixel is either visible or not visible. In a 24-bit transparent PNG, 8 of those bits can be devoted to describing the transparency of the pixel, allowing 256 possible levels of translucency all the way from completely transparent (0) to completely opaque (255).

Including Images in Your Content

The text content of a web page is part of the XHTML document, surrounded by tags that indicate the meaning and purpose of each portion of words. Images, on the other hand, are external files and not actually part of the document at all. An image is referenced from an XHTML document with the img element (or the object element, though img is more common and reliable). Rendering a web page that includes images is a two-stage process; first the markup is downloaded, and then the external images are downloaded. Wherever the img element occurs in the document, the browser will fetch the referenced file from the web server and render it on the page in place of the element.

img

The inline img element (an abbreviation of "image," as you might have guessed) is considered a *replaced element*; the element itself is not rendered. It's also an empty element with no text content, so it must be self-closed with a trailing slash (/>). The img element requires a src attribute to define the source of the graphic file as the URL (either absolute or relative) where that file resides on a web server.

An alt attribute is also required, providing an alternative text equivalent of the image. The alternative text will be displayed if the image is unavailable or if the browser is incapable of displaying images, and it can offer improved accessibility for the visually impaired. Listing 5-1 shows an img element with only the src and alt attributes, the bare minimum required to be valid.

Listing 5-1. *The Simplest Incarnation of the img Element*

```
<img src="/images/pizza.jpg" alt="A pizza with sausage and olives" />
```

Required Attributes

- `src`: Specifies the URL where the graphic file resides on a web server

- `alt`: Provides an alternative text equivalent of the image

Optional Attributes

- `width`: Specifies the width of the image in pixels

- `height`: Specifies the height of the image in pixels

- `ismap`: Declares that the image is used for a server-side image map

- `usemap`: Identifies a client-side image map to be used

- `longdesc`: Specifies the URL of an extended text description of the image

Standard Attributes

- `class`

- `dir`

- `id`

- `lang`

- `style`

- `title`

- `xml:lang`

The alt Attribute

All instances of the `img` element must carry an `alt` attribute to provide a text alternative for when the picture can't be seen. It could be that the reader is visually impaired, they're using a device that doesn't display the image, or the image file couldn't be found at the source URL. Including a brief alternative text description preserves some of your image's communicative intent when the image itself isn't visible. An `alt` attribute can contain up to 1,024 characters (including spaces), but shorter is better. If the image is particularly complex and demands a wordy explanation, you should provide that via the `longdesc` attribute, which we'll cover shortly.

The text value of an `alt` attribute should serve as a replacement for the image when the image isn't available. If your page features a photo of your cat asleep in a grocery bag, the appropriate `alt` text might be "my cat in a bag" or "my gray cat sleeping in a brown paper bag" or even "my gray striped tabby asleep in a brown paper grocery bag on my kitchen table." These all describe the content of the picture to help your readers conjure the image in their minds even if they can't see it on their screens. Figure 5-5 shows an example of how Internet Explorer for Windows reacts if a referenced image can't be found on the server. The value of the `alt` attribute is displayed in place of the missing image, offering at least a sense of what it depicts.

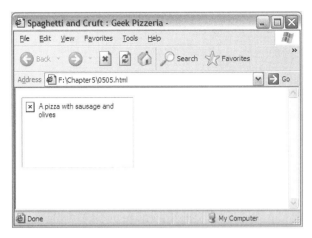

Figure 5-5. *A graphical browser will display the alternative text if the image fails to download.*

An `alt` attribute should be a meaningful substitute for the image, so avoid unhelpful `alt` texts such as "company logo." Tell your visitors the name of the company, not just that your anonymous company has some sort of logo they're unable to see. If you like, you can specify that the missing image is, in fact, a logo with `alt` text such as "CorpCo, Inc., logo" or something similar. It still replaces the image as well as passing on the extra information that it's a logo. Images that are pictures of text should include that text in their `alt` attributes.

A well-written `alt` attribute might inform the reader that the missing image is a logo, a photograph, an illustration, a portrait, a landscape, a thumbnail, a close-up, a chart, a map, and so on, but you should avoid restating the obvious: "a picture of my cat" tells the reader what it's a picture of but doesn't tell them much else about the scene that picture captures. The `alt` attribute is a descriptive or functional replacement for the image, so you should try to describe the subject if possible, not just the image itself. And you shouldn't use the image file name as the value of `alt`; mycat.jpg tells the reader nothing meaningful about the picture.

Internet Explorer for Windows, the most common browser on the most common operating system today, inexplicably displays the contents of an `alt` attribute as a *tooltip*, a small text bubble that appears when the user's mouse lingers over the image (shown in Figure 5-6).

Figure 5-6. *Internet Explorer for Windows improperly displays the value of the alt attribute as a tooltip below the mouse cursor.*

Because of this, many web designers in years past misused the `alt` attribute to inject the kind of supplemental information they wanted to appear in a tooltip: "my favorite picture" or "my cat's name is Neena." These statements don't describe the image or take its place, so they're not really proper values for `alt`. And since only Internet Explorer for Windows shows the `alt` value in a tooltip, that information isn't seen by anyone who is using a different browser.

The `title` attribute, on the other hand, will be displayed as a tooltip in most graphical browsers, and that is the more correct place to include a description of the image's contextual purpose, with the attribute acting as a caption, or indeed a title. When both `alt` and `title` are present, as in Listing 5-2, Internet Explorer will display the `title` text rather than the `alt` text.

Listing 5-2. *An img Element with Descriptive alt and title Attributes*

```
<img src="/images/pizza.jpg" title="Our famous Pizza Napoli" ➥
alt="A whole pizza topped with green olives and melted mozzarella cheese" />
```

Even worse than improper `alt` text, some web designers omit the `alt` attribute entirely just to avoid unwanted tooltips in Internet Explorer. An `img` element without an `alt` attribute, in addition to being invalid XHTML, is also inaccessible. A screen reader or text browser might simply state "[IMAGE]" without any further information or may read/display the URL from the `src` attribute. Omitting the `alt` attribute could render an important image meaningless.

Informative `alt` text is especially critical when using images in links or as buttons to submit forms. Such images are functional, not merely informative. If an image features text acting as a link phrase, it's absolutely essential that the link is made accessible by including the same phrase in an `alt` attribute. Figure 5-7 shows an example of a site's navigation consisting of linked images. A visitor with keen eyesight who is able to download the images can get around just fine, even without `alt` attributes.

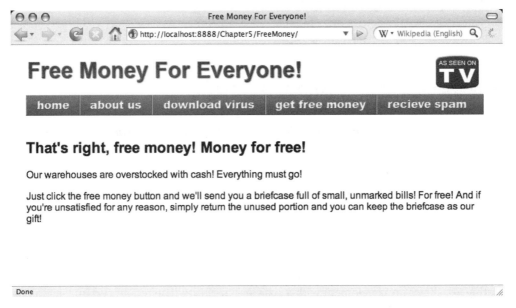

Figure 5-7. *This site's navigation consists of linked image buttons. This is how it appears in Firefox.*

However, Figure 5-8 shows the same site as it appears in Lynx, a text-only web browser that displays the image file name when the `alt` attribute is missing. Without `alt` attributes for the images, the site's navigation is practically useless.

Inline images that are decorative (meaning they're just for show and aren't informative as content) still require `alt` attributes. But rather than describing their ornamental function, simply including an empty `alt` attribute (`alt=""`) will "hide" those nonessential images; it's as if the image doesn't exist at all if its description is blank. As an added bonus, Internet Explorer won't show tooltips for images with an empty `alt` attribute.

■**Note** Many people use the incorrect phrase *alt tag* to refer to the `alt` attribute. This is confusing and misleading since `alt` is not a *tag* at all; it's an *attribute* of the `img` element.

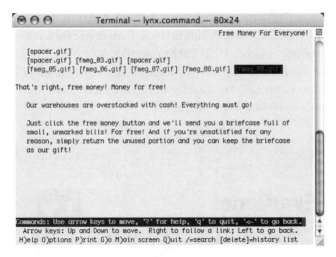

Figure 5-8. *Images without alt attributes are indicated by the file name in Lynx. This site has become nigh impossible to navigate, forcing the visitor to guess where each link might lead.*

longdesc

The optional `longdesc` attribute (shortened from "long description") contains a URL pointing to another page with a more detailed description of the image when that description is too lengthy for the `alt` attribute. It's especially handy for charts and graphs that might graphically present complex data that would otherwise need to be shown in a table. Listing 5-3 shows an `img` element with a `longdesc` attribute. The referenced image is a pie chart, something rather difficult to explain in a brief `alt` attribute.

Listing 5-3. *An img Element with a longdesc Attribute*

```
<img src="/images/piechart.gif" alt="A pie chart showing the proportional ➥
popularities of different pizza toppings" longdesc="/toppings.html" />
```

Figure 5-9 shows the pie chart, as well as the same information presented in a table. The tabular data can be accessed and understood by people who otherwise wouldn't be able to see and interpret the visual chart. You'll learn about using tables to structure complex tabular data in Chapter 7.

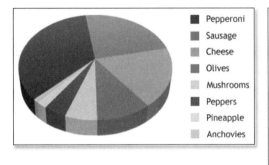

Topping	Percentage
Various pizza toppings and the percentage of customers surveyed who ranked them as their favorite.	
Pepperoni	35%
Sausage	24%
Cheese	18%
Olives	10%
Mushrooms	6%
Peppers	4%
Pineapple	2%
Anchovies	1%

Figure 5-9. *The pie chart graphic side by side with its tabular text equivalent*

width and height

Images will appear at their natural dimensions when rendered in a browser window. But because images are downloaded *after* the markup and text, the browser won't know the dimensions of the image until it has been completely downloaded as well. The browser will reflow text to accommodate the image once its dimensions are known, which can be jarring if your visitor has already started reading the text. Including width and height attributes in an img element will tell the browser to reserve space for the image and draw the text where it should the first time around.

If the width and height attributes aren't the same as the image's natural dimensions, the browser will scale the image to fit to those attributes. However, you should usually avoid resizing images this way. When a web browser scales an image larger than its natural dimensions, it will appear blocky, showing off the individual pixels. If it's scaled smaller, it may still look sharp, but the file size will be larger than necessary and take longer to download. Ideally, the width and height attributes should match the image's natural width and height, and you should do your resizing with a graphic editing program better equipped for the task.

▓**Note** You can also use the CSS width and height properties to describe an image's dimensions. When an img element that includes a width or height attribute is further styled by CSS, the CSS dimensions will override the XHTML attributes.

---

usemap and ismap

An *image map* is an image where certain areas have been designated as hyperlinks, rather than the entire image being contained in a single link. The usemap attribute identifies the specific map element to use when rendering a *client-side* image map. The ismap attribute declares that this image will be used as a *server-side* image map (which is an inherently inaccessible device that should usually be avoided). You'll learn more about the inner workings of image maps when you learn about hyperlinks in Chapter 6.

Deprecated Presentational Attributes

Older versions of HTML included a number of optional attributes for the img element that have since been deprecated in favor of CSS. None of these is valid in XHTML, but we're listing them here so you'll recognize these attributes and know how to achieve their effects with modern CSS:

- align: Specifies how the image should be aligned with adjacent text using the values left, right, top, middle, and bottom. Left or right alignment is achieved with the float property in CSS; top, middle, and bottom alignments are achieved with the vertical-align property.

- border: Specifies the width of the border that will surround images that act as hyperlinks. This has been supplanted by the border-width property in CSS.

- hspace: Specifies the horizontal space on the left and right sides of the image, replaced by the CSS margin-left and margin-right properties.

- vspace: Specifies the vertical space at the top and bottom of the image, replaced by the CSS margin-top and margin-bottom properties.

■**Note** You may encounter a lowsrc attribute within img elements in some older documents. This attribute designated a smaller file that would be downloaded first before the final image was downloaded. However, it's an outdated, proprietary attribute that was supported only by older versions of Netscape Navigator. The lowsrc attribute is invalid and shouldn't be used.

Images in Context

The img element is inline, so it will appear alongside any adjacent text on the same line, with the bottom edge of the image resting on the same invisible baseline. Listing 5-4 shows an img element within a paragraph of text (designated by the p element).

Listing 5-4. *An img Element Inline with Text in a Paragraph*

```
<p><img src="/images/pizza.jpg" width="180" height="110" ➥
alt="A close-up of one of our delicious pizzas" />
We handcraft our pizzas on the spot using only the best ingredients,
and then we bake them to perfection in our rustic wood-fired brick oven.</p>
```

Figure 5-10 shows how this would appear in a graphical browser. The bottom edge of the inline image rests on the same baseline as the text.

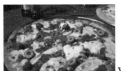
We handcraft our pizzas on the spot using only the best ingredients, and then we bake them to perfection in our rustic wood-fired brick oven.

Figure 5-10. *The image is inline with its neighboring text when displayed in a browser. (Photo by Jeremy Keith.)*

If the image, the text, or both are separately contained by block-level elements (such as a div or p element), the standard block behavior takes over, and the browser will draw the appropriate line breaks. Listing 5-5 shows the same content, but this time the img element is outside the paragraph, wrapped in its own div element.

Listing 5-5. *An img Element Within a Block-Level div, Followed by a Paragraph*

```
<div><img src="/images/pizza.jpg" width="180" height="110" ➥
alt="A close-up of one of our delicious pizzas" /></div>

<p>We handcraft our pizzas on the spot using only the best ingredients,
and then we bake them to perfection in our rustic wood-fired brick oven.</p>
```

Figure 5-11 shows the result in a graphical browser, with the image (or rather the div that contains it) and paragraph rendered on separate lines.

When deciding whether an img element should appear inside or outside the element containing adjacent text, consider the meaning of the image. Is the image part of the same thought or idea being expressed by the text? If so, it may belong within the paragraph. If the image represents an idea that stands alone, then the text can also stand alone in an element of its very own.

We handcraft our pizzas on the spot using only the best ingredients, and
then we bake them to perfection in our rustic wood-fired brick oven.

Figure 5-11. *The div and p elements are both block-level, so each appears on its own line.*

■**Caution** Remember that the body element can have only block-level elements as children. An img is an
inline element, so it cannot be a direct child of the body; it must be held in some block-level container to keep
your XHTML valid.

When two or more images appear together, they behave the same as other inline elements;
they will line up next to each other on the same baseline, just like words do. And like words,
images will automatically wrap to multiple lines if they're too wide to fit on one.

Wrapping Text Around an Image

You've no doubt seen it in hundreds of books, magazines, and newspapers: an image
placed in a column of text where the text wraps around the image and continues on its
way, like a stream flowing around a boulder. In previous versions of HTML, this was
accomplished with the now-deprecated align attribute, but today you can achieve the
same effect with the float property in CSS.

The float property accepts one of three values: left, right, or none. When an element
is "floated," it will be shifted as far to one side (left or right) as possible until its edge comes
up against the edge of its containing block (or until it collides with another floating element).
Any text or elements that come afterward will then flow upward around the floated element.
The default none value is most useful for overriding any float properties that have been
granted to an element by another rule in your style sheet.

In Listing 5-6, you see the markup for an image followed by a block of text (both are
contained in a single paragraph). The img element features a class attribute that will make
it easy to apply CSS.

Listing 5-6. *An Image in a Paragraph of Text*

```
<p><img src="/images/pizza.jpg" width="180" height="110" class="figure" ➥
alt="A close-up of one of our delicious pizzas" />
Spaghetti &#38; Cruft opened our doors in 1999, bringing great pizza and
pasta to the heart of the city's trendy Riverbend district. We handcraft
our pizzas on the spot using only the best ingredients, and then we bake them to
perfection in our rustic wood-fired brick oven. We sell pizza by the slice
or by the pie and even offer catering for any occasion all around the
neighborhood.</p>
```

The image belongs to the `figure` class, and Listing 5-7 shows the CSS rule for that class, declaring that the element should float to the left.

Listing 5-7. *The CSS Rule for the figure Class*

```
.figure {
  float: left;
}
```

Figure 5-12 shows the combined result. The image floats to the left side of the paragraph, and the following text flows upward around it.

Figure 5-12. *The image floats to the left, allowing the text to wrap around it.*

An inline image rests on the same baseline as its neighboring text, but when that image is floated to one side, its top edge now rests at the top of the line it appears on, descending below the baseline. In the previous example, you'll notice that the wrapped text rubs directly against the right edge of the image, making it harder to read. To create a bit of spacing, you can apply margins to the floating image by expanding the CSS rule, as in Listing 5-8.

Listing 5-8. *Adding Margins to the figure Class Rule*

```
.figure {
  float: left;
  margin-right: 1em;
  margin-bottom: .5em;
}
```

Only the right and bottom sides need margins in this case because the top and left sides don't collide with any text. Leaving those sides with the default margin value of 0 will make those edges press right against the invisible edge of the containing paragraph. You can see in Figure 5-13 that the floating image now has a bit more room to breathe; the margins extend the influence of the image's float, and the text now wraps around the margins as well.

Spaghetti & Cruft opened our doors in 1999, bringing great pizza and pasta to the heart of the city's trendy Riverbend district. We handcraft our pizzas on the spot using only the best ingredients, and then we bake them to perfection in our rustic wood-fired brick oven. We sell pizza by the slice or by the pie and even offer catering for any occasion all around the neighborhood.

Figure 5-13. *Applying some margins to the floating image separates it from the text.*

Background Images

Using the CSS background-image property, you can add decorative imagery to your page and still avoid mixing presentation with your content—images that are meaningful content belong with your other content. Almost any element in XHTML can be assigned a background image, and the contents of the element will overlay that background. The background image will *tile* in both directions by default, beginning at the top-left corner of the element and replicating itself horizontally and vertically to fill the space, like the tiles on a kitchen floor.

Listing 5-9 shows a CSS rule that will apply a background image to the body element. The image is specified by its URL, contained in parentheses and denoted by the url keyword.

Listing 5-9. *A Background Image Applied to the body Element*

```
body {
  background-image: url(/images/background.gif);
}
```

The image tiles to fill the window when a graphical browser renders the document, as you can see in Figure 5-14.

Spaghetti & Cruft opened our doors in 1999, bringing great pizza and pasta to the heart of the city's trendy Riverbend district. We handcraft our pizzas on the spot using only the best ingredients, and then we bake them to perfection in our rustic wood-fired brick oven. We sell pizza by the slice or by the pie and even offer catering for any occasion all around the neighborhood.

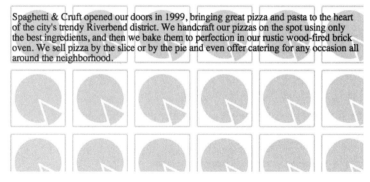

Figure 5-14. *The background image tiles in both directions, repeating as many times as necessary to fill the element's area.*

You can modify the default tiling with the `background-repeat` property, specifying whether the image should be repeated only horizontally, only vertically, or not at all. Listing 5-10 expands the previous CSS rule, declaring that the background image should be repeated horizontally along the x-axis.

Listing 5-10. *Adding a background-repeat Declaration*

```
body {
  background-image: url(/images/background.gif);
  background-repeat: repeat-x;
}
```

You can see in Figure 5-15 that the image now repeats across the top of the page but not downward.

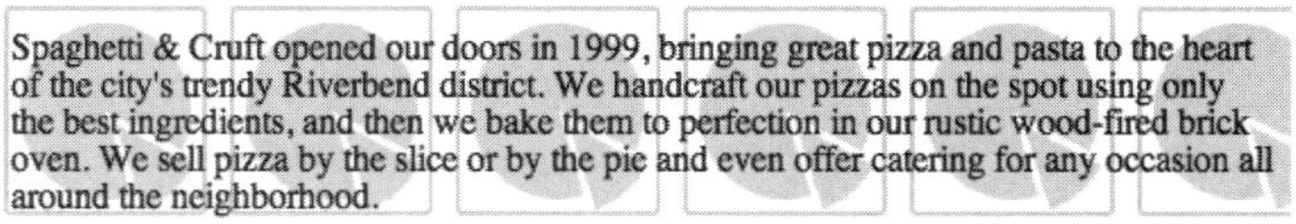

Spaghetti & Cruft opened our doors in 1999, bringing great pizza and pasta to the heart of the city's trendy Riverbend district. We handcraft our pizzas on the spot using only the best ingredients, and then we bake them to perfection in our rustic wood-fired brick oven. We sell pizza by the slice or by the pie and even offer catering for any occasion all around the neighborhood.

Figure 5-15. *The background now tiles horizontally but not vertically.*

Likewise, a value of `repeat-y` will tile the image vertically but not horizontally. Listing 5-11 shows the revised CSS.

Listing 5-11. *The Value repeat-y Will Tile the Image Vertically*

```
body {
  background-image: url(/images/background.gif);
  background-repeat: repeat-y;
}
```

Figure 5-16 shows the result. The image now tiles vertically along the y-axis.

Spaghetti & Cruft opened our doors in 1999, bringing great pizza and pasta to the heart of the city's trendy Riverbend district. We handcraft our pizzas on the spot using only the best ingredients, and then we bake them to perfection in our rustic wood-fired brick oven. We sell pizza by the slice or by the pie and even offer catering for any occasion all around the neighborhood.

Figure 5-16. *Now the background tiles vertically but not horizontally.*

The default value of background-repeat is repeat, which you can use to override another value in another rule if necessary. You can also disable tiling altogether with the value no-repeat, as shown in Listing 5-12.

Listing 5-12. *The no-repeat Value Prevents the Image from Tiling*

```
body {
  background-image: url(/images/background.gif);
  background-repeat: no-repeat;
}
```

Figure 5-17 shows the effect of the no-repeat value; the image appears only once and doesn't tile in either direction.

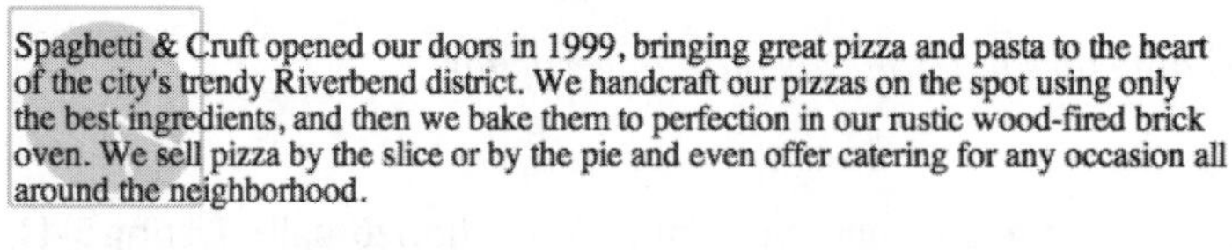

Spaghetti & Cruft opened our doors in 1999, bringing great pizza and pasta to the heart of the city's trendy Riverbend district. We handcraft our pizzas on the spot using only the best ingredients, and then we bake them to perfection in our rustic wood-fired brick oven. We sell pizza by the slice or by the pie and even offer catering for any occasion all around the neighborhood.

Figure 5-17. *The background image appears only once and is not repeated.*

If your background image is much larger than the element it decorates, the element's dimensions act like a window defining the portion of the background that can be seen. In Figure 5-18, the background image is much larger than the element it has been applied to (a div in this case), so part of the image is hidden.

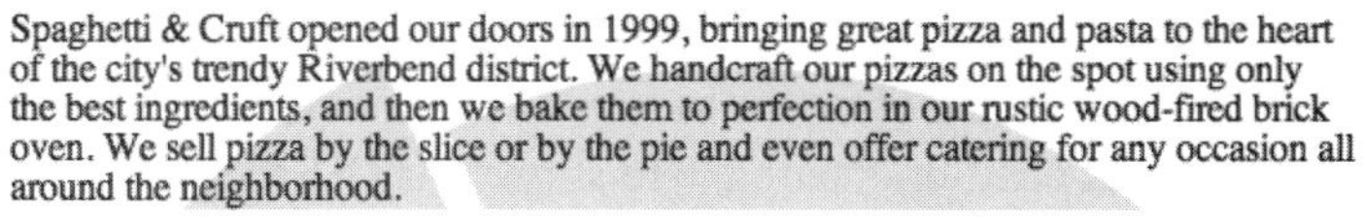

Spaghetti & Cruft opened our doors in 1999, bringing great pizza and pasta to the heart of the city's trendy Riverbend district. We handcraft our pizzas on the spot using only the best ingredients, and then we bake them to perfection in our rustic wood-fired brick oven. We sell pizza by the slice or by the pie and even offer catering for any occasion all around the neighborhood.

Figure 5-18. *Only part of the background image is visible because it's much larger than the element to which it has been applied.*

If the element expands—if more content is added, if the text size is increased, or if the element is resized with CSS—more of the image becomes visible, as in Figure 5-19.

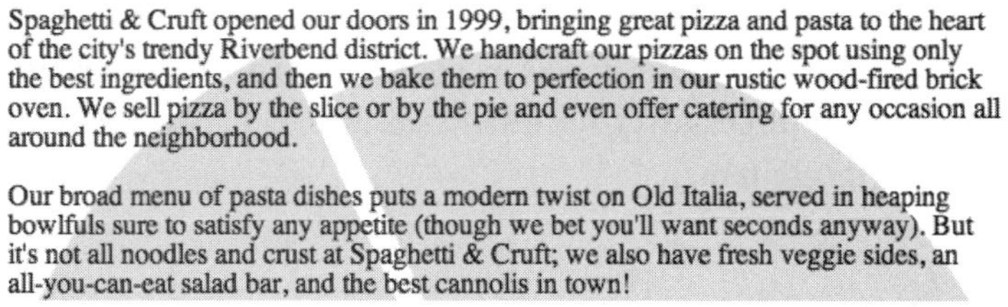

Spaghetti & Cruft opened our doors in 1999, bringing great pizza and pasta to the heart of the city's trendy Riverbend district. We handcraft our pizzas on the spot using only the best ingredients, and then we bake them to perfection in our rustic wood-fired brick oven. We sell pizza by the slice or by the pie and even offer catering for any occasion all around the neighborhood.

Our broad menu of pasta dishes puts a modern twist on Old Italia, served in heaping bowlfuls sure to satisfy any appetite (though we bet you'll want seconds anyway). But it's not all noodles and crust at Spaghetti & Cruft; we also have fresh veggie sides, an all-you-can-eat salad bar, and the best cannolis in town!

Figure 5-19. *Adding another paragraph expands the parent element, revealing more of the background image.*

Text can be difficult to read when it overlays a complicated background image or when there's insufficient contrast between the foreground and background colors. Be wise in your use of background images, ensuring they don't interfere too much with the readability of your content.

Also be sure to specify a solid background color (with the CSS background-color property) that provides enough contrast with the foreground text color in the event the image doesn't display. Most modern browsers default to black text on a white background. If your design uses light-colored text against a dark background image, you should also declare a dark background color—background images are rendered on top of background colors, but the solid color will be displayed when the image isn't available.

Positioning a Background Image

By default, a background image is placed at the top-left corner of the element, which is also where the tiling begins if the image is allowed to tile. The CSS background-position property controls the placement of a background image. If the image is meant to repeat, the value of background-position will mark the beginning of the tiling pattern.

The property takes two values, one for the horizontal position and one for the vertical position. The horizontal value always comes before the vertical, and if only one value is given, it will be taken as the horizontal position. Listing 5-13 shows the CSS to place a background image at the bottom of the right side of a div element.

Listing 5-13. *Adding a background-position Declaration*

```
div {
  background-image: url(/images/background.gif);
  background-repeat: no-repeat;
  background-position: right bottom;
}
```

Figure 5-20 shows the result—the image is positioned in the element's bottom-right corner. In this example, the div element is only as tall as its contents, so its bottom edge won't reach the bottom of the window—unless declared otherwise, the height of an element is always dictated by the height of its contents.

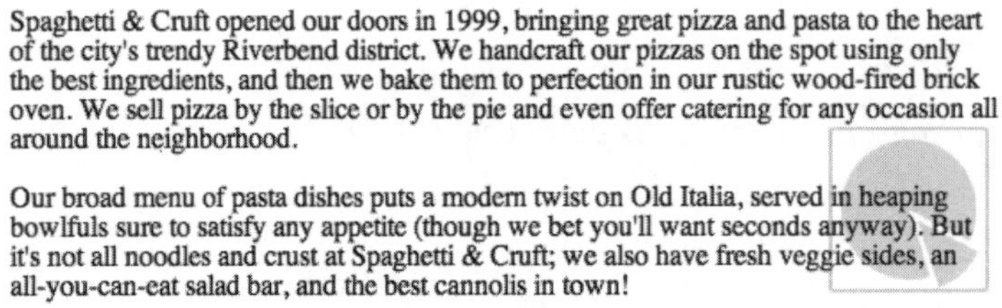

Spaghetti & Cruft opened our doors in 1999, bringing great pizza and pasta to the heart of the city's trendy Riverbend district. We handcraft our pizzas on the spot using only the best ingredients, and then we bake them to perfection in our rustic wood-fired brick oven. We sell pizza by the slice or by the pie and even offer catering for any occasion all around the neighborhood.

Our broad menu of pasta dishes puts a modern twist on Old Italia, served in heaping bowlfuls sure to satisfy any appetite (though we bet you'll want seconds anyway). But it's not all noodles and crust at Spaghetti & Cruft; we also have fresh veggie sides, an all-you-can-eat salad bar, and the best cannolis in town!

Figure 5-20. *The image now appears in the bottom-right corner and still doesn't repeat.*

You can specify a value for background-position in a few ways: keywords, lengths, and percentages. The keywords to use are left, center, or right for the horizontal position and top, center, or bottom for the vertical. Note that you can use the keyword center for either horizontal or vertical positioning; vertically, center will be half the element's height, and horizontally, center is half the element's width.

A length is simply any number with any unit of measure, such as 10px, 20mm, or 3.5em, and the two values needn't use the same unit. No unit is required for lengths of 0. After all, 0px is the same as 0in or 0em—zero is always zero. Listing 5-14 shows two lengths for the background-position property, placing the image 40 pixels from the left and 3 em units from the top.

Listing 5-14. *Using Lengths for background-position*

```
body {
  background-image: url(/images/background.gif);
  background-repeat: no-repeat;
  background-position: 40px 3em;
}
```

Figure 5-21 shows the rendered result, with the image positioned 40 pixels from the left side and 3 ems from the top, just as declared in the CSS.

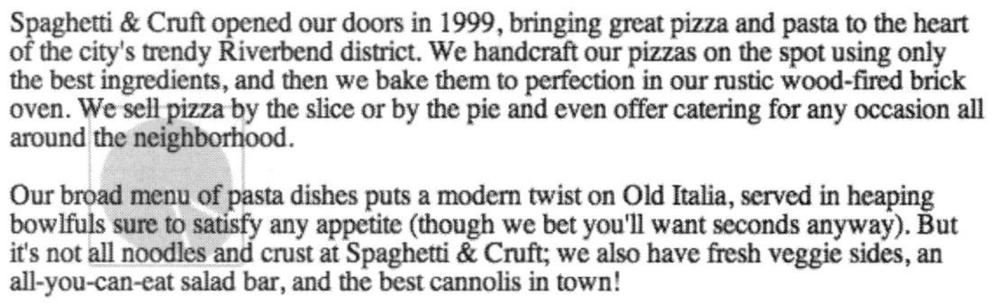

Spaghetti & Cruft opened our doors in 1999, bringing great pizza and pasta to the heart of the city's trendy Riverbend district. We handcraft our pizzas on the spot using only the best ingredients, and then we bake them to perfection in our rustic wood-fired brick oven. We sell pizza by the slice or by the pie and even offer catering for any occasion all around the neighborhood.

Our broad menu of pasta dishes puts a modern twist on Old Italia, served in heaping bowlfuls sure to satisfy any appetite (though we bet you'll want seconds anyway). But it's not all noodles and crust at Spaghetti & Cruft; we also have fresh veggie sides, an all-you-can-eat salad bar, and the best cannolis in town!

Figure 5-21. *The background image is positioned exactly where the CSS told it to be.*

When you position a background image with percentages, you must factor in the size of the image as well as the size of the element it decorates. A background image positioned 75% from the left side of the element will move the reference point 75% from the left side of the image as well. This especially makes sense when centering a background at 50%; the background is placed at a point halfway across the element and halfway across the image, as illustrated in Figure 5-22.

This isn't true for lengths based on other units of measure; nonpercentage lengths always measure the distance from the top and left sides of the element to the top and left sides of the image, as Figure 5-23 illustrates.

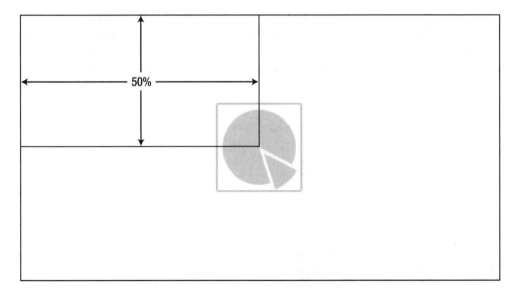

Figure 5-22. *A background image positioned 50% from the left and 50% from the top will be perfectly centered, measuring the size of both the element and the image.*

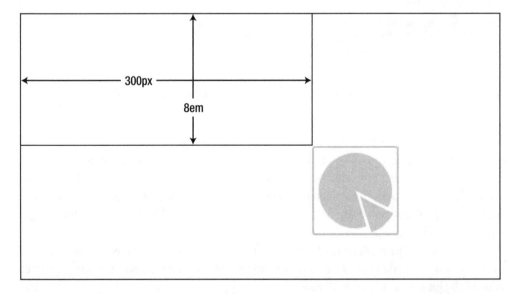

Figure 5-23. *Nonpercentage lengths position the top-left corner of the background image at the precise point specified in your CSS. This example shows the result of background-position: 300px 8em;.*

Summary

Imagery can be instrumental in a well-designed web page and is just one more way to make your site unique and identifiable. But images can also convey meaning in ways words can't. You can embed meaningful images into your content with the inline img element, always including an alternative text equivalent to improve accessibility for people and devices that can't see the image. You should separate presentational images from content by using CSS and the background-image property. CSS also gives you the power to control the placement and repetition of background images and the ability to influence the placement of inline images to integrate them into the flow of your page design.

The three popular file formats for compressing images for the web are JPEG, GIF, and PNG. The format you choose will depend on the image—use JPEG for colorful photos, use GIF or 8-bit PNG for text and illustrations with solid colors or for transparency, and use 24-bit PNG for alpha transparency.

You'll make frequent use of the elements and techniques you've explored in this chapter and the previous one to give your content meaning and to make your pages visually attractive. But the web wouldn't be the web without one essential component: the hyperlink. Chapter 6 will introduce you to hyperlinks and show you how to transform your documents into living, working parts of the World Wide Web.

Summary

CHAPTER 6

■ ■ ■

Linking to the Web

This chapter shows you how to use links to provide a connection between different documents. Links are one of the most important features that make the World Wide Web so powerful. The real power comes from the fact that you can easily link to both your own documents as well as to other external documents found on the web. Using links, you can point to other documents, graphics, and programs from within your document. Learning about links requires you to revisit the use of URLs, which you first saw in Chapter 1. By default, a link shows up as underlined text within your document. When you hover over the link, the default cursor changes to a different cursor, indicating it is a link. When you select the link, the browser navigates to where the link is pointing.

The Anchor Tag

The use of links is based around a single tag: the anchor tag. The anchor tag has only a few attributes, but it provides a lot of functionality, as you'll see. The basic syntax of the anchor element is as follows:

```
<a href="http://urlgoeshere.com">Text to display</a>
```

<a>

You use the anchor element to mark any markup that causes the user's browser to navigate to a different location when interacted with. The text between <a></a> is presented to the user. In a visual browser, the text is typically underlined. Other types of browsers vary in their use, depending on the agent itself. When the user clicks on the link, the browser is directed to the document that is specified by the href attribute.

Required Attributes

No attributes are required for the <a> tag.

Optional Attributes

- `charset`: Specifies a character set used in the encoding of the target URL.

- `coords`: Specifies coordinates used to define a shape in a client-side image map.

- `href`: Specifies the URL that you wish the browser to open when the user clicks on the link. This is the most commonly used attribute for the anchor tag.

- `hreflang`: Specifies the base language used in the URL specified by the `href` attribute.

- `rel`: Specifies the relationship between the current document and the target URL. Possible values include `alternate`, `stylesheet`, `start`, `next`, `prev`, `contents`, `index`, `glossary`, `copyright`, `chapter`, `section`, `subsection`, `appendix`, `help`, and `bookmark`.

- `rev`: Specifies the relationship between the target URL and the current document. Possible values include `alternate`, `stylesheet`, `start`, `next`, `prev`, `contents`, `index`, `glossary`, `copyright`, `chapter`, `section`, `subsection`, `appendix`, `help`, and `bookmark`.

- `shape`: Defines the type of region for mapping in the current `<area>` tag in an image map. Possible values include `circle`, `default`, `poly`, and `rect`.

- `type`: Specifies the MIME type of the target URL. Refer to Chapter 3 for details on the MIME types.

Standard Attributes

- `accesskey`

- `class`

- `dir`

- `id`

- `lang`

- `style`

- `tabindex`

- `title`

- `xml:lang`

Event Attributes

- `onblur`

- `onclick`

- `ondblclick`

- `onfocus`

- `onkeydown`

- `onkeypress`

- `onkeyup`

- `onmousedown`

- `onmousemove`

- `onmouseover`

- `onmouseup`

The anchor element has several attributes, but the most commonly used attribute is the `href` attribute.

Using the <a> Tag

This section shows examples of how to use the anchor (`<a>`) tag in different ways. Other sections that follow show some of the more advanced features in combination with CSS.

Linking to Other Documents

The most common use of the anchor tag is to simply link to another document. Let's start by linking to another document from within a document. A typical application of the anchor tag would be when you publish an XHTML document on the Internet and then link your document to other documents (see Listing 6-1).

Listing 6-1. *Using the Anchor Element*

```
<!DOCTYPE html
PUBLIC "-//W3C//DTD XHTML 1.0 Strict//EN"
"http://www.w3.org/TR/xhtml1/DTD/xhtml1-strict.dtd">
<html>
    <head>
        <title>Using Links</title>
    </head>
    <body>
      <p>
        <a href="http://www.google.com">Search</a>
      </p>
    </body>
</html>
```

This sample uses the `<a>` tag along with the `href` attribute to provide users the ability to do a search using Google. Clicking on the text or image located between the opening `<a>` tag and the closing `</a>` tag will result in the link being activated. If the link element has focus, users can also press the Enter key to invoke the link. The `href` provides the location—in this case, `http://www.google.com`—where the browser should navigate to, as shown in Figure 6-1.

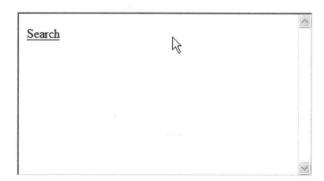

Figure 6-1. *The anchor tag is used in a simple web page.*

Listing 6-1 provides the full URL to the requested document. The full URL is referred to as an absolute path. When you wish to link to a document that is stored in a different location from yours, you need to use an absolute link so that the browser knows exactly where to retrieve the document from. The absolute link provides the domain, at a minimum, and can include a directory and the specific file (document) you're looking to link to.

When you want to link to other documents that are on your domain, you have the option of using a relative link. A relative link uses a shortcut so that you don't need to specify the domain and possibly the directory path of the document you wish to link to. Relative paths are based on where the original document is located. Links that are located within the same directory as the document don't have any path. To access a directory that is in the same directory as your document, you use the directory name followed by a slash and then the file name: `images\filename`. To access a document or file that is up one level from the current document, add two periods: `../filename`. Notice in Listing 6-2 that `href` doesn't contain any domain or file path information.

Listing 6-2. *Using Relative Links*

```
<!DOCTYPE html
PUBLIC "-//W3C//DTD XHTML 1.0 Strict//EN"
"http://www.w3.org/TR/xhtml1/DTD/xhtml1-strict.dtd">
<html>
    <head>
        <title>Using Links - Relative Links</title>
    </head>
    <body>
        <p>
            Options:<br />
            <a href="home.html">Home</a><br />
            <a href="news.html">News</a><br />
            <a href="menu.html">Menu</a><br />
            <a href="locations.html">Locations</a>
        </p>
    </body>
</html>
```

Also, notice that several links have been added within the same document, thus providing several options for users to select from. How, for example, does the browser know where to look for the document titled `home.html`? With relative links, the browser makes the assumption that since you didn't provide an alternate place to retrieve the document from, it must be located in the same domain and file path where it found the current document. In this case, it looks for the document named `home.html` in the same location that it loaded the original document.

■**Tip** It's a good idea to use relative links to navigate between the documents on your site. Doing so makes it much easier should you decide to change the location of your documents, which would cause part of the URL name to change.

Oftentimes, as your site gets larger and you have different types of files, such as XHTML files, images, and CSS, you may find yourself placing these files in different folders to help in organization. In Chapter 11, we'll show you how to build an entire site, and we'll provide some practical advice on how to set up your site. Using relative links could prove to be difficult, as you may have files in directories other than the one that your document exists in. You can use two periods followed by a slash (../) to instruct the browser that it needs to move up one level in the directory path.

```
<a href="../home/index.html>Home Page</a>
```

Based on the href in this example, the browser will move up a level from the level that the current linking document is in. The browser will then change to the home folder and lastly load the document index.html.

FIXING LINKS

When you create a link in your document, it might not always work. For example, you might create a link in your document, click on the link, and get an error. There are a couple things you can do when links don't work:

- *Check the URL*: The URL may have changed since you first created it, so verify it by cutting and pasting the link into your browser manually.

- *Check the spelling, capitalization, and the file name (including the extension) of the link*: All it takes is one incorrect character to cause your link to fail.

One sure way to get the correct URL is to open the link in a browser and cut and paste it into your document.

Linking to Non-XHTML Documents

So far, you've seen how to link to other XHTML documents. It's also possible to link to non-XHTML data that you can find on the Internet. One common use is to provide links to an FTP site in order to make it easy for users to download a file. For example, the following link allows users to open their browser to the Microsoft FTP site:

```
<a href="ftp://ftp.microsoft.com">Microsoft FTP Site</a>
```

When users click on the link, it will connect them to the Microsoft FTP site, as shown in Figure 6-2.

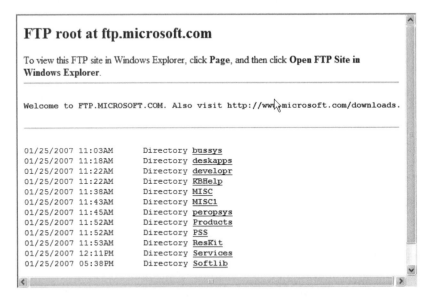

FTP root at ftp.microsoft.com

To view this FTP site in Windows Explorer, click **Page**, and then click **Open FTP Site in Windows Explorer**.

Welcome to FTP.MICROSOFT.COM. Also visit http://www.microsoft.com/downloads.

```
01/25/2007 11:03AM      Directory bussys
01/25/2007 11:18AM      Directory deskapps
01/25/2007 11:22AM      Directory developr
01/25/2007 11:22AM      Directory KBHelp
01/25/2007 11:38AM      Directory MISC
01/25/2007 11:43AM      Directory MISC1
01/25/2007 11:45AM      Directory peropsys
01/25/2007 11:52AM      Directory Products
01/25/2007 11:52AM      Directory PSS
01/25/2007 11:53AM      Directory ResKit
01/25/2007 12:11PM      Directory Services
01/25/2007 05:38PM      Directory Softlib
```

Figure 6-2. *The user's browser at the Microsoft FTP site*

You can also use this same technique to link to other non-XHTML files on the Internet. For example, if you have a .pdf document that you wish to make available on your website, you could simply use a link similar to the following:

```
<a href="menu.pdf">Download Menu in PDF (500k)</a>
```

If a document isn't a standard HTML/XHTML document, it's considered good practice to make it clear to users what size and type of document it is. The example specifies that it is a .pdf document and is 500k. This provides users with enough information to decide whether their computer supports the file type and if the file is too large to download. When users click on the Download Menu link, the browser presents them with one or both of the following options:

- Save the file to the local machine.

- Open the file.

If users select to save the file, the browser will prompt for a location and then download the file and save it to the local machine. If they select to open the file, the browser will retrieve the menu.pdf file and use the file extension to try to determine what application to use to open the file. If the browser doesn't know how to handle the file, it will display some type of error message, depending on the platform, or it will prompt the users to determine what type of application the file should be associated with. You can use the technique presented here for any file type. One word of caution: be careful when linking directly to certain types of files, such as .exe files, because malicious people sometimes place computer viruses or destructive files on their websites.

Linking to E-Mail Addresses

One of the most common ways to use the anchor element besides linking to other XHTML documents is to automatically link to an e-mail address. This is a good way to make sure that users send e-mail to the correct person. When using the `<a>` tag for e-mail, you use the `href` in the following fashion:

```
<a href="mailto:webmaster@mywebpage.com?subject=Feedback">Feedback</a>
```

By default, when users follow the link, the browser opens a new window with the default e-mail application. If there is no default e-mail application, nothing will happen. In the example, the e-mail address webmaster@mywebpage.com is inserted automatically into the To line of the e-mail application. The `?subject=Feedback` places the text following the `?subject=` into the subject line of the e-mail client, if the e-mail application supports this functionality. In this case, the text *Feedback* is placed in the subject line. Figure 6-3 displays what Microsoft Outlook looks like after clicking on the `mailto:` link.

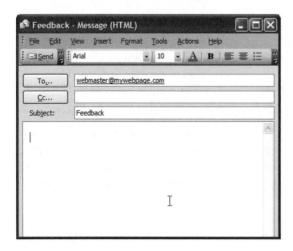

Figure 6-3. *Outlook after a mailto: link was selected*

■Tip Using an anchor element to link to an e-mail address is somewhat discouraged. When you embed your e-mail address within a document, you're making your address available to anyone who can read your document. Some people collect these e-mail addresses using special programs and use them for sending out spam. At the same time, you really want to give your users the ability to e-mail you with questions and comments. You can use forms (as you'll see in Chapter 8) to allow your users to communicate with you, or you can use an obfuscation technique to confuse the programs harvesting e-mail addresses. You must weigh the pros and cons when deciding whether you want to put a direct e-mail address in your documents. Do you care if you get spam? Does your e-mail server do a decent job of filtering it out? These are the types of questions you'll want to think about.

Using an Image As a Link

You learned about the `<img>` tag in Chapter 5, so now you can put it to good use. Listing 6-3 shows how you can combine the `<img>` tag along with the `<a>` tag to make an image into a link.

Listing 6-3. *XHTML That Uses an Image Tag Within an Anchor*

```
<!DOCTYPE html
PUBLIC "-//W3C//DTD XHTML 1.0 Strict//EN"
"http://www.w3.org/TR/xhtml1/DTD/xhtml1-strict.dtd">
<html>
    <head>
        <style type="text/css">
            img {border: none;}
        </style>
        <title>Using Links - Image Links</title>
    </head>
    <body>
        <p>
            <a href="mailto:webmaster@mywebpage.com">
            <img src="email_btn.gif" alt="Email Webmaster" /></a>
        </p>
    </body>
</html>
```

The only real trick here is to be sure to put the `<img>` tags within the anchor tags. This makes the entire image a link. Also, notice that you can add a style to remove the default border on the image, as shown in Figure 6-4.

Figure 6-4. *A browser displaying an image link*

You can use any image you'd like to create links. Typically, people create an image that looks like a button and use it as a link. One thing to consider when using an image is that any text you want to use must be part of the image itself. You also might want to use an animated .gif file to make your site a bit more fun. An animated .gif file uses a sequence of images to make an image animated. Be careful not to use too many animated .gif files, because you don't want to distract from the content or make your document look comical. Another common practice is to use an image in place of using text altogether. For example, you might do this in a toolbar or in other cases where a picture or set of pictures may flow better with your entire document.

A better option than using the `<img>` tag is to use CSS. CSS provides more flexibility and keeps the presentation separate from the rendering. The "Adding CSS to the Anchor Tag" section provides an example.

Using IDs

One of the neat features that the anchor allows you to do is to link to a specific location within a document. For instance, in a sample restaurant website, you could have one document that is simply a list of definitions for cooking terms. Then the menu document could link directly to the terms to allow users to find information about a term they may not be familiar with. When they click on the link for the term, the retrieved page will open up. This way, users don't have to search for a specific term in a document. In order to set up an ID, you first must assign a value to the `id` attribute:

```
<a id="filet">Definition goes here</a>
```

Now that you've set up an ID, you need to be able to link directly to it. You do that by specifying the URL like you normally would, but you also include a pound sign followed by the ID (#id) that you wish to link to. For example, to link to the definition of *filet* in the `definitions.html` document, you'd use the following code:

```
<a href="http://www.mywebsite/definitions.html#filet"></a>
```

Many times you may want to link to content within the same page. For example, you may have a list of steps or rules that you want to provide details about further down in the document. You can use the `id` attribute here as well. Another common use of the `id` attribute is to make top and bottom links on the document when the document is extremely long. Listing 6-4 shows you how to use a link to allow users to quickly jump to the top of the document once they scroll down to the bottom.

Listing 6-4. *Using the id Attribute to Link to an Internal Document*

```
<!DOCTYPE html
PUBLIC "-//W3C//DTD XHTML 1.0 Strict//EN"
"http://www.w3.org/TR/xhtml1/DTD/xhtml1-strict.dtd">
<html>
    <head>
        <title>Using IDs Within the Same Doc</title>
    </head>
    <body>
        <p>
            <a id="top">

            ..

            ..

            ..

            ..
        </p>
        <p>
            <a href="#top">Return to top</a>
        </p>
    </body>
</html>
```

This code isn't complete. We tried to conserve space and showed you where there would be a lot more content within the document. When users click on the link Return to top, the browser finds the ID top and returns users to the top of the page.

Adding CSS to the Anchor Tag

In keeping with the theme of showing a little CSS with each chapter, this section shows you a couple of common CSS techniques developers often use to keep a particular color scheme or theme for their website. By default, the browser underlines your links and makes them specific colors so they stand out to users. However, the default colors may not fit in well with your visual layout. You can change the look of the link by using CSS to change the <a> tag, as Listing 6-5 shows.

Listing 6-5. *Using CSS with the Anchor Tag*

```
<!DOCTYPE html
PUBLIC "-//W3C//DTD XHTML 1.0 Strict//EN"
"http://www.w3.org/TR/xhtml1/DTD/xhtml1-strict.dtd">
<html>
    <head>
        <style type="text/css">
            a:link { color: red; text-decoration: none }
            a:visited { color: green; text-decoration: none}
            a:hover {color: blue; text-decoration: underlined}
            a:active {color: black; text-decoration: none}
            a:focus {color: yellow; text-decoration: underlined}
        </style>
        <title>Using CSS with Anchors</title>
    </head>
    <body>
        <p>
            <a href="mailto:webmaster@mywebsite.com">Send Feedback</a>
        </p>
    </body>
</html>
```

In this code, you use CSS to apply specific styles to the different states available for a link. This code uses a new concept called *pseudo classes*. You use pseudo classes in combination with a selector to apply a style to a specific condition or portion of an element. The format of a pseudo class looks like this:

```
selector:pseudo-class {property: value}
```

When a link (link) has never been selected, it shows up with a text color of red. If a user has already clicked on the link (visited), it shows up as green. As the user clicks (active) on the link, it turns black, and when the user moves the mouse over the link (hover), it turns blue. Lastly, this code adds a style for the focus pseudo class. When the user uses a keyboard shortcut or tabs to the link, the link control gains focus, turns yellow, and becomes underlined. When styling links, it is important to remember to use the focus pseudo class for users who use alternative pointing devices or a keyboard. Figure 6-5 shows a link that displays red text prior to a user clicking on it.

When the user hovers over the link, it turns blue and is underlined, as shown in Figure 6-6.

Figure 6-5. *The link prior to a user clicking on it*

Figure 6-6. *The link turns blue when someone hovers over it.*

Keep in mind that you can apply many different styles to the link, visited, hover, and active pseudo classes in order to provide a custom look and feel. The order in which you apply the styles is important. An easy way to remember the order is with the saying LoVe HAte: link, visited, hover, and active.

You can use CSS to create some really cool effects. By using a background, a border, and several other attributes, you can make a menu that changes colors as the user moves over a link. Listing 6-6 builds on the original menu built back in Listing 6-2. By simply applying a new style, you can completely change the look and feel.

Listing 6-6. *Using CSS to Create a Changing Background Color*

```
<!DOCTYPE html
PUBLIC "-//W3C//DTD XHTML 1.0 Strict//EN"
"http://www.w3.org/TR/xhtml1/DTD/xhtml1-strict.dtd">
<html>
    <head>
        <style type="text/css">
            a {color: black;
                font: 12px Arial,Helvetica,sans-serif;
                text-decoration: none;
                border: 2px solid black;
                display: block;
                width: 200px;
                padding: 3px 10px;
                background: #dcdcdc;}
```

```
            a:hover, a:active, a:focus {
                background: #4169E1;
                font-weight: bold;}
        </style>
        <title>Using Links - Changing Backgrounds</title>
    </head>
    <body>
        <p>
            Options:<br/>
            <a href="home.html">Home</a><br />
            <a href="news.html">News</a><br />
            <a href="menu.html">Menu</a><br />
            <a href="locations.html" >Locations</a>
        </p>
    </body>
</html>
```

Figure 6-7 shows the much-improved version of the menu. By adjusting the styles, you can dramatically change how the links are presented. Not only have you changed the background color, but you've also changed the weight of the font to make the text stand out for the selected link. Also, notice that you can add attributes to make the menu items more usable for those users who aren't using a mouse. The a:active and a:focus attributes now provide the same functionality as when using a mouse. As users tab through the controls using their keyboard, it is obvious which menu item has focus.

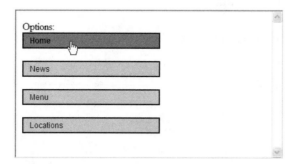

Figure 6-7. *The much-improved menu*

Back when we discussed how to use the <img> tag within the anchor, we mentioned that there is a better way to do the same thing with CSS. Listing 6-7 is similar to Listing 6-6, except instead of changing the background color, you're changing the background image. This provides for some professional-looking buttons, as Figure 6-8 shows. The bold code in Listing 6-7 shows the differences from the previous version. Here you remove the background color, adjust the height and width to match the bitmaps, adjust the padding, and supply the images to the background-image attribute.

Listing 6-7. *Using CSS to Create Professional-Looking Buttons*

```
<!DOCTYPE html
PUBLIC "-//W3C//DTD XHTML 1.0 Strict//EN"
"http://www.w3.org/TR/xhtml1/DTD/xhtml1-strict.dtd">
<html>
    <head>
        <style type="text/css">
            a {color: black;
                font: 12px Arial,Helvetica,sans-serif;
                text-decoration: none;
                display: block;
                width: 200px;
                height: 22px;
                padding-top:8px;
                text-align:center;
                background-image: url('btnOn.gif');}
            a:hover {
                background-image:url('btnOff.gif');
                font-weight: bold;}
        </style>
        <title>Using Links with Background Images</title>
    </head>
    <body>
        <p>
            Options:
            <a href="home.html">Home</a><br />
            <a href="news.html">News</a><br />
            <a href="menu.html">Menu</a><br />
            <a href="locations.html">Locations</a>
        </p>
    </body>
</html>
```

Listing 6-7 provides for some professional-looking buttons, as Figure 6-8 shows.

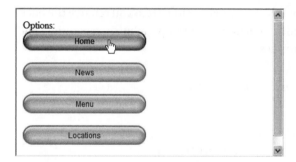

Figure 6-8. *Using the background-image attribute to create rollover buttons*

This code is pretty cool and simple. You can find many different websites that provide free buttons or the ability to generate bitmaps for buttons. A couple of good places to start are http://www.freebuttons.com and http://www.netdenizen.com/buttonmill.

Creating Image Maps

An image map allows you to break an image into specific regions that can be used as links within the same document or to other documents. When users move their cursor over a part of an image that has a hotspot, the cursor changes to indicate it's a link, and the alt attribute is displayed. Image maps have specific locations and allow for the selection of a state. They then link to a document based on the selection.

Image maps are not commonly used, because they tend to embed behavior and layout information within a document, and their functionality is not always intuitive to the readers of your document. When using image maps, you need to be careful that your interface is intuitive to users. If it isn't, they won't have any idea that the links exist. Some documents even add a small instruction above or below the image indicating what to do.

To use an image map, start by having an image that you wish to add hotspots to and a map that specifies the required links and coordinates. Figure 6-9 shows a circle and a square. In the "Usage" section, you'll learn how to use an image map to let the user decide whether they want a round or square pizza.

Using an image map requires the use of two new tags: <map> and <area>. The <map> tag is used as a container to a list of <area> tags. You can put as many <area> tags within a <map> tag as you need. Some of the more complicated maps can contain a hundred or more <area> tags.

Figure 6-9. *The image used for an image map*

<map>

The <map> tag specifies a client-side image map with clickable regions.

Required Attributes

- id: Specifies a unique ID for the map element

Optional Attributes

- name: Specifies a unique name for the map element

Standard Attributes

- class

- dir

- id

- lang

- style

- title

- xml:lang

Event Attributes

- accesskey

- onblur

- onclick

- ondblclick

- onfocus

- onkeydown

- onkeypress

- onkeyup

- onmousedown

- onmousemove

- onmouseout

- onmouseover

- onmouseup

- tabindex

<area>

You use the area element to specify a region in an image map.

Required Attributes

- alt: Specifies the text to be used as an alternate for the area

Optional Attributes

- coords: Specifies the coordinates of the clickable area within a map. If the shape attribute equals rect, then the format is left, top, right, and bottom. If the shape attribute equals circ, then the format is center x, center y, and radius. If the shape attribute equals poly, then the format is x1, y1, x2, y2, . . . xn, yn.

- `href`: A URL that specifies the link of the area.

- `nohref`: Excludes an area from an image map using the values `true` and `false`.

- `shape`: Specifies the shape of an area. Valid values are `circle`, `poly`, and `rect`.

Standard Attributes

- `accesskey`

- `class`

- `dir`

- `id`

- `lang`

- `style`

- `tabindex`

- `title`

- `xml:lang`

Event Attributes

- `onblur`

- `onclick`

- `ondblclick`

- `onfocus`

- `onkeydown`

- `onkeypress`

- `onkeyup`

- `onmousedown`

- `onmousemove`

- onmouseout

- onmouseover

- onmouseup

■Tip The name attribute has been deprecated on the <map> tag in XHTML 1.0 and removed in subsequent versions. However, browsers tend not to work well with maps that don't have a name attribute, because the browsers handle content as text/html unless overridden with content negotiation. Therefore, it's best to continue to use the name attribute for the time being.

Usage

The best way to see how an image map works is to build one. Let's start by creating the map container within the body element and giving it the id of map. Later, when you want to link the map to the image, you'll use the value specified in the id attribute. Next, you need to specify the actual hotspots using the area tag. You have two different links (round pizza and square pizza), so you need to use two different area elements. When specifying the square pizza, choose a shape of rect and specify its left, top, right, and bottom. When specifying the round pizza, use a shape of circ, which requires a center point and a radius. Also, notice that you provide an href that your application will navigate to should the user click on the region as well as the alt text. In order to specify the coordinates, use an image-editing program, such as Microsoft Paint, shown in Figure 6-10. Hover over the areas indicated to get their coordinates. For the circle, you need to get the center point and calculate the radius.

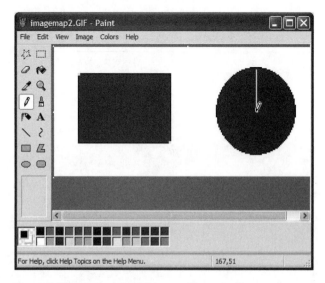

Figure 6-10. *Determining the coordinates of an area*

■**Tip** Many tools are available (some for free) that will aid in the generation of an image map. For example, you can find one at `http://www.kolchose.org/simon/ajaximagemapcreator/`.

Once you've defined the `<map>` and `<area>`s within your document, you need to hook the map to the image you wish to apply it to. This is actually pretty simple. All you need to do is use the `usemap` attribute within the `<img>` tag and specify the `id` of the map you wish to use. Listing 6-8 puts it all together.

Listing 6-8. *Using an Image Map*

```
<!DOCTYPE html
PUBLIC "-//W3C//DTD XHTML 1.0 Strict//EN"
"http://www.w3.org/TR/xhtml1/DTD/xhtml1-strict.dtd">
<html>
    <head>
        <style type="text/css">
            img {border-style: none}
        </style>
        <title>Image Maps</title>
    </head>
    <body>
        <p>
            <map id="map" name="map">
                <area shape="rect" href="square.html"
                  coords="20,27 97,76" alt="Order
                    Square Pizza" />
                <area shape="circle" href="round.html"
                  coords="167,51 35" alt="Order
                    Round Pizza" />
            </map>
            <img usemap="#map" src="imagemap.gif"
              alt="Choose square or round pizza! "/>
        </p>
    </body>
</html>
```

Figure 6-11 shows the image map in action. In this case, the cursor over the circle indicates that the user wants to order a round pizza. Notice that the `alt` text is displayed, and the pointer has changed to indicate a link is available. If a user clicks on it, the browser will navigate to whatever link is specified.

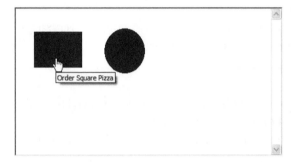

Figure 6-11. *Hovering over an image map*

An additional shape, poly, allows for the ultimate in flexibility. When using the poly shape, you need to specify a space-delimited list of points that make up the outline of the polygon. For example, this code shows how to make an oddly shaped polygon:

```
<area shape="poly" href="poly.html" coords=" ="140,210, 190,257, 140,305 110,260"

    alt="A Polygon">
```

■**Tip** When using an image map, you may want to also use CSS to specify that the image doesn't have a border. If you don't, a blue border will be placed around the image.

Summary

This chapter has shown you how to create links using the anchor tag. You saw how to create links to documents that are within the same site as well as to documents on other sites. Next, you learned how you can use image maps to break an image into multiple areas that you can use to link to multiple documents. Finally, you learned some of the basics of styling your links to make them fit into a theme for an entire website or just to have fun. When changing any styles related to the anchor tag, you should consider the effects it will have from a usability point of view. Users are accustomed to the normal link behavior, so any new behavior needs to be easy to follow and understand. In Chapter 7, you'll learn how to store tabular data using tables.

CHAPTER 7

■■■

Using Tables

This chapter details the use of tables in your documents. Tables are useful when trying to capture data that is *tabular* in nature—that is, data that is best kept in a table format or within rows and columns. Tables are common within web documents, but they aren't always used in the correct fashion. The goal of this chapter is to show you how to use CSS as much as possible to separate the look and feel of tables from the actual data within them. CSS is mature enough that you can style tables exclusively with CSS, thus allowing the separation you're striving to maintain.

The Basics of Tables

You can easily set up a basic table in your document. A table consists of three elements: table, tr, and td. Listing 7-1 shows the code for a typical table.

Listing 7-1. *Basic Tag Layout of a Table*

```
...
<table>
  <tr>
    <td>Row 1 Cell 1</td>
    <td>Row 1 Cell 2</td>
    <td>Row 1 Cell 3</td>
  </tr>
  <tr>
    <td>Row 2 Cell 1</td>
    <td>Row 2 Cell 2</td>
    <td>Row 2 Cell 3</td>
  </tr>
</table>
...
```

Figure 7-1 shows what this basic table looks like within a visual web browser. You can see that it creates a set of columns and rows, similar to a spreadsheet.

| Row 1 Cell 1 | Row 1 Cell 2 | Row 1 Cell 3 |
| Row 2 Cell 1 | Row 2 Cell 2 | Row 2 Cell 3 |

Figure 7-1. *A basic table within a web browser*

The <table> tag marks the beginning and end of the table. The table element must be within the body of the document. The <tr> tag set marks the beginning and end of a row and is found within the table element. Lastly, the <td> tag set marks each cell within the row. The content of the cell exists between the opening and closing <td> tags. You can pretty much put any content you want in a cell—text, bitmaps, links, and other tables are all possibilities. You can add as many rows and cells as you want within a table. Each cell, as well as the table itself, can size itself automatically based on the data it contains.

When creating a large table, consider the rendering time. In other words, take into account the time it takes to create the table and place it into the document and onto your browser. In order for a table to size itself automatically, it must read all the data that goes into the cells to determine how wide to make each cell. As you'll see later in the "<colgroup>" section, you can provide the table with hints on how wide to make each column, thereby speeding up the rendering process. The next few sections provide the attributes for the basic tags used for creating tables.

<table>

The <table> tag set defines where a table starts and ends. You can place table headers, rows, cells, and other tables within a table.

Required Attributes

The <table> tag doesn't have any required attributes.

Optional Attributes

- border: Specifies the width of a table's border in pixels.

- cellpadding: Specifies the amount of space between the cell walls and the content in pixels or as a percent.

- cellspacing: Specifies the amount of space between cells in pixels or as a percent.

- `frame`: Specifies how the outer borders of a table should be displayed. You use this attribute along with the `border` attribute. Possible values are `above`, `below`, `border`, `box`, `hsides`, `lhs`, `rhs`, `void`, and `vsides`.

- `rules`: Specifies the horizontal and vertical divider lines. You use this attribute along with the `border` attribute. Possible values are `all`, `cols`, `groups`, `none`, and `rows`.

- `summary`: Specifies a summary of the tables for special browsers that provide speech-synthesizing and nonvisual capabilities. If you need to use a table for layout purposes, you shouldn't use the `summary` attribute, as it will confuse the nonvisual browser user.

- `width`: Specifies the width of the table in pixels or as a percent. The use of the CSS property `width` is the preferred method.

Standard Attributes

- `class`

- `dir`

- `id`

- `lang`

- `style`

- `title`

- `xml:lang`

Event Attributes

- `onclick`

- `ondblclick`

- `onkeydown`

- `onkeypress`

- `onkeyup`

- `onmousedown`

- `onmousemove`

- onmouseout

- onmouseover

- onmouseup

<tr>

The <tr> tag marks the start of a new row in a table.

Required Attributes

There are no required attributes for the <tr> tag.

Optional Attributes

- align: Specifies the alignment of the text within a cell. Possible values are center, char, justify, left, and right. The use of the CSS property text-align is the preferred method.

- char: Specifies which character the text should be aligned on. This requires the use of the align attribute with the value set as char.

- charoff: Specifies in pixels or as a percentage how far the alignment should be adjusted to the first character to align on. This requires the use of the align attribute with the value set as char.

- valign: Specifies the text alignment in vertical cells. Possible values are baseline, bottom, middle, and top.

Standard Attributes

- class

- dir

- id

- lang

- style

- title

- xml:lang

Event Attributes

- `onclick`

- `ondblclick`

- `onkeydown`

- `onkeypress`

- `onkeyup`

- `onmousedown`

- `onmousemove`

- `onmouseout`

- `onmouseover`

- `onmouseup`

`<td>`

The `<td>` tag marks the start of a new cell within a row in a table.

Required Attributes

No attributes are required for the `<td>` tag.

Optional Attributes

- `abbr`: Specifies a shortened version of the content in a cell. You use this optional attribute to provide nonvisual browsers a shortened version of long content.

- `align`: Specifies the alignment of cell content. Possible values are `center`, `char`, `justify`, `left`, and `right`. The use of the CSS property `text-align` is the preferred method.

- `axis`: Places a cell into conceptual categories. These categories form an axis in an n-dimensional space. User agents can then give users access to the categories.

- `char`: Specifies which character the text should be aligned on. This requires the use of the `align` attribute with the value set as `char`.

- charoff: Specifies in pixels or as a percentage how far the alignment should be adjusted to the first character to align on. This requires the use of the align attribute with the value set as char.

- colspan: Specifies the number of columns this cell should occupy.

- rowspan: Indicates the number of rows this cell should occupy.

- scope: Specifies if a cell provides header information for the rest of the row that contains it or for the rest of the column. Valid values are col, colgroup, row, and rowgroup.

- valign: Specifies the vertical alignment of cell content. Possible values are baseline, bottom, middle, and top.

Standard Attributes

- class

- dir

- id

- lang

- style

- title

- xml:lang

Event Attributes

- onclick

- ondblclick

- onkeydown

- onkeypress

- onkeyup

- onmousedown

- onmousemove

- onmouseout

- onmouseover

- onmouseup

Coding a Basic Table

In keeping with the restaurant theme used throughout the book, the code in Listing 7-2 creates a table that contains price information for different pizzas.

Listing 7-2. *The Code for a Basic Table*

```
<!DOCTYPE html
PUBLIC "-//W3C//DTD XHTML 1.0 Strict//EN"
"http://www.w3.org/TR/xhtml1/DTD/xhtml1-strict.dtd">
<html xmlns="http://www.w3.org/1999/xhtml">
  <head>
    <title>A Basic Table</title>
  </head>
  <body>
    <table border="1" summary="Prices for types of pizza by size">
      <tr>
        <td scope="col">Pizza Type</td>
        <td scope="col">Small</td>
        <td scope="col">Medium</td>
        <td scope="col">Large</td>
      </tr>
      <tr>
        <td scope="row">Thin Crust</td>
        <td>3.99</td>
        <td>4.99</td>
        <td>6.99</td>
      </tr>
      <tr>
        <td scope="row">Deep Dish</td>
        <td>4.99</td>
        <td>6.99</td>
        <td>8.99</td>
      </tr>
      <tr>
```

```
        <td scope="row">Stuffed Crust</td>
        <td>5.99</td>
        <td>7.99</td>
        <td>9.99</td>
      </tr>
    </table>
  </body>
</html>
```

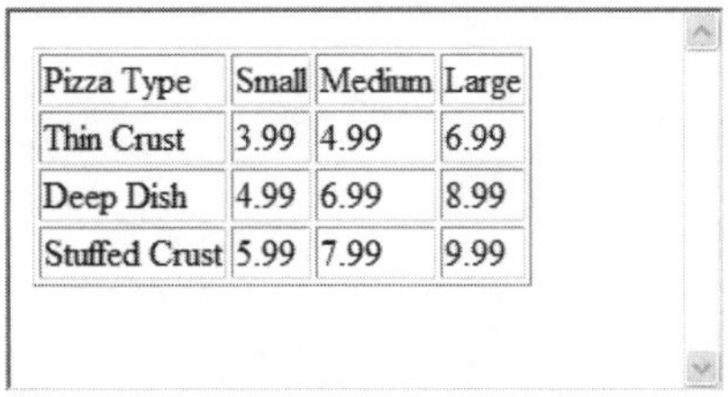

This table associates the prices of the pizzas with their type and size. You start with the `<table>` tag, and then you use the `<tr>` tag to create rows. You create a row for each type of pizza in the restaurant, and you create cells within each row to hold the different prices. This table is a perfect way to store the tabular data.

You should also specify a `summary` property in the `table` element. The `summary` attribute is one of several attributes that you'll see throughout this chapter that provide information to nonvisual browsers. They allow these browsers to interpret a document properly. We are introducing some the accessibility attributes early on to impress the importance of considering nonvisual browsers when creating your documents. In this case, the `summary` attribute describes what data is in the table. The `summary` attribute is not rendered for visual browsers. The `summary` attribute really shines when you have a complex table that is not obvious, but be careful to not overuse this attribute because it can lead to redundancy.

Also, notice that this table makes use of the `scope` attribute. The `scope` attribute is an optional attribute that helps nonvisual browsers interpret the layout of the data within a table. In this case, we specified that some of the `<td>` tags apply to the entire column. For example, the text *Small* is meant for the entire column it is in, and the prices below it are for a small pizza. Along the same lines, we listed several different types of pizzas and specified the `scope` attribute as `row`, since each cell in the row represents the price for that type of pizza. Figure 7-2 shows the results in a web browser.

Pizza Type	Small	Medium	Large
Thin Crust	3.99	4.99	6.99
Deep Dish	4.99	6.99	8.99
Stuffed Crust	5.99	7.99	9.99

Figure 7-2. *The pizza table displayed in a web browser*

Notice that the table has set its own size for each cell and that each cell is left-aligned by default. Later, you'll learn how to change the cell alignment and set the width using CSS. Wouldn't it be nice if you could put a title on the table so users know what it is? This is where the `caption` element comes in.

\<caption\>

The \<caption\> tag is used to assign a title to a table. In a visual browser, it places a caption or title above the table itself. It is not contained within a row or cell. You should place the \<caption\> tag after the \<table\> tag. You can specify a single caption per table.

Required Attributes

The \<caption\> tag doesn't have any required attributes.

Optional Attributes

There are no optional attributes for the \<caption\> tag.

Standard Attributes

- class

- dir

- id

- lang

- style

- title

- xml:lang

Event Attributes

- onclick

- ondblclick

- onkeydown

- onkeypress

- onkeyup

- onmousedown

- onmousemove

- onmouseout

- onmouseover

- onmouseup

Usage

In Listing 7-3, the bold code shows how to add a caption to the pizza table.

Listing 7-3. *Adding a Caption to a Table*

```
<!DOCTYPE html
PUBLIC "-//W3C//DTD XHTML 1.0 Strict//EN"
"http://www.w3.org/TR/xhtml1/DTD/xhtml1-strict.dtd">
<html xmlns="http://www.w3.org/1999/xhtml">
  <head>
    <title>A Basic Table with Caption</title>
  </head>
  <body>
    <table border="1" summary="Prices for types of pizza by size">
      <caption>Our Pizza Selections</caption>
      <tr>
        <td scope="col">Pizza Type</td>
        <td scope="col">Small</td>
        <td scope="col">Medium</td>
        <td scope="col">Large</td>
      </tr>
      <tr>
        <td>Thin Crust</td>
        <td>3.99</td>
        <td>4.99</td>
        <td>6.99</td>
      </tr>
      <tr>
        <td>Deep Dish</td>
        <td>4.99</td>
        <td>6.99</td>
        <td>8.99</td>
      </tr>
```

```
    <tr>
      <td>Stuffed Crust</td>
      <td>5.99</td>
      <td>7.99</td>
      <td>9.99</td>
    </tr>
  </table>
</body>
</html>
```

Figure 7-3 shows the result. Notice that the caption is displayed outside the table and centered over the table.

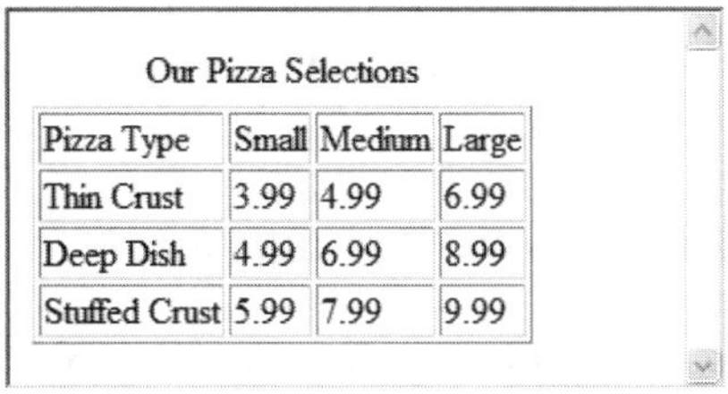

Figure 7-3. *The pizza table displayed with a caption*

<th>

Now let's make one more change to the table by adding a header row. Sometimes you want to mark cells in your table as being a header and not part of the data itself. You may also want to consider using the abbr attribute to provide an abbreviated version of any long headers. This provides nonvisual browsers a shorter alternative to use.

You can use the <th> tag in place of the <td> tag to mark a cell as a header. A header cell is normally bold and centered within the cell for visual browsers.

Required Attributes

There are no required attributes for the <th> tag.

Optional Attributes

- abbr: Specifies a shortened version of the content in a cell as text.

- align: Specifies the alignment of cell content. Possible values are center, char, justify, left, and right.

- axis: Places a cell into conceptual categories, which form an axis in an n-dimensional space. User agents can then give users access to the categories.

- char: Specifies which character the text should be aligned on. This requires the use of the align attribute with the value set as char.

- charoff: Specifies in pixels or as a percentage how far the alignment should be adjusted to the first character to align on. This requires the use of the align attribute with the value set as char.

- colspan: Specifies the number of columns this cell should occupy as a number.

- headers: Specifies a space-separated list of header cells that provide header information for the current data cell. You must set the cell names by their ID. The headers attribute helps nonvisual user agents render header information about data cells.

- rowspan: Indicates the number of rows this cell should occupy as a number.

- scope: Specifies whether a cell provides header information for the rest of the row that contains it or for the rest of the column. Valid values are col, colgroup, row, and rowgroup.

- valign: Specifies the vertical alignment of cell content. Possible values are baseline, bottom, middle, and top.

Standard Attributes

- class

- dir

- id

- lang

- style

- title

- xml:lang

Event Attributes

- onclick

- ondblclick

- onkeydown

- onkeypress

- onkeyup

- onmousedown

- onmousemove

- onmouseout

- onmouseover

- onmouseup

Listing 7-4 shows how to use the <th> tag in the pizza-pricing table to mark the pizza sizes as headers.

Listing 7-4. *Adding a Header Cell to a Table*

```
<!DOCTYPE html
PUBLIC "-//W3C//DTD XHTML 1.0 Strict//EN"
"http://www.w3.org/TR/xhtml1/DTD/xhtml1-strict.dtd">
<html xmlns="http://www.w3.org/1999/xhtml">
  <head>
    <title>Using the table header attribute</title>
  </head>
  <body>
    <table border="1" summary="Prices for types of pizza by size">
     <caption>Our Pizza Selections</caption>
      <tr>
        <th scope="col">Pizza Type</th>
        <th scope="col">Small</th>
        <th scope="col">Medium</th>
        <th scope="col">Large</th>
      </tr>
```

```
      <tr>
        <td scope="row">Thin Crust</td>
        <td>3.99</td>
        <td>4.99</td>
        <td>6.99</td>
      </tr>
      <tr>
        <td scope="row">Deep Dish</td>
        <td>4.99</td>
        <td>6.99</td>
        <td>8.99</td>
      </tr>
      <tr>
        <td scope="row">Stuffed Crust</td>
        <td>5.99</td>
        <td>7.99</td>
        <td>9.99</td>
      </tr>
    </table>
  </body>
</html>
```

In Figure 7-4, you can see that the cells marked with the `<th>` tag really stand out as headers, since they are bold and centered within their cells.

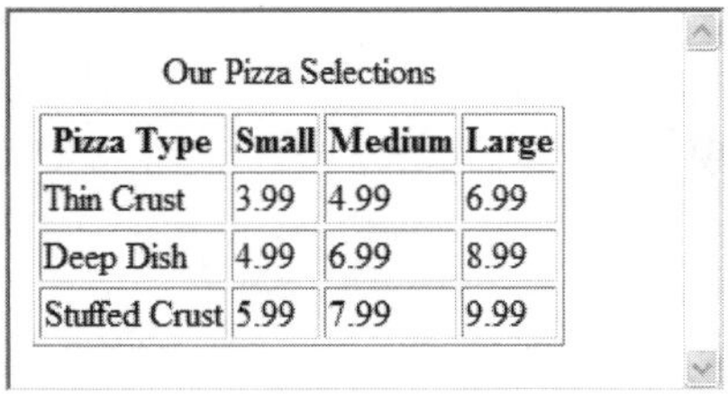
Our Pizza Selections

Pizza Type	Small	Medium	Large
Thin Crust	3.99	4.99	6.99
Deep Dish	4.99	6.99	8.99
Stuffed Crust	5.99	7.99	9.99

Figure 7-4. *The pizza table displayed with headers*

Advanced Use of Tables

The first part of this chapter introduced you to the basics of creating tables. This section introduces you to some of the more advanced attributes, as well as a few more elements that you can use within a table. First, we'll cover the `colspan` and `rowspan` attributes (see Listing 7-5). The `colspan` attribute allows you to merge multiple cells into one large cell. You specify how many columns you want a single cell to occupy. The `rowspan` attribute does the same thing but goes across multiple rows instead of cells.

Listing 7-5. *Code for Adding rowspan and colspan to a Basic Table*

```
<!DOCTYPE html
PUBLIC "-//W3C//DTD XHTML 1.0 Strict//EN"
"http://www.w3.org/TR/xhtml1/DTD/xhtml1-strict.dtd">
<html xmlns="http://www.w3.org/1999/xhtml">
  <head>
    <title>Using colspan and rowspan</title>
  </head>
  <body>
    <table border="1" summary="Prices for types of pizza by size">
      <caption>Our Pizza Selections</caption>
      <tr>
        <th rowspan="5" scope="row">Pizza<br />Type</th>
        <th colspan="4" scope="col">Size</th>
      </tr>
      <tr>
        <th></th>
        <th scope="col">Small</th>
        <th scope="col">Medium</th>
        <th scope="col">Large</th>
      </tr>
      <tr>
        <td scope="row">Thin Crust</td>
        <td>3.99</td>
        <td>4.99</td>
        <td>6.99</td>
      </tr>
      <tr>
        <td scope="row">Deep Dish</td>
        <td>4.99</td>
        <td>6.99</td>
        <td>8.99</td>
      </tr>
      <tr>
        <td>Stuffed Crust</td>
        <td>5.99</td>
        <td>7.99</td>
        <td>9.99</td>
      </tr>
    </table>
  </body>
</html>
```

Tip When you create a table that has an empty cell, you should consider placing a nonbreaking space entity ( ) in it as a placeholder for the data. If you don't use the nonbreaking space entity, the table won't display properly when using Windows Internet Explorer. It will be missing the cell border if you've set one.

Figure 7-5 displays the results of this code. Notice how much more effective the headings are when you merge them using rowspan and colspan attributes. This makes the table look better visually, but more importantly, the data is grouped properly within the document.

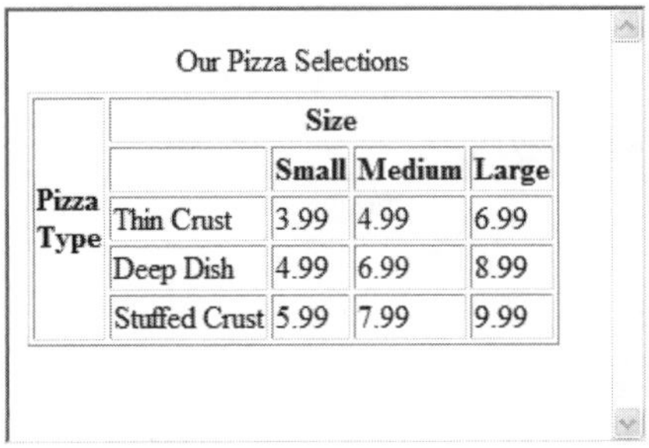

Figure 7-5. *The pizza table displayed with descriptive headers*

So far, you've seen the most common way to create a table, but you can also use the thead, tfoot, and tbody elements to create rows and cells within a table. The order in which these elements appear within a table element is important. They must appear in this order: thead, tfoot, and tbody. These elements allow you to group together the similar markup in your document and apply styles more easily to content within the thead, tfoot, and tbody elements. However, this approach hasn't caught on because of the lack of compatibility amongst the browsers in the past and because of the wealth of HTML from the past where people didn't use these elements. However, this is starting to change, and most modern browsers now work with these elements.

\<tbody\>

The \<tbody\> tag set defines where a table body starts and ends. It is contained within a table element. The thead, tfoot, and tbody elements allow you to group rows within a table easily.

Required Attributes

The \<tbody\> tag doesn't have any required attributes.

Optional Attributes

- `align`: Specifies the alignment of the text within a cell. Possible values are `center`, `char`, `justify`, `left`, and `right`.

- `char`: Specifies which character the text should be aligned on. This requires the use of the `align` attribute with the value set as `char`.

- `charoff`: Specifies in pixels or as a percentage how far the alignment should be adjusted to the first character to align on. This requires the use of the `align` attribute with the value set as `char`.

- `valign`: Specifies the vertical alignment of cell content. Possible values are `baseline`, `bottom`, `middle`, and `top`.

Standard Attributes

- `class`

- `dir`

- `id`

- `lang`

- `style`

- `title`

- `xml:lang`

Event Attributes

- `onclick`

- `ondblclick`

- `onkeydown`

- `onkeypress`

- `onkeyup`

- `onmousedown`

- onmousemove

- onmouseout

- onmouseover

- onmouseup

\<thead>

The \<thead> tag set defines where a table header starts and ends. It is contained within a table element. A standards-compliant browser repeats the headings at the top of each page when printing on paper.

Required Attributes

There are no required attributes for the \<thead> tag.

Optional Attributes

- align: Specifies the alignment of the text within a cell. Possible values are center, char, justify, left, and right.

- char: Specifies which character the text should be aligned on. This requires the use of the align attribute with the value set as char.

- charoff: Specifies in pixels or as a percentage how far the alignment should be adjusted to the first character to align on. This requires the use of the align attribute with the value set as char.

- valign: Specifies the vertical alignment of cell content. Possible values are baseline, bottom, middle, and top.

Standard Attributes

- class

- dir

- id

- lang

- style

- title

- xml:lang

Event Attributes

- onclick

- ondblclick

- onkeydown

- onkeypress

- onkeyup

- onmousedown

- onmousemove

- onmouseout

- onmouseover

- onmouseup

■Tip Internet Explorer doesn't automatically display the content specified in the <thead> or <tfoot> on each page when printing to paper. A workaround to this issue is to use CSS and set the table-header-group and table-footer-group properties like this:

```
thead { display: table-header-group; }
tfoot { display: table-footer-group; }
```

<tfoot>

The <tfoot> tag set defines where a table footer starts and ends. It is contained within a table element.

Required Attributes

There are no required attributes for the <tfoot> tag.

Optional Attributes

- `align`: Specifies the alignment of the text within a cell. Possible values are `center`, `char`, `justify`, `left`, and `right`.

- `char`: Specifies which character the text should be aligned on. This requires the use of the `align` attribute with the value set as `char`.

- `charoff`: Specifies in pixels or as a percentage how far the alignment should be adjusted to the first character to align on. This requires the use of the `align` attribute with the value set as `char`.

- `valign`: Specifies the vertical alignment of cell content. Possible values are `baseline`, `bottom`, `middle`, and `top`.

Standard Attributes

- `class`

- `dir`

- `id`

- `lang`

- `style`

- `title`

- `xml:lang`

Event Attributes

- `onclick`

- `ondblclick`

- `onkeydown`

- `onkeypress`

- `onkeyup`

- `onmousedown`

- onmousemove

- onmouseout

- onmouseover

- onmouseup

Usage

Listing 7-6 shows how the code from Listing 7-1 would look using this alternative style.

Listing 7-6. *An Alternate Way to Create Rows and Cells Within a Table*

```
<!DOCTYPE html
PUBLIC "-//W3C//DTD XHTML 1.0 Strict//EN"
"http://www.w3.org/TR/xhtml1/DTD/xhtml1-strict.dtd">
<html xmlns="http://www.w3.org/1999/xhtml">
  <head>
    <title>Using an alternate way to create a table</title>
  </head>
  <body>
    <table border="1" summary="This table provides the pricing information
      for pizzas">
      <thead>
        <tr>
          <th>Pizza Type</th>
          <th>Small</th>
          <th>Medium</th>
          <th>Large</th>
        </tr>
      </thead>
      <tfoot>
        <tr>
          <td scope="row"># Pieces</td>
          <td>8</td>
          <td>12</td>
          <td>16</td>
        </tr>
      </tfoot>
```

```
        <tbody>
          <tr>
            <td scope="row">Thin Crust</td>
            <td>3.99</td>
            <td>4.99</td>
            <td>6.99</td>
          </tr>
          <tr>
            <td scope="row">Deep Dish</td>
            <td>4.99</td>
            <td>6.99</td>
            <td>8.99</td>
          </tr>
          <tr>
            <td scope="row">Stuffed Crust</td>
            <td>5.99</td>
            <td>7.99</td>
            <td>9.99</td>
          </tr>
        </tbody>
      </table>
    </body>
</html>
```

Figure 7-6 shows the result. Breaking up the table in this fashion allows you to easily style the table by group using CSS. Notice that we're still using the `<th>` tag. The thead element is used to structurally group the elements only.

Pizza Type	Small	Medium	Large
Thin Crust	3.99	4.99	6.99
Deep Dish	4.99	6.99	8.99
Stuffed Crust	5.99	7.99	9.99
# Pieces	8	12	16

Figure 7-6. *The pizza table displayed using thead, tbody, and tfoot elements*

<colgroup>

We'll cover one last set of elements in this section. Previously, we mentioned that you can provide hints to the browser about how you want it to display your document. Using the `colgroup` and `col` elements allows you to be specific to help speed up the rendering. These elements aren't really used much in the real world but are presented here for completeness.

You use the `colgroup` element to define a group of `<cols>` tags. You should use the element only within a `table` element. You use this element to group columns and to ease styling with CSS.

Required Attributes

No attributes are required for the `<colgroup>` tag.

Optional Attributes

- `align`: Specifies the alignment of the text within a cell. Possible values are `center`, `char`, `justify`, `left`, and `right`.

- `char`: Specifies which character the text should be aligned on. This requires the use of the `align` attribute with the value set as `char`.

- `charoff`: Specifies in pixels or as a percentage how far the alignment should be adjusted to the first character to align on. This requires the use of the `align` attribute with the value set as `char`.

- `span`: Specifies the number of columns the `<colgroup>` should occupy.

- `valign`: Specifies the vertical alignment of cell content. Possible values are `baseline`, `bottom`, `middle`, and `top`.

- `width`: Specifies the width of the table in pixels or as a percent.

Standard Attributes

- `class`

- `dir`

- `id`

- `lang`

- style

- title

- xml:lang

Event Attributes

- onclick

- ondblclick

- onkeydown

- onkeypress

- onkeyup

- onmousedown

- onmousemove

- onmouseout

- onmouseover

- onmouseup

<col>

The <col> tag defines the attribute values for one or more columns in a table. You can use the <col> tag to specify whatever attributes you want to be in common for each column.

Required Attributes

There are no required attributes for the <col> tag.

Optional Attributes

- align: Specifies the alignment of the text within a cell. Possible values are center, char, justify, left, and right.

- char: Specifies which character the text should be aligned on. This requires the use of the align attribute with the value set as char.

- `charoff`: Specifies in pixels or as a percentage how far the alignment should be adjusted to the first character to align on. This requires the use of the `align` attribute with the value set as `char`.

- `span`: Specifies the number of columns the `<col>` should occupy.

- `valign`: Specifies the vertical alignment of cell content. Possible values are `baseline`, `bottom`, `middle`, and `top`.

- `width`: Specifies the width of the table in pixels or as a percentage.

Standard Attributes

- `class`

- `dir`

- `id`

- `lang`

- `style`

- `title`

- `xml:lang`

Event Attributes

- `onclick`

- `ondblclick`

- `onkeydown`

- `onkeypress`

- `onkeyup`

- `onmousedown`

- `onmousemove`

- `onmouseout`

- `onmouseover`

- `onmouseup`

Usage

Listing 7-7 shows the typical use of the `colgroup` and `col` elements.

Listing 7-7. *The Basic Syntax of Using the colgroup and col Elements*

```
...
<table>
  <colgroup>
    <col width="33"/>
    <col width="33"/>
    <col width="34"/>
  </colgroup>
  <tr>
    <td>Row 1 Cell 1</td>
    <td>Row 1 Cell 2</td>
    <td>Row 1 Cell 3</td>
  </tr>
  <tr>
    <td>Row 2 Cell 1</td>
    <td>Row 2 Cell 2</td>
    <td>Row 2 Cell 3</td>
  </tr>
</table>
...
```

Typically, each `<col>` represents one cell within the table. Note that when you use a `span` attribute, it applies to the number of cells identified by the span. Any attributes that you set in the `<col>` will be the default throughout the table. You can also set attributes at a higher level in the `colgroup` element.

Using CSS to Add Style to Your Tables

This section shows some of the basic ways you can style your tables in order to align the text in a specific way, add colors, and change the border. You can use most of the CSS functionalities to customize your tables to fit your needs.

Adding Borders

Up to this point, we cheated a little and placed some of the look and feel into the XHTML document by using the `border` attribute of the `table` element. Here we'll go back and show you the proper way of using CSS to style your border (see Listing 7-8).

Listing 7-8. *Adding a Border Using CSS*

```
<!DOCTYPE html
PUBLIC "-//W3C//DTD XHTML 1.0 Strict//EN"
"http://www.w3.org/TR/xhtml1/DTD/xhtml1-strict.dtd">
<html xmlns="http://www.w3.org/1999/xhtml">
  <head>
    <title>Using CSS for Borders</title>
    <style type="text/css">
      td, th {border-style: groove;}
      table {border-style: groove;}
    </style>
  </head>
  <body>
    <table summary="Prices for types of pizza by size">
      <thead>
        <tr>
          <th scope="col">Pizza Type</th>
          <th scope="col">Small</th>
          <th scope="col">Medium</th>
          <th scope="col">Large</th>
        </tr>
      </thead>
      <tbody>
        <tr>
          <td scope="row">Thin Crust</td>
          <td>3.99</td>
          <td>4.99</td>
          <td>6.99</td>
        </tr>
        <tr>
          <td scope="row">Deep Dish</td>
          <td>4.99</td>
          <td>6.99</td>
          <td>8.99</td>
        </tr>
        <tr>
          <td scope="row">Stuffed Crust</td>
          <td>5.99</td>
          <td>7.99</td>
          <td>9.99</td>
```

```
        </tr>
      </tbody>
    </table>
  </body>
</html>
```

Listing 7-8 removes the `border` attribute from the `table` element and adds a style to the document for the table as well as each cell. You use the `border-style` property to change the default to a grooved look, as Figure 7-7 shows. Many other styles are available from the `border-style` property: `none`, `hidden`, `dotted`, `dashed`, `solid`, `double`, `groove`, `ridge`, `inset`, and `outset`.

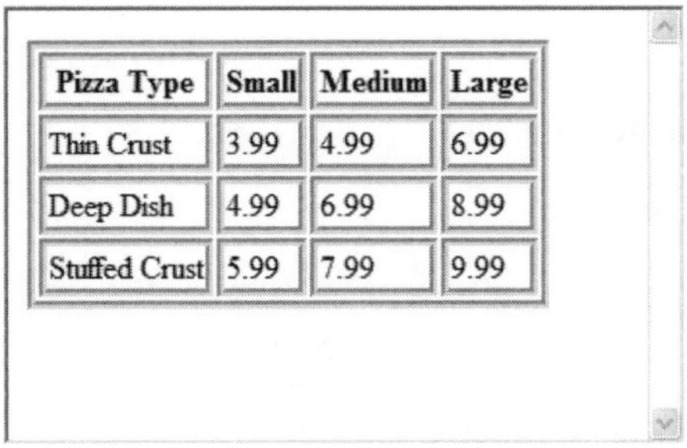

Figure 7-7. *Using CSS to specify the border*

CSS gives you complete control over how the border is rendered in the browser. You can also select the color and width of the table's appearance using the following CSS in place of the bold code shown in Listing 7-8:

```
<style type="text/css">
  td {border:2px solid red;}
  table {border:2px solid red;}
</style>
```

This code uses a shortcut property to set several properties (the border size, style, and color) at one time. You can review Appendix D to see more of the properties that are available under CSS.

Aligning Text in a Table

Up to this point, we've used the default style for all the text. Of course, you can use the `text-align` property in CSS to align a cell in the following ways: `left`, `right`, `center`, and `justify`. In the sample pizza table, it would be nice to right-align the prices and left-align the descriptions of the pizzas (as they are by default). You can do this using the bold code in Listing 7-9. You can pretty much use any of the CSS text properties to decorate your text to change the color, font, direction, and many other attributes.

Listing 7-9. *Text Alignment Within a Table*

```
<!DOCTYPE html
PUBLIC "-//W3C//DTD XHTML 1.0 Strict//EN"
"http://www.w3.org/TR/xhtml1/DTD/xhtml1-strict.dtd">
<html xmlns="http://www.w3.org/1999/xhtml">
  <head>
    <title>Adding Text Alignment</title>
    <style type="text/css">
      td {border:1px solid black;}
      table {border:1px solid black;}
      td.number{text-align: right;color: blue;}
      td.text{text-align: left;}
    </style>
  </head>
  <body>
    <table summary="This table provides the pricing information for pizzas">
     <caption>Our Pizza Selections</caption>
      <thead>
        <tr>
          <th scope="col">Pizza Type</th>
          <th scope="col">Small</th>
          <th scope="col">Medium</th>
          <th scope="col">Large</th>
        </tr>
      </thead>
      <tbody>
        <tr>
          <td class="text" scope="row">Thin Crust</td>
          <td class="number">3.99</td>
          <td class="number">4.99</td>
          <td class="number">6.99</td>
        </tr>
        <tr>
          <td class="text" scope="row">Deep Dish</td>
          <td class="number">4.99</td>
          <td class="number">6.99</td>
          <td class="number">8.99</td>
        </tr>
```

```
        <tr>
          <td class="text" scope="row">Stuffed Crust</td>
          <td class="number">5.99</td>
          <td class="number">7.99</td>
          <td class="number">9.99</td>
        </tr>
      </tbody>
    </table>
  </body>
</html>
```

Figure 7-8 shows the table with the numbers properly aligned. The `color` property sets the text color to red in order to make the price stand out from the table.

Our Pizza Selections			
Pizza Type	**Small**	**Medium**	**Large**
Thin Crust	3.99	4.99	6.99
Deep Dish	4.99	6.99	8.99
Stuffed Crust	5.99	7.99	9.99

Figure 7-8. *Using CSS to change the text alignment of the pizza table*

Adding Padding to Cells

The pizza table as it stands now is a bit crowded; the cells and text are rather scrunched together. You can use CSS to "pad" space on each of the sides around the text itself. The shortcut property `padding` allows you to set each of the sides individually, or you can set a single value for all the sides. You can set the padding to a specific value (in pixel, em, or ex measurements) or as a percentage of the closest element. For example, Listing 7-10 shows you how to set a padding of 10 pixels inside each cell.

Listing 7-10. *Using CSS to Pad Each Side of a Cell the Same Amount*

```
...
    <style type="text/css">
      td {border:1px solid black;}
      table {border:1px solid black;}
      td.number{text-align: right;color: blue;padding: 10px;}
      td.text{text-align: left;padding: 10px;}
    </style>
...
```

Listing 7-11 shows you how to set the padding of each side separately.

Listing 7-11. *Using CSS to Pad Each Side of a Cell a Different Amount*

...

```
<style type="text/css">
  td {border:1px solid black;}
  table {border:1px solid black;}
  td.number{text-align: right;color: blue;padding: 2px,6px,2px,6px;}
  td.text{text-align: left;padding: 2px,6px,2px,6px;}
</style>
```

...

You can use a single entry of the padding property and apply it to all four sides, or you can apply individual entries to the top, right, bottom, and left. Figure 7-9 shows the effect that the padding has on the table.

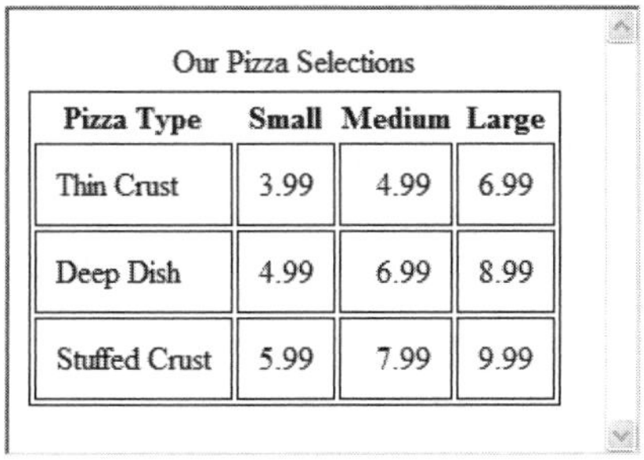

Figure 7-9. *Using CSS to change the padding of the pizza table*

Notice in Figure 7-9 that each cell in the table has its own border, making the table look rather odd. You can use the CSS property border-collapse to control this, as Listing 7-12 shows.

Listing 7-12. *Using the collapse Property to Merge Cell Borders*

```
<style type="text/css">
  td, th {border-style: groove;}
  table {border-style: groove;border-collapse: collapse;}
</style>
```

The border-collapse property has two possible values: separate and collapse. Specifying separate shows the border of each individual data cell, and specifying collapse allows each data cell to share borders, as shown in Figure 7-10.

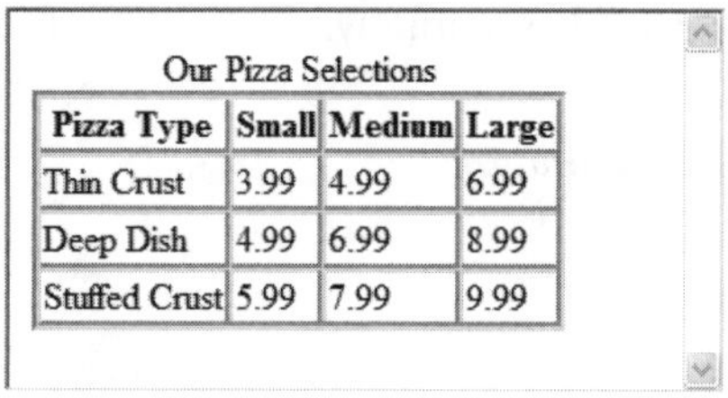

Figure 7-10. *Using border-collapse to merge the borders in each cell*

Adding Backgrounds to Tables

You can use CSS to change the background color of a table. One common and interesting technique is to alternate between two different colors to provide a striped look reminiscent of mainframe reports generated years ago (see Listing 7-13).

Listing 7-13. *Using a CSS Background with a Table*

```
<!DOCTYPE html
PUBLIC "-//W3C//DTD XHTML 1.0 Strict//EN"
"http://www.w3.org/TR/xhtml1/DTD/xhtml1-strict.dtd">
<html xmlns="http://www.w3.org/1999/xhtml">
  <head>
    <title>Using CSS for Backgrounds</title>
    <style type="text/css">
      td, th {border-style: groove;}
      table {border-style: groove;border-collapse: collapse;}
      tr.hlRow td, th {background-color: #eee;}
      tr.regRow td {background-color: #fff;}
    </style>
  </head>
<body>
    <table summary="This table provides the pricing information for pizzas">
      <thead>
        <tr class="hlRow">
          <th scope="col">Pizza Type</th>
          <th scope="col">Small</th>
          <th scope="col">Medium</th>
          <th scope="col">Large</th>
        </tr>
      </thead>
      <tbody>
```

```
      <tr class="regRow">
        <td scope="row">Thin Crust</td>
        <td>3.99</td>
        <td>4.99</td>
        <td>6.99</td>
      </tr>
      <tr class="hlRow">
        <td scope="row">Deep Dish</td>
        <td>4.99</td>
        <td>6.99</td>
        <td>8.99</td>
      </tr>
      <tr class="regRow">
        <td scope="row">Stuffed Crust</td>
        <td>5.99</td>
        <td>7.99</td>
        <td>9.99</td>
      </tr>
    </tbody>
  </table>
</body>
</html>
```

Figure 7-11 shows the results of running Listing 7-13. Notice how every other row has a different background color, making the table easier to read than if it were a single color. Using CSS, you can define two classes: one for highlighted rows (hlRow) and one for normal rows (regRow). In these classes, you define what color you want the background to be. Next, you simply assign the class to each <tr>, as shown in the bold code in Listing 7-13.

Pizza Type	Small	Medium	Large
Thin Crust	3.99	4.99	6.99
Deep Dish	4.99	6.99	8.99
Stuffed Crust	5.99	7.99	9.99

Figure 7-11. *Using background-color to produce a striped table*

Another common technique is to add a background image to a table. You can achieve this using some of the CSS background attributes, as shown in Listing 7-14.

Listing 7-14. *Using the Background Attributes*

```
<style type="text/css">
  td, th {border-style: groove;}
  table {border-style: groove;border-collapse: collapse;}
  table {background-image: url(pizza.gif);background-repeat repeat;}
</style>
```

Here you set the background of the table to the image called *pizza.gif*, which the table will repeat to fill the background. It is also common to use the CSS background shortcut property, which looks something like this:

```
table { background: #000000 url(pizza.gif) repeat fixed top;}
```

This accomplishes the same thing, but it allows you to set many attributes in one shot. First, you choose the background color of the table, then the image you want (if any). You choose whether you want the image to repeat, whether you want it to be fixed or scroll with the rest of the page, and the starting position of the image. For more details on using the background property, see Appendix D. When adding images to any background, consider the readability. If the image is too dark or busy and the text color is dark, the data within the table may become difficult to read.

Summary

This chapter has shown you how to create tables to hold tabular data. In the past and even still today, it is common to see tables used as an aid in visual browsers when laying out documents. This is not a good practice and should be avoided. Using CSS, in combination with the div and span elements you saw in Chapter 4, is the preferred way to present your documents. When using tables, be sure to keep accessibility in mind, and use the special attributes to accommodate those using a nonvisual browser. In Chapter 11, you'll see how you can create a layout for your document from scratch. But first, in the next chapter, you'll learn to create your own forms that will allow users to enter their own data into your documents.

CHAPTER 8

Building Forms

We've referred to the web as a conduit for the movement of information, distributing ideas around the world to anyone who wants to find them. It's this far-reaching scope and wide-open range that makes the web so philosophically magnificent and fascinating. But information doesn't flow only downhill. Your visitors might arrive at your website to passively absorb, but, if allowed, they can also participate in the exchange of information, offering their own ideas and reactions.

But how can you receive such feedback from your visitors? The simplest, most common, and perhaps most powerful means of moving ideas uphill onto the web is through a form. In the analog world, a form is simply a printed document with predefined, labeled blanks where people can write information. Forms standardize the formatting of data for easier handling; when a clerk knows exactly where to look to find a customer's name on a slip of paper, it saves precious time and makes their job that much easier. But if you take this concept a step further, a web form becomes more than just a stodgy way to force your formatting expectations onto your visitors. Forms are the means by which an anonymous user becomes an active participant.

If you've ever used a web search engine, made an online purchase, created a personalized login to a website, or posted a comment to an online forum, you've already seen and used web forms; the web simply wouldn't be what it is without them. They're ubiquitous and a fundamental cornerstone of online living, so you'll inevitably need to include forms in some of the pages you build. This chapter explores the XHTML elements you'll need to construct functional, usable, and accessible forms for your web pages, as well as a few ways to use CSS to make your web forms visually appealing.

How Forms Work

Defined in simplest terms, a *form* is any section of a web page where a user can input information (though sometimes form elements are used to display information rather than collect it). Your visitors can enter text into blank fields, make choices by checking boxes, select options from menus, and then click a button to send it all away for processing. These interactive devices are called *controls*, and their contents are the controls' *values*.

To modify the value of a control, your visitor must first bring the control into *focus* so it becomes active and primed to accept input. A control is usually given focus by clicking it with a mouse or using the Tab key to move the cursor from one control to the next. Entering a value requires typing text or performing some other deliberate action (clicking a mouse button, pressing the Enter key, and so on). Your visitor can then shift their browser's focus to another control, enter another value, and continue in that fashion until all the controls have been modified.

A form isn't really complete until it's submitted. The information that was entered will be transmitted to the server in a *form data set* consisting of all the form controls and their values. The job of processing the data set falls to a *form handler:* a script or program that has been designed to interpret and utilize the submitted data. Many form handlers are also designed to validate the entered values, making sure all the required information has been entered and properly formatted.

Handling submitted form data is something entirely different; it involves complex matters of scripting, programming, database design, and application design, and it can even delve into issues of encryption, privacy, and security. Such advanced topics are well beyond the scope of a book about front-end XHTML and CSS. Instead, the rest of this chapter focuses on the markup you'll need to be familiar with to assemble forms for display and use.

■**Caution** The on-screen rendering of various form elements can be quite different between different browsers and operating systems. Most of the images you'll see throughout this chapter have been captured using Firefox 2.0 for Macintosh OS X. These same form elements might look different in another browser or on another platform, so don't be too surprised if what you see on your own computer isn't the same as what you see in this book. The actual functionality of all of these elements is identical in every browser, even if their default appearance isn't.

The Components of a Form

The entirety of a form is wrapped within a single form element that acts as a container for the specialized elements that generate form controls. These controls are the text fields, checkboxes, menus, and buttons your visitors will use to enter their information or make their selections. When the form is submitted, all the values of its various controls are sent as name/value pairs to a form handler as part of a data set. Therefore, each control must carry a name attribute so it can be correctly paired with its value.

form

As the name of the element implies, form defines the portion of an XHTML document that can receive input from the user. This is a block-level element that acts as a container for other specialized form elements, as well as any other elements needed to give the form structure. But even though form is a block-level element, its contents must be held in block-level containers of their own; like the body element, a form cannot have inline children. To include multiple, separate forms within a single document, each must be contained by its own form element—you can't nest a form within a form.

The form element requires an action attribute in its opening tag, whose value is the URL of the form handler. That form handler may be a document or script elsewhere on the website, a back-end application, or the very same document the form resides in if its data will be handled exclusively on the client side by JavaScript or if the XHTML document has been integrated with some kind of scripting language such as PHP, Ruby, ASP, or ASP.NET.

A method attribute is optional and can accept two values, get or post, to indicate the particular HTTP method to use when the form is submitted. When the method value is get, the submitted data set will be appended to the form handler's URL (from the action attribute) in a *query string* consisting of all the form's name/value pairs. The form handler can then interpret and process that URL, extracting values from the exposed query string. A method of post sends the data set directly to the form handler application (not in a visible URL query string) for processing at the server.

The get method should be used to request static data from the server for temporary use (for example, searching the web for a definition of the word *idempotent*), especially when the URL—including its query string—might be reused. The post method is most often used to send data to the server where it will be saved for use in the future (for example, submitting a comment to a weblog) or when a URL with a visible query string isn't desirable for reasons of security and privacy. The default form method is get, which will be assumed if the method attribute isn't included.

■**Note** HTTP stands for HyperText Transfer Protocol, which is the set of program rules used for transferring electronic data over the web. The two basic methods of HTTP are "get" to send data from a server to a client and "post" to send data from a client to a server. Whenever you download something from a web server, be it an XHTML document, a cascading style sheet, a video, an image, and so on, your web browser sends a request to "get" that file. Many forms use the opposite "post" method, sending data from your browser to the server.

Listing 8-1 shows the XHTML markup for a simple form, including the action and method attributes in the opening <form> tag. This example contains two input elements (a text field and a submit button) and a text label wrapped in a label element. You'll learn more about these elements later in this chapter.

Listing 8-1. *Simple Form with a Text Control and a Submit Button*

```
<form method="post" action="/cgi-bin/formhandler.cgi">
  <p><label for="email">Enter your E-mail address to subscribe ➥
    to our mailing list.</label></p>
  <p><input type="text" name="email" id="email" />
  <input type="submit" name="subscribe" value="Subscribe" /></p>
</form>
```

Figure 8-1 shows how this will appear in a visual web browser with default styling.

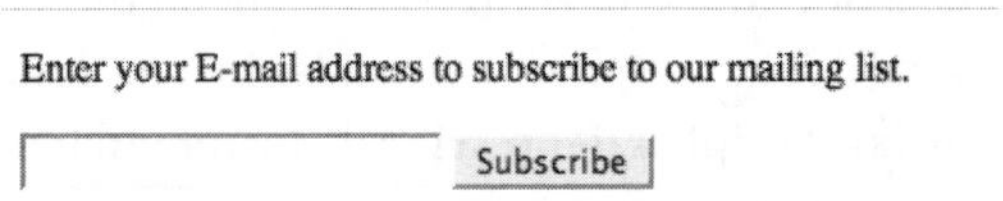

Enter your E-mail address to subscribe to our mailing list.

[   ] Subscribe

Figure 8-1. *The same simple form as it appears in Firefox for Mac OS X. The button may look different in another browser, but it always works the same way.*

■**Tip** The `label` element is extremely important in forms. It provides a text label for an individual form control that can be read by assistive technologies to improve the form's accessibility. You'll learn about it in detail later in this chapter.

Required Attributes

- `action`: Specifies the URL of the form handler, which is the script or application that will process the submitted form data

Optional Attributes

- `accept`: Includes a comma-separated list of accepted file MIME types when files are being posted through the form (via an `input type="file"` control).

- `accept-charset`: Specifies the accepted character encoding for data submitted through the form. When this attribute is missing, the accepted character encoding is assumed to be the same as that of the parent document.

- enctype: Specifies the content type used to post the form. The default value for this attribute is `application/x-www-form-urlencoded`, and a value of `multipart/form-data` should be used if the submitted form will include files uploaded via an `input type="file"` control.

- method: Specifies which HTTP method will be used to submit the form data, either `get` or `post`.

Standard Attributes

- `class`

- `dir`

- `id`

- `lang`

- `name`

- `style`

- `title`

- `xml:lang`

input

Many common form controls can be created with the inline `input` element, and each type of input control is defined with a corresponding `type` attribute. Because the `input` element is inline, several can appear side by side, but all must be held in a block-level container (remember that the `form` element cannot have inline children). The `input` element is also an empty element, so it can hold no text content, can hold no other elements, and must be closed with a trailing slash (`/>`). An `input` element is replaced by a functional form control when a browser renders the document.

Required Attributes

- name: Identifies the control so it can be matched with its value when the form is submitted. A markup validator may not generate an error if this attribute is missing, but it's required in order to successfully handle the form.

Optional Attributes

- `alt`: Specifies an alternative text description (only for `input type="image"`).

- `accept`: Includes a comma-separated list of accepted file MIME types (only for `input type="file"`).

- `accesskey`: Assigns a keyboard shortcut to a control for easier and quicker access through keyboard navigation. The value of this attribute is the character corresponding to the access key. The exact keystroke combination needed to activate an access key varies between browsers and operating systems.

- `checked="checked"`: When present, sets an initial checked state for checkboxes or radio buttons (only for `input type="checkbox"` and `input type="radio"`). Remember that *all* attributes *must* have a quoted value in XHTML, so it must appear as `checked="checked"`, as redundant as that seems.

- `disabled="disabled"`: When present, disables the control so it cannot receive focus or be modified. The value of a disabled control is not submitted. Many visual browsers will display disabled controls in a "grayed-out" style.

- `ismap="ismap"`: Declares that the control is a server-side image map (only for `input type="image"`).

- `maxlength`: Specifies the maximum number of characters that can be entered in a text field (only for `input type="text"` or `input type="password"`).

- `readonly="readonly"`: Specifies that the control may only display a value and cannot be modified. This differs from `disabled` in that a read-only control can still receive focus and its value is still submitted with the form (only for `input type="text"` or `input type="password"`).

- `size`: Specifies the width of a text, password, or file control when displayed (only for `input type="text"`, `input type="password"`, or `input type="file"`). The value of this attribute is a number of characters, so the actual rendered width will depend on the font size. By default, most browsers will display text and password fields around 20 or 25 characters wide.

- `src`: Specifies the source URL of an image file (only for `input type="image"`).

- `tabindex`: Specifies the control's position in the tabbing order when active controls are cycled through using the Tab key.

- `type`: Specifies the type of form control the element will create. The default value is `text`.

- `usemap`: Specifies the URL of a client-side image map (only for `input type="image"`).

- `value`: Specifies the initial value of a control before it has been modified by the user.

Standard Attributes

- `class`

- `dir`

- `id`

- `lang`

- `style`

- `title`

- `xml:lang`

Note that many of the optional attributes available for the `input` element are specific only to certain types of form inputs (as indicated by the `type` attribute). Next we'll go through each of the different input types in more detail, one by one.

input type="text"

This type of `input` element creates a single-line field in which your visitor can type whatever text you might require, such as a name, address, or short answer to a question. It usually appears in visual browsers as a white, rectangular box with a slightly inset border. These single-line text fields are best for very short bits of text, no more than a few words. If the entered text exceeds the width of the field, the excess characters will run off to the left of the control so the latter text is shown but the first portion appears truncated. Rest assured that the complete text is still there; it's just not all visible. Longer, multiline passages of text can be entered into the specialized `textarea` element, covered later in this chapter.

An `input type="text"` element may carry an optional `maxlength` attribute, defining the maximum number of characters (including spaces) that can be entered. Unfortunately, web browsers offer no indication that a text field has a maximum allowed length; when you reach the limit, it simply stops accepting anything you type. If you paste an overlong string of text into a field with a `maxlength` attribute, the text will be truncated. If you need to use a `maxlength` attribute on a text field (for example, a username field to log in to a system that allows usernames to be 12 characters long only), it's helpful to indicate the maximum length in a note near the form control.

An optional value attribute allows you to set the initial text of the field, which a user can delete, modify, or leave alone, and the default value will be submitted with the form. It's primarily useful for automatically "prepopulating" forms with stored information that a user can edit. Text fields that are meant to be blanks where new information can be entered should, in fact, be blank when initially rendered.

Listing 8-2 shows the XHTML markup to create a text field control, including a maxlength attribute and a note about the maximum allowed length. The field has been prepopulated in this example using the value attribute.

Listing 8-2. *A Text Field with a Prepopulated value Attribute*

```
<p><label for="zip">Change your ZIP code <em>(maximum 5 characters)</em></label>
<input type="text" id="zip" name="zip" size="5" maxlength="5" value="94710" /></p>
```

Figure 8-2 shows how this would look in a browser (again, this is Firefox 2.0 on Mac OS X; other browsers might differ slightly).

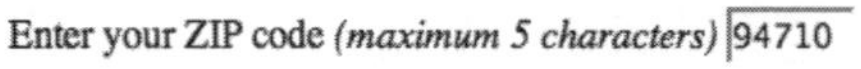

Enter your ZIP code *(maximum 5 characters)* 94710

Figure 8-2. *The text field as it appears in a browser with default styling. The value of the value attribute is displayed in the field when the page loads.*

This example also has an optional (and presentational) size attribute, defining the width of the field as a number of characters. By default, most browsers will display text fields around 20 or 25 characters wide. You can also modify the width of a text field with the CSS width property using any unit you like (ems, pixels, a percentage, and so on).

input type="password"

This control is similar to a text field; it's a single-line field and will usually appear as a rectangular box with a white background and an inset border. But unlike a regular text field, a password field obscures the entered text, usually as a series of asterisks (*) or solid dots. This offers a bit of added security and privacy, preventing someone from peering over your shoulder to sneak a peek at your secret password when you're logging into a secure system. But this is very light security, protecting your password from a casual glance only. A properly secured form should be encrypted when it's submitted to the server; don't count on just visually obscuring passwords to keep a determined crook at bay.

As with a text field, a password field can carry `maxlength` and `size` attributes. It also accepts a `value` attribute, but it's probably not a good idea to prepopulate a secure password, is it?

Listing 8-3 shows an `input type="password"` with a `maxlength` attribute. The maximum length is noted in the control's label.

Listing 8-3. *A Password Form Control*

```
<div>
<label for="password">
  Enter your password <em>(maximum 12 characters)</em>
</label>
<input type="password" name="password" id="password" maxlength="12" />
</div>
```

Figure 8-3 shows how a graphical browser renders the markup, with the entered text obscured as a string of asterisks—some browsers obscure passwords as dots instead.

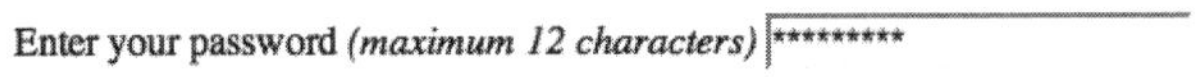

Enter your password *(maximum 12 characters)* |*********

Figure 8-3. *Text entered into a password field is obscured to prevent sneaky onlookers from reading it.*

▐**Note** *Encryption* is a means of mathematically scrambling data so that anyone who attempts to intercept it will not be able to read or use the information. Unscrambling, or *decrypting*, encrypted data requires an *encryption key* that should be extremely difficult to guess. Any sensitive information, such as passwords and credit card numbers, sent over the web through a form should be encrypted to protect the security and privacy of your users. Encryption is usually done on the server side and is much too complicated to be addressed in detail in this book.

---

input type="checkbox"

A checkbox control is a choice toggle in the form of a small square filled with a check mark (or sometimes an *x*) when the control is selected. Checkboxes are used when several options are available and more than one can be selected, in the sense of "check all that apply." Each checkbox `input` may have a `value` attribute corresponding to whatever the selected option is, and this value will be passed along behind the scenes when the form is submitted. Without a specific value, all that will submit is the state of the box—a value of "on" if it's checked or nothing at all if it's not checked (which is inferred to mean "off"). In some cases, this is enough information (when combined with the name or a unique id attribute for each checkbox), so an explicit value attribute might not always be necessary.

Once checked, a checkbox can be unchecked by simply selecting it again. Furthermore, it can be "prechecked" using the checked attribute. This attribute doesn't carry a value; its value is determined by the attribute's very existence. If the attribute is present, the box is checked; if it's not present, then the box is not checked. In previous versions of HTML, the checked attribute could be *minimized*, appearing with no value at all. However, *all* attributes in XHTML *must* have a value, so checked should appear as checked="checked" to be valid; attribute minimization is not allowed in XHTML. The value must match the attribute name in this case—checked="yes" wouldn't be correct.

Listing 8-4 shows an example of several checkbox input elements, one of which has been checked by default. They all include a value attribute to pass along more information than a simple "checked" or "unchecked" status would offer. These options are marked up in an unordered list for added structure.

Listing 8-4. *A Set of Multiple-Choice Options Using Checkbox Controls*

```
<p>Choose your toppings:</p>
<ul>
  <li>
    <label for="top1">
      <input type="checkbox" id="top1" name="top1" ➡
      value="pepperoni" checked="checked" />
      Pepperoni
    </label>
  </li>
  <li>
    <label for="top2">
      <input type="checkbox" id="top2" name="top2" value="xcheese" />
      Extra cheese
    </label>
  </li>
  <li>
    <label for="top3">
      <input type="checkbox" id="top3" name="top3" value="onions" />
      Onions
    </label>
  </li>
  <li>
    <label for="top4">
      <input type="checkbox" id="top4" name="top4" value="mushrooms" />
      Mushrooms
    </label>
```

```
    </li>
    <li>
      <label for="top5">
        <input type="checkbox" id="top5" name="top5" value="olives" />
        Olives
      </label>
    </li>
</ul>
```

You can see how this will appear in a browser in Figure 8-4. The default list item bullets can be removed with CSS, as you learned in Chapter 4. Once again, this image is from Firefox 2.0 on Mac OS X. Checkboxes will look different in other browsers.

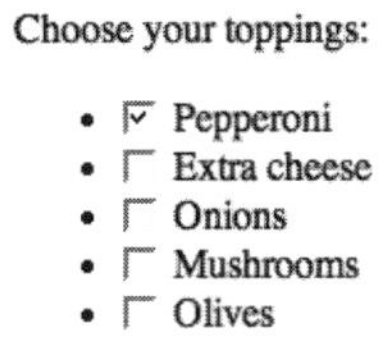

Choose your toppings:

- ☑ Pepperoni
- ☐ Extra cheese
- ☐ Onions
- ☐ Mushrooms
- ☐ Olives

Figure 8-4. *The list of checkboxes as it might appear in a browser with default styling*

input type="radio"

A radio button control is somewhat like a checkbox, but only one option in a set can be selected. Radio buttons get their name from the station preset buttons on old-fashioned car radios; since you can listen to only one radio station at a time, pushing one button in would cause the previous button to pop back out. The radio buttons in a web form work the same way; selecting a button will automatically deselect whichever one in the list was previously selected. Hence, radio buttons are ideal when you need to offer a multiple-choice list of options where only one choice is allowed (unlike checkboxes, which allow several choices). Once a radio button has been checked, it cannot be unchecked unless another button in the set is checked in its stead. To define a set of radio buttons, each one must share the same value of the name attribute.

As with checkboxes, each radio button control can carry a value attribute to pass along additional information about the selected option, and in this case a value is strongly recommended. In the absence of a value attribute, the submitted value would simply be "on" without any other indication of which option was selected. Also like checkboxes, a radio button can be preselected by including the checked="checked" attribute. However, only one radio button in a set may be preselected.

Listing 8-5 shows a set of radio buttons, each with the same name attribute and with id and value attributes to differentiate the options.

Listing 8-5. *A Set of Radio Buttons*

```
<p>Choose the size of your pizza:</p>
<ul>
  <li>
    <label for="small">
      <input type="radio" name="size" id="small" value="small" /> Small
    </label>
  </li>
  <li>
    <label for="medium">
      <input type="radio" name="size" id="medium" value="medium" /> Medium
    </label>
  </li>
  <li>
    <label for="large">
      <input type="radio" name="size" id="large" value="large" /> Large
    </label>
  </li>
</ul>
```

Figure 8-5 shows this set of radio buttons rendered in Firefox 2.0 for OS X. As with most other form controls, radio buttons may appear different in other browsers. In this example, one of the options has been selected, filling the circle with a solid dot. Changing the selection will automatically uncheck the previous choice.

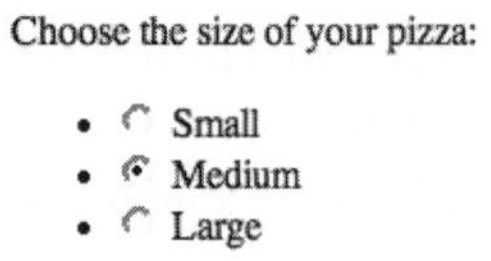

Choose the size of your pizza:

- ◯ Small
- ◉ Medium
- ◯ Large

Figure 8-5. *The set of radio buttons as it might be rendered in a visual browser, now with one option selected*

input type="file"

The file input type creates a special file upload control—usually consisting of a text field alongside a "browse" button—allowing the user to locate a file on their computer's hard drive or local network, either by entering the exact file path in the text field or by clicking the button to invoke their operating system's built-in file browser. Once a user locates a file by browsing for it, the local file path is displayed in the text field. As with other text fields, an optional size attribute can specify the width of the file field as a number of characters.

The chosen file will be uploaded to the web server when the form is posted. An `input type="file"` control can include an optional `accept` attribute whose value is a comma-separated list of the accepted file types (specified by their MIME types; see Appendix D for the full list). If you're asking your users to upload an image, for example, the `accept` attribute can limit accepted formats to only image types or can even restrict it to only GIFs and PNGs; any other file type will be rejected. If your form includes file controls, you should include an `accept` attribute in the opening `<form>` tag as well.

Listing 8-6 presents the markup for a file control, including an `accept` attribute that limits uploaded files to GIF, JPEG, or PNG.

Listing 8-6. *A file Control That Includes a size Attribute*

```
<p>Upload a picture of your favorite pizza!</p>
<p><input type="file" size="40" accept="image/gif, image/jpeg, image/png" /></p>
```

Figure 8-6 shows how this looks in Firefox 2.0 for Mac OS X. A file has been selected by browsing the local hard drive, and its path appears in the text field. Only the first portion is visible because the full path is longer than what the text field can display.

Upload a picture of your favorite pizza!

/Users/craig/Pictures/iPhoto Library/Originals/200   Browse...

Figure 8-6. *The file control as it appears in Firefox 2.0 for OS X*

FILE CONTROLS IN SAFARI

Most visual web browsers display a file control as a text field with a button to its right, with the notable exception of Apple's Safari for Macintosh OS X. As you can see here, Safari doesn't show a writable text field, instead offering only the browse option with the button on the left side of the control (the button reads Choose File rather than Browse as in most other browsers). To the right of the button, Safari displays only the name of the selected file (once the file has been selected) instead of the full path. Along with the file name, Safari will also display a small icon to indicate the type of file, if the type is known. As is usually the case, the functionality of the control is identical even if its presentation isn't.

Upload a picture of your favorite pizza!

Choose File   🖼 pizza.jpg

input type="submit"

Quite simply, an input type="submit" control creates a button that will submit the entire form data set—all the data entered in the various controls—when clicked. The control's value attribute sets the text that will be displayed on the rendered button, which usually defaults to "Submit" or "Submit Query" if a value attribute isn't present. Once the button is clicked and the form is submitted, the form handler (specified in the form element's action attribute) takes over to process the data.

You can see the XHTML markup for a simple login form with a submit button in Listing 8-7. In this example, the value of "Log In" will appear on the rendered button rather than the default text.

Listing 8-7. *A Simple Login Form with a Submit Button*

```
<p><label for="username">Your Username:</label>
  <input type="text" id="username" name="username" /></p>
<p><label for="password">Your Password:</label>
  <input type="password" id="password" name="password" /></p>
<p><input type="submit" name="login" value="Log In" /></p>
```

Figure 8-7 shows the rendered form, from Firefox 2 on Mac OS X once again; form buttons will appear quite different in other browsers.

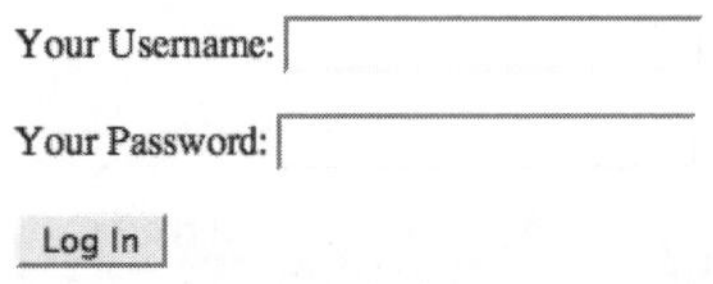

Figure 8-7. *The submit button's default text is replaced by the text from the input's value attribute.*

input type="reset"

This control resets the entire form, blanking out anything that has been entered and setting all controls back to their initial values. Reset buttons were much more common in the past, but a few years of practical usability testing has shown them to rarely be of much value. It's far too likely that a user will *accidentally* reset the form and irretrievably lose all the information they've carefully entered—especially frustrating when there's no mechanism to undo such a mistake. These days reset buttons are generally discouraged; if you decide to use them, do so with caution.

As with a submit button, the reset button's value attribute determines the text that will display, usually defaulting to "Reset" in the absence of a value attribute.

input type="button"

A button control is just that: a generic button. It has no inherent function; it merely serves as a clickable widget that can trigger a client-side script. The button's text can be set via the `value` attribute and will typically default to "Button" if no value is provided. Instead of embedding these scripted buttons in your markup, it's usually preferable to use client-side JavaScript to generate the control. After all, the button won't function without a client-side script to imbue it with purpose, and a control that works only with a script needn't be displayed if the script isn't available.

input type="image"

An image control behaves essentially like a submit button; activating the control will submit the form. But an `input type="image"` control allows you to substitute the standard button with a more decorative graphic. As with other images in XHTML, an image control requires a `src` attribute to specify the image file's URL and an `alt` attribute to provide an alternative text description when the image isn't available (see Chapter 5 for more about the `alt` attribute). Alternative text is especially vital for image form controls to ensure that the form can be successfully completed, even when the image can't be seen. Without a useful `alt` attribute, people using text browsers or screen readers will have difficulty identifying the button, making it nearly impossible for them to submit the form. You wouldn't want to turn away a paying customer simply because they can't see your Buy Now button, would you?

When your visitor uses a mouse (or other pointing device) to click an image control, the precise location of that click is included in the data set as X and Y coordinates (with the control identified by its `name` attribute). A script or form handler can use this information to determine exactly which part of the button was clicked and thus treat an image control like an image map (which you learned about in Chapter 6), with different regions of the button triggering different actions. However, since this requires the button to be clicked by a pointing device, people using their keyboard to submit the form will be at a disadvantage. It's preferable to use separate, distinct submit or image controls to trigger those different actions rather than a single image button.

You can see the markup to insert an image control in Listing 8-8 and the rendered result in Figure 8-8.

Listing 8-8. *Using input type="image" in Place of input type="submit"*

```
<p><input type="image" name="post" src="post.png" alt="Post your comment" /></p>
```

Figure 8-8. *An image control inserts a graphical button that might be more (or sometimes less) attractive than the standard button style.*

input type="hidden"

As you might suspect, a hidden input will not be displayed. It exists simply as a vehicle to pass along extra data with the submitted form that a user needn't see or modify—such as an order number or internal tracking ID—via the element's `value` attribute.

button

The `button` element works just like a submit, reset, or button `input` type, or even an `input type="image"` control—activating a `button` element (with the click of a mouse or press of a key) will submit or reset the form or trigger a scripted response.

The `button` element is inline and requires a `type` attribute (with a value of `submit`, `reset`, or `button`), and like other form controls, a `button` may appear only within a `form`. However, unlike the `input` element, a `button` element is not empty; it can contain text or other elements, offering many more design and semantic options than a simple `input` element. In fact, a button *must* hold some content, because an empty `button` element will have no default label. Web developer Aaron Gustafson offers an informative overview of the `button` element's usefulness and flexibility in his article "Push My Button" (`http://www.digital-web.com/articles/push_my_button/`).

You can see an example of the `button` element in Listing 8-9, which includes a bit of emphasized text and an image.

Listing 8-9. *A button Element Containing Text and an Image*

```
<div>
  <button type="submit" name="continue">
    <strong>Continue to the next page</strong>
    <img src="next.png" width="28" height="20" alt="" />
  </button>
</div>
```

When a browser renders this on-screen (as shown in Figure 8-9), the entire element becomes an active push button to submit the form. By default, a `button` element will have the same appearance as an `input` button but can be easily styled with CSS (whereas some browsers such as Safari will not allow `input` buttons to be styled at all).

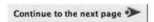

Figure 8-9. *The button as it appears in Firefox for OS X*

Required Attributes

- `type`: Specifies the type of button control the element will create—`submit`, `reset`, or `button`

Optional Attributes

- `accesskey`: Assigns a keyboard shortcut to the control for easier and quicker access through keyboard navigation. The value of this attribute is the character corresponding to the access key. The exact keystroke combination needed to activate an access key varies between browsers and operating systems.

- `disabled="disabled"`: When present, disables the button so it cannot be activated. Many browsers will display disabled controls in a "grayed-out" style.

- `tabindex`: Specifies the control's position in the tabbing order when active controls are cycled through using the Tab key.

- `value`: Specifies a value that may be passed along with the submitted form data.

Standard Attributes

- `class`

- `dir`

- `id`

- `lang`

- `name`

- `style`

- `title`

- `xml:lang`

select

The inline `select` element creates a selection control, which is a menu of options from which to choose. The control either may be displayed as a single line that can "drop down" and expand to show all the options or may occupy multiple lines as specified by the optional `size` attribute. A single-line selection control, often called a *drop-down menu*, will show the selected option when in its collapsed, inactive state, with a small arrow icon at its right end as a visual cue that the control can be expanded. In graphical browsers, selections in a multiline select are usually highlighted with a different background color.

A single-line selection control will allow only one option to be chosen. Adding the attribute multiple="multiple" will automatically convert the select element to a multi-line control and allow the user to choose more than one option by holding down the Shift, Control, or Command key while making their choices. In the absence of a size attribute, some browsers will expand the menu to show 10 or 20 options or to show all of them if there are only a few. This is inconsistent and unreliable across various browsers, so you should always include a size attribute when multiple selections are allowed.

When the form is submitted, the chosen option (or options) will be passed as the value of the selection control. A name attribute is required for the select element in order to identify it and to preserve the connection between the control and its value.

The display and behavior of a single-line selection control can be somewhat unpredictable, largely dependent on the browser and operating system. If the control appears near the bottom of the screen, the menu will usually expand upward rather than downward to prevent the expanded menu from extending past the lower edge of the computer screen. A menu might expand in both directions if the selected option is near the middle of the list. When expanded, a selection control will overlap other content on the page and can even escape the boundaries of the browser window.

When the list of options is exceptionally long, a vertical scroll bar will appear in the expanded menu, allowing the user to scroll up or down to see the entire list. The number of items visible in the expanded list can change depending on the size of the screen or browser window, automatically determined by the browser and operating system. A multiline select element will display a vertical scroll bar if the number of options exceeds the number of visible lines.

The width of a selection control is determined by the longest option in the list. The element's natural width can be modified with the CSS width property, and any text that exceeds that width will appear truncated, but most browsers will automatically expand the width of the opened menu. Ideally, each option in the list should have a short text label of no more than a few words.

The select element is not empty, instead acting as a container for one or more option or optgroup elements, which you'll learn about next. The select element must contain at least one option. Listing 8-10 shows a select element containing three options. Without a multiple attribute, this control defaults to a single-line selection.

Listing 8-10. *A select Element Containing Three option Elements*

```
<select name="size">
  <option>Small</option>
  <option>Medium</option>
  <option>Large</option>
</select>
```

You can see what this control will look like in Figure 8-10, closed on the left and expanded on the right. As with most other form controls, different browsers present the select element in different styles (this is Firefox 2 for Mac OS X).

Figure 8-10. *The same selection control in both inactive and active states*

Adding a multiple="multiple" attribute, as in Listing 8-11, converts the control from a single-line drop-down menu to a multiline box, allowing the user to choose more than one option.

Listing 8-11. *A select Element with a multiple Attribute*

```
<select name="toppings" size="3" multiple="multiple">
  <option>Extra cheese</option>
  <option>Mushrooms</option>
  <option>Olives</option>
</select>
```

Figure 8-11 shows the result: a scrolling box displaying the options. No scroll bar is needed in this case because there are only three options, which is the same number of lines specified in the size attribute.

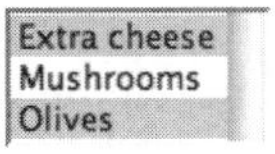

Figure 8-11. *The menu is automatically converted to a scrolling box when multiple selections are allowed.*

Required Attributes

- name: Identifies the control so that it can be associated with its value when the form is submitted. A markup validator may not generate an error if this attribute is missing, but it's required to successfully handle the form.

Optional Attributes

- `disabled="disabled"`: When present, disables the control so it cannot receive focus. The value of a disabled control is not submitted. Many visual browsers will display disabled controls in a "grayed-out" style.

- `multiple="multiple"`: Indicates that multiple options may be selected.

- `tabindex`: Specifies the control's position in the tabbing order when active controls are cycled through using the Tab key.

Standard Attributes

- `class`

- `dir`

- `id`

- `lang`

- `style`

- `title`

- `xml:lang`

option

Each option in a `select` element is contained by an `option` element. It's a nonempty element (requiring a closing `</option>` tag) but can contain only a text label that will be displayed in the `select` menu, with each option appearing on its own line within the menu. An `option` element cannot contain any other elements, only text. That text content is also the value that will be sent with the form unless a different value is specified in a `value` attribute.

An option can be preselected by including a `selected` attribute (whose value in XHTML is also `selected`, as in `selected="selected"`). More than one option can be preselected in this way, but only when the parent selection control has a `multiple` attribute.

The `option` elements in Listing 8-12 have been given `value` attributes that will be submitted in place of the element's text content. This way a back-end system can receive whatever cryptic values it has been programmed to handle while the user still sees sensible text labels. The first option has an empty `value` attribute, since that option acts only as a label for the control and should not be submitted with the form (it has also been preselected by adding a `selected` attribute). A validation script could automatically detect that this control was submitted with no value and reply with a message urging the user to make a selection.

Listing 8-12. *A select Element Containing option Elements*

```
<select name="size">
  <option value="" selected="selected">pick a size...</option>
  <option value="1">Small</option>
  <option value="2">Medium</option>
  <option value="3">Large</option>
</select>
```

Required Attributes

No attributes are required for the `option` element.

Optional Attributes

- `disabled="disabled"`: When present, disables the option so it cannot be selected. Many browsers will display disabled options in a "grayed-out" style.

- `label`: Provides a shorter alternative text label, displayed in place of the element's contents to improve accessibility when the regular value is too verbose. Unfortunately, this attribute isn't widely supported by current browsers or assistive technologies.

- `selected="selected"`: Indicates an initially selected option.

- `value`: Specifies a value that may be passed along with the submitted form data. If no `value` attribute is present, the selected `option` element's contents are passed as the value of the selection control.

Standard Attributes

- `class`

- `dir`

- `id`

- `lang`

- `name`

- `style`

- `title`

- `xml:lang`

optgroup

One or more option elements can be sorted into related sections or categories by wrapping them in a containing optgroup element, so named because it's a "group of options." An option group can contain only option elements; no other elements are allowed, and you cannot nest an optgroup within an optgroup.

In visual browsers, the value of the required label attribute will be displayed as a title at the top of the group with the options indented beneath it. All browsers display optgroup labels in some distinctive fashion, but the exact style varies widely. Firefox and Internet Explorer render them in a boldfaced and italicized font, while Safari renders them boldfaced and in a gray color. Opera departs even further, displaying optgroup labels as white text on a black background.

The optional disabled attribute will effectively disable the entire group, preventing the user from selecting any of those options. The optgroup label itself is not a selectable option.

You can see an example of optgroup markup in Listing 8-13, which groups different pizza toppings into logical categories. While the "Other" category is a group of one, this is still perfectly logical and semantically correct in the context of the menu.

Listing 8-13. *A select Element Containing Multiple Option Groups*

```
<select name="extra">
  <option value="" selected="selected">Choose one extra topping</option>
  <optgroup label="Meat">
    <option>Pepperoni</option>
    <option>Sausage</option>
    <option>Canadian Bacon</option>
    <option>Anchovies</option>
  </optgroup>
  <optgroup label="Fruits/Veggies/Fungi">
    <option>Onions</option>
    <option>Peppers</option>
    <option>Olives</option>
    <option>Mushrooms</option>
    <option>Pineapple</option>
  </optgroup>
  <optgroup label="Other">
    <option>Extra cheese</option>
  </optgroup>
</select>
```

Figure 8-12 shows the same selection control in two different browsers, Firefox and Opera. You can see that it looks very different in each, but the functionality is the same.

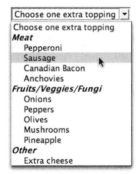

Figure 8-12. *The control in Firefox 2 for Mac OS X (left) and Opera 9 for Mac OS X (right). Although the labels appear very different, both browsers do make them clearly distinguishable from the options beneath them.*

Required Attributes

- `label`: Specifies a text label or title for the option group, usually displayed in some distinctive style to set it apart from the selectable options

Optional Attributes

- `disabled="disabled"`: When present, disables the entire group so none of its options can be selected. Many visual browsers will display disabled options in a "grayed-out" style.

Standard Attributes

- `class`

- `dir`

- `id`

- `lang`

- `name`

- `style`

- `title`

- `xml:lang`

textarea

The textarea element creates a multiline field for entering passages of text too lengthy for a single-line text field (input type="text"). Its size is defined by the required rows and cols attributes, with the value of rows being the vertical number of text rows and cols being the number of characters (or columns, which gives the attribute its shortened name, *cols*) on a horizontal line. Since the size of the box is based on the size of the text, a larger or smaller font size will obviously influence the dimensions of the textarea element. The text area's dimensions can be further modified by the CSS width and height properties, overriding the rows and cols attributes. Vertical and horizontal scroll bars will appear if the amount of text entered into a textarea exceeds what can fit within its given dimensions.

This is a nonempty element that requires a closing tag. It can contain only text, which will be displayed as the control's initial value, and a user can easily delete or edit that initial text. Any initial text within a textarea element will be displayed with all white space intact, including tabs and returns. If the element has no initial text content, the control will be empty when a browser renders it.

By default, most visual browsers render the text within a text area in a monospace typeface—one in which every character is the same width, such as Courier—but this can be modified with CSS if you prefer (and you'll learn how later in this chapter). Listing 8-14 shows a textarea element containing some text as its initial value.

Listing 8-14. *A textarea Element Containing Initial Text*

```
<textarea name="message" rows="6" cols="50">
Dear Mario and Luigi,
Your crust is divine, your sauce both sweet and spicy.
Your WiFi is strong and stable where the coffee shop's is dicey.
</textarea>
```

Figure 8-13 shows how this is rendered. Some browsers will automatically reserve some space for a scroll bar along the box's right edge, though the box will not actually become scrollable until it has been filled with enough text to warrant it. Once again, this is from Firefox 2 for Mac OS X.

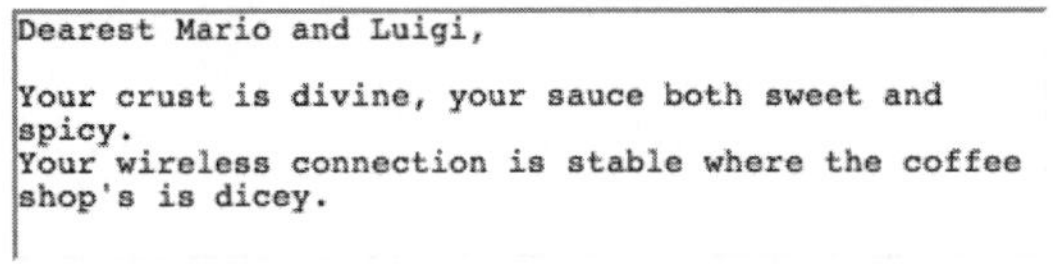

Figure 8-13. *The textarea control as seen in a graphical browser. Note that the text within it appears in a monospace typeface by default.*

Required Attributes

- `cols`: Specifies the number of characters to display on a single horizontal line, thus defining the width of the rendered box. Text will automatically wrap to new lines as needed or will invoke a horizontal scroll bar if a long line of text doesn't include word spaces to facilitate wrapping.

- `name`: Identifies the control so that it can be associated with its value when the form is submitted. A markup validator may not generate an error if this attribute is missing, but it's required in order to successfully handle the form.

- `rows`: Specifies the number of lines of text to display before scrolling vertically, thus defining the height of the rendered box. The browser will automatically produce a vertical scroll bar when the length of the text exceeds this given height.

Optional Attributes

- `accesskey`: Assigns a keyboard shortcut to the control for easier and quicker access through keyboard navigation. The value of this attribute is the character corresponding to the access key. The exact keystroke combination needed to activate an access key varies between browsers and operating systems.

- `disabled="disabled"`: When present, disables the control so that it cannot receive focus and its value cannot be modified. Many browsers will display disabled controls in a "grayed-out" state. The value of a disabled control is not submitted.

- `readonly="readonly"`: Specifies that the control may only display a value and cannot be modified. This differs from `disabled` in that a read-only control can still receive focus and its value is still submitted with the form.

- `tabindex`: Specifies the control's position in the tabbing order when active controls are cycled through using the Tab key.

Standard Attributes

- `class`

- `dir`

- `id`

- `lang`

- `style`

- title

- xml:lang

Structuring Forms

Now that you've been introduced to all the myriad of form controls you'll need, you might be wondering just how to put them all together. Controls are merely component parts, and the form in its entirety is more than the sum of its controls. A usable and accessible form needs a meaningful structure, just as the rest of your document does. And because the form element may contain almost any structural markup, you have a broad XHTML arsenal at your disposal.

When you construct a form, as with any other content, you should think about the meaning and purpose of the content and wrap it in the most semantically appropriate tags. A list of options with checkboxes or radio buttons should probably be marked up as a list and each option held in a separate list item (the li element). If the ordering of those options is significant—option 1, option 2, option 3, and so on—the list should probably be an ordered one (using the ol element). If your form is split into distinct sections, perhaps each section could be wrapped in a div element with a heading (h1 through h6) as its title. If each control in that form represents a separate thought, it may be sensible to place them in paragraphs (the p element).

With that in mind, remember that forms are not actually read like static content. They exist to engage the user—to open the door and invite your visitors in. Think about the meaning behind the information you're requesting of them, and consider the often-tedious procedure of stepping through a series of controls and entering data into them. Arrange and organize your form with an eye toward optimal usability and accessibility.

In addition to the headings, paragraphs, lists, and tables you already know, a few special elements are specifically designed for use with forms.

fieldset

The block-level fieldset element encompasses a set of related controls, collecting them into a logical group. The field set can in turn contain any other structural markup needed to further arrange and support each control (paragraphs, lists, and so on), and even nested fieldset elements to establish groups within groups (though nesting should be kept to a minimum). By default, most visual web browsers will display a thin border around a field set, though the exact appearance of the border will vary from browser to browser. We'll show you how you can remove this default border with CSS later in this chapter.

You'll recall that controls within a form element must appear within a block-level container, since form cannot have inline children. The fieldset element is just such a container, and it has more semantic value than the semantically neutral div element;

if you're inclined to use a div to group controls, a fieldset might be a better choice. Consider the meaning and purpose of the controls, and gather them into field sets appropriately.

A fieldset element must contain a legend element (covered in more detail next) to provide a title for the set of fields.

Listing 8-15 demonstrates the markup for a simple form, much like the one you saw in Listing 8-1 way back at the beginning of this chapter. This time, the two form controls have been wrapped in a fieldset element to bind them together and establish their semantic relationship.

Listing 8-15. *A Simple Form with a Field Set Containing Two Controls*

```
<form method="post" action="/cgi-bin/formhandler.cgi">
  <fieldset>
    <legend>Subscribe to our mailing list</legend>
    <label for="email">Enter your E-mail address</label>
    <input type="text" id="email" name="email" />
    <input type="submit" name="subscribe" value="Subscribe" />
  </fieldset>
</form>
```

You can see how this appears in a graphical browser in Figure 8-14. The border is automatically drawn by the browser, along with a small amount of padding to create space between the border and its contents. Both the border and padding can be adjusted with CSS.

Figure 8-14. *The form as it appears in Firefox for Mac OS X*

Required Attributes

No attributes are required for the fieldset element.

Optional Attributes

The fieldset element doesn't have any optional attributes.

Standard Attributes

- class

- dir

- id

- lang

- style

- title

- xml:lang

legend

The legend element provides a text title or caption for a field set and hence may appear only within a fieldset element. Legend text should be chosen with care and should be succinct and descriptive. It's an inline element that can contain only text and other inline elements, but most browsers will position a legend so that it overlaps the field set's top border (as shown in Figure 8-15), deviating slightly from typical inline behavior.

Unfortunately, the legend element is notoriously difficult to style consistently with CSS. You might be able to alter its font family, size, weight, and color, but attempting to apply a background, margins, and padding or to reposition the legend via CSS will be problematic in some common browsers. As a general rule, it's often best to allow browsers to render field set legends in their own default styling and keep the CSS artistry to a minimum.

Listing 8-16 shows a field set featuring a legend element, in this case acting as both a title to announce the purpose of the controls and some instructional text to help the visitor figure out what to do. An accesskey attribute has also been added, creating a keyboard shortcut to aid accessibility. Activating the access key will let a user jump directly to this section of the web page without the need to scroll. Not all web browsers support access keys inherently, and those that do might have very different implementations of the functionality.

Listing 8-16. *A legend Element Featuring an accesskey Attribute*

```
<fieldset>
  <legend accesskey="T">Choose additional toppings</legend>
  <ul>
    <li>
      <label for="top1">
        <input type="checkbox" id="top1" name="top1" value="peppers" />
        Peppers
      </label>
    </li>
```

```
    <li>
      <label for="top2">
        <input type="checkbox" id="top2" name="top2" value="xcheese" />
        Extra cheese
      </label>
    </li>
    <li>
      <label for="top3">
        <input type="checkbox" id="top3" name="top3" value="mushrooms" />
        Mushrooms
      </label>
    </li>
    <li>
      <label for="top4">
        <input type="checkbox" id="top4" name="top4" value="olives" />
        Olives
      </label>
    </li>
  </ul>
</fieldset>
```

Figure 8-15 illustrates how a legend is rendered in Firefox for Mac OS X, and most other visual browsers will display it much like this. The text is vertically centered over the field set's top border and has a slight gap of white space on each side. One interesting oddity is that Internet Explorer for Windows colors legend elements blue by default, but you can alter this with CSS if you prefer.

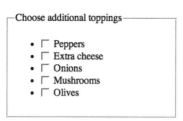

Figure 8-15. *The legend element as seen in Firefox with default styling. This rendering is fairly typical, though you might see slight variations in some browsers.*

Required Attributes

No attributes are required for the legend element.

Optional Attributes

- accesskey: Assigns a keyboard shortcut to the element for easier and quicker access through keyboard navigation. The value of this attribute is the character corresponding to the access key, though the exact keystroke combination needed to activate an access key varies between browsers and operating systems.

Standard Attributes

- class

- dir

- id

- lang

- style

- title

- xml:lang

label

Perhaps the most useful and meaningful element for structuring forms, the inline label element creates a text label for a specific control. A label element may contain both the control and its text label, in which case the connection between the two elements is implied by context. Alternatively, the label element may carry an optional for attribute whose value corresponds to the control's unique id, explicitly declaring the connection between the two elements. The for attribute, though not technically required, is strongly recommended. Even if the label element encloses both the text and the control, the for and id attributes reinforce the connection.

When a label is properly associated with a control, many browsers will make the entire label area clickable to give focus to the specified control (Safari and OmniWeb are the most notable exceptions). This feature especially improves the usability of checkboxes and radio buttons, because the text label enlarges the clickable area, and those controls can present very small targets for a mouse pointer to land on. It's possible for more than one label to share the same for value, in which case all those labels are associated with the same control and any of them will give focus to that control when clicked (except in Safari or OmniWeb, of course).

When laying out a form, labels for text fields and selection menus typically appear above or to the left of the control, while labels for checkboxes and radio buttons should appear to the control's right. These aren't rules dictated by web standards, just usability conventions established over time.

Listing 8-17 expands the same mailing list subscription form, this time adding some more structural markup. Options to choose either plain text or HTML e-mails appear in a nested field set, since those controls are a subset of the complete set of controls. They're in an unordered list because it's a list of two options in no particular order, so that markup makes good sense. Labels have been added to identify the e-mail address text field as well as the radio buttons for choosing a format, and all are explicitly connected to their controls with for attributes. It might look like a lot of extra markup for such a simple form, but the benefits gained in improved usability, accessibility, and meaningful structure are worth it.

Listing 8-17. *A Form Structured with Field Sets and Labels*

```
<form method="post" action="/cgi-bin/formhandler.cgi">
  <fieldset>
    <legend>Subscribe to our mailing list</legend>
      <p>
        <label for="email">Your E-mail address</label>
        <input type="text" name="email" id="email" />
      </p>
      <fieldset>
        <legend>Select your preferred format</legend>
        <ul>
          <li>
            <label for="text">
             <input type="radio" name="pref" value="text" id="text" /> Plain text
            </label>
          </li>
          <li>
             <label for="html">
               <input type="radio" name="pref" value="html" id="html" /> HTML
             </label>
          </li>
        </ul>
      </fieldset>
    <p><input type="submit" id="subscribe" value="Subscribe" /></p>
  </fieldset>
</form>
```

You can see how this form looks in Figure 8-16. Alas, it's not very pretty when rendered with the browser's default styles. But you have the power of CSS on your side, and you'll learn just a few ways to improve the looks of your forms in the next section.

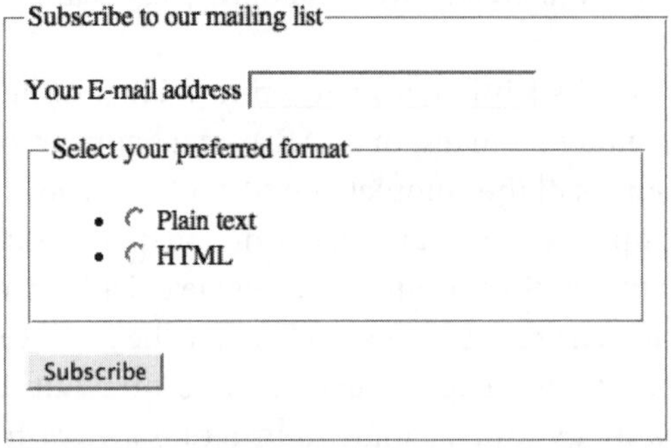

Figure 8-16. *The form isn't the most attractive thing when rendered with a browser's default style sheet, but its markup is semantically sound and will be accessible to a wider range of people and devices.*

Required Attributes

No attributes are required for the label element.

Optional Attributes

- for: Explicitly associates the label with a single control when the attribute's value matches the control's unique id

Standard Attributes

- class

- dir

- id

- lang

- style

- title

- xml:lang

INDICATING REQUIRED FIELDS

Not every control in every form is essential for the form's completion. Some fields may be required while others will be optional, so it's polite and advisable to clearly indicate the difference. In the relatively short life of the World Wide Web thus far, it has become a convention to indicate required fields with an asterisk (*), a small graphical dot, or the word *required* next to the control.

In addition to an indicator of some sort, it's recommended that you include an informational statement to introduce that notation to anyone who might not be familiar with it. A sentence such as "Required fields are marked with *" at the beginning of the form will suffice. If a particular form has no optional fields, it could become redundant to indicate every single control as required, so simply stating that "All fields are required" might be preferable. An instructional statement probably isn't necessary if required fields are individually tagged with the word *required*.

Some web designers opt for indicating required fields with an italicized or boldfaced label, but this cue is essentially visual and hence problematic for nonsighted users. If you choose to alter the presentation of label text to indicate required fields, do so by wrapping the text in an em or strong element so that even nonvisual devices can suitably emphasize it. If you use an image as a required field indicator, adding alt="required" will assist nonsighted users. Don't indicate required fields visually through CSS alone; the indicator has real meaning and so belongs in the XHTML markup.

You shouldn't indicate required fields purely through the use of color either; color-blind users might be unable to distinguish them, and unsighted users will obviously run into problems. If you do use color (in combination with some other cue), don't use red because a red label typically indicates an error.

Styling Forms with CSS

As we've said before, form controls will appear slightly different in just about every browser on the planet. This is true partly because they're not strictly web elements; they're basic elements of any graphical user interface. Many web browsers that run on desktop computers don't possess any ingrained presentation logic for rendering form controls. Rather, they call upon the local operating system to display those controls in whatever visual style is native to that operating system.

Safari, OmniWeb, and Camino for Macintosh OS X all rely on that operating system's standard rendering of form controls, so buttons, checkboxes, and selection menus in those browsers appear in glassy, candy-coated splendor. Internet Explorer is such a deeply entrenched part of the Windows operating system that form controls will look completely different under Windows XP than they do in the same browser running under Windows Vista. Mozilla Firefox, a browser that is available for Windows, Macintosh, and Linux, renders form controls in very different ways on each of those platforms. The same is also true of Opera, another fine cross-platform browser.

Figure 8-17 shows the same form in both Safari for Mac OS X and Internet Explorer 6 for Windows XP. Compared to the images of Firefox you've seen throughout this chapter, you can see just how differently these controls are presented.

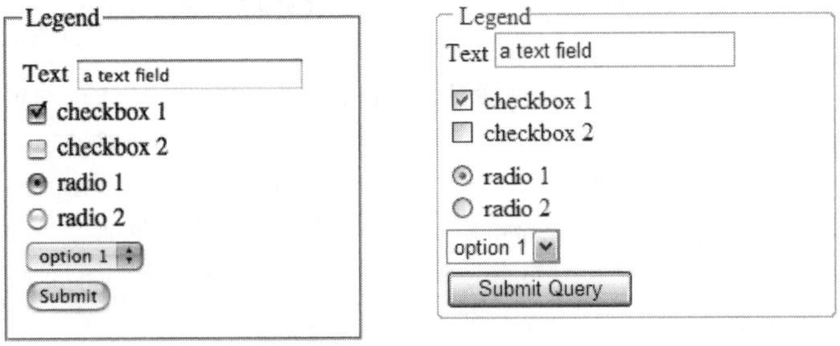

Figure 8-17. *A comparison of a text field, checkboxes, radio buttons, a selection menu, and a submit button as rendered by two very different browsers, Safari on the left and Internet Explorer on the right*

In the end, web designers must accept the inescapable fact that forms will never look the same in every browser. With that acceptance comes a Zen-like relinquishing of control. In many cases, it's simply best to leave form controls alone and allow the browsers to display them in whatever style they will. This is not to say that form controls can *never* be styled, just that sometimes perhaps they *shouldn't* be.

A person who regularly uses a particular browser on a particular operating system tends to grow accustomed to a consistent presentation of form-related interface elements. They'll become trained to recognize text fields, drop-down menus, and buttons in that familiar style because they see them every day. Deviating too far from that norm—by making a submit button look like a text link, for example—may simply breach your visitors' expectations and make the form more difficult to use ("I'm looking for the submit button, but all I can find is a text link!").

Despite these admonitions against overly styling form controls and despite warnings that not all browsers will honor CSS applied to those controls, it's still often possible to affect their design. Many browsers do, in fact, allow extensive alteration of a form control's appearance; its coloring, typography, borders, and background can all be modified through CSS. Browsers that don't honor those style properties will simply display the control in its default style. In the terms of modern best practices, this is known as *graceful degradation*: devices that support the CSS will display the control as designed, while those that don't support the CSS . . . won't. The control still functions just as it should.

As a rule of thumb, redesigning form controls should be kept to a minimum, and those form controls should still look like what they are. A text field needs to look like a text field, and a button should look like a button.

■**Tip** Roger Johansson has explored the rendering of form elements in a wide range of browsers on several operating systems, including tests of how those browsers honor or disregard CSS rules applied to those elements. See his article "Styling form controls with CSS, revisited" (`http://www.456bereastreet.com/archive/200701/styling_form_controls_with_css_revisited/`) for more information, complete with eye-opening demonstrations.

With all of that said, a web designer can easily, through artful application of CSS, influence the overall layout and design of the form and the page in which it resides. The presentation of the controls themselves may sometimes be beyond the designer's reach, but the elements around them are fair game for styling.

Removing the Border from Field Sets

The majority of graphical web browsers display a field set with a border and a bit of padding by default. The border exists for a reason—to visually indicate the boundaries of the group— but it's not always a desirable part of a visual design. Luckily it's easily removed with CSS, as shown in Listing 8-18.

Listing 8-18. *The border Property with a Value of none*

```
fieldset {
  border: none;
}
```

The none keyword instructs the browser to override any default or inherited values for border color, width, or style. The border property is CSS *shorthand*, automatically applying the same value to all four sides of an element without the need to call out each side individually. There is also an equivalent padding shorthand property, shown in Listing 8-19, affecting the padding on all four sides of a box with a single declaration.

Listing 8-19. *The padding Property with a Value of 0*

```
fieldset {
  border: none;
  padding: 0;
}
```

You can see the result in Figure 8-18. This is the same form you saw in Figure 8-16, only now the field sets vanish into white space. Those elements still exist in the markup, bringing all their semantic and accessibility benefits with them, but their presentation has been altered to reduce visual clutter. The bullets have also been removed from the unordered list, as you learned about in Chapter 4, and the list items have been shifted to the left to align with the other elements.

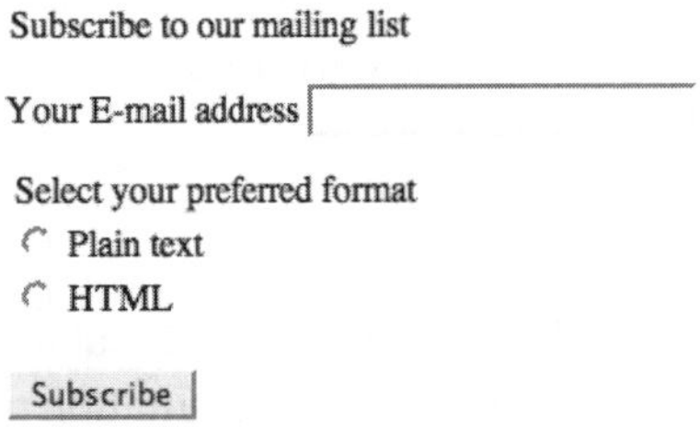

Figure 8-18. *The form as it appears without borders or padding around the field sets*

Aligning Labels

Being an inline element, a `label` will be only as wide as its text contents, and that text will align to the left by default just as any ordinary text would. But what if your form has a stack of several controls with labels of different widths? By default, it will look something like Figure 8-19. Surely there must be some way to tidy this up.

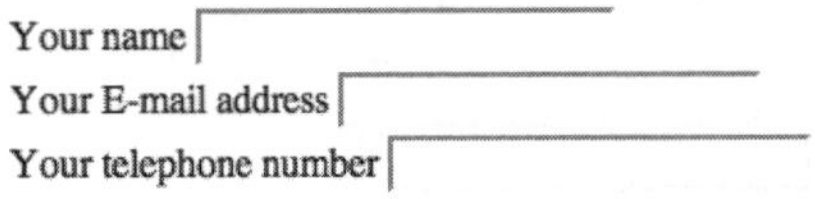

Figure 8-19. *Labels of different widths will be staggered.*

Inline elements can be treated as block-level elements with the CSS declaration `display: block`. However, that will also cause them to appear on their own line (as any other block-level element would) rather than to the left of the control. If the label is also floated to the left, the text field can then flow up onto the same line. It so happens that any floated element is automatically treated as a block-level element, so the `display: block` declaration isn't even necessary in combination with `float: left`.

Once the labels have become floating blocks, giving each of them the same width will push their related text fields to the right, aligning them in a neat column. The text will still be aligned to the left of the label, resulting in varying gaps of white space between the labels and their controls. You can align the text to the right instead, and a small margin will put some distance between the labels and their controls. Listing 8-20 shows the final CSS rule, converting all `label` elements within the element with the ID "info" (which might be a `div`, a `fieldset`, or even the `form` itself) to floating blocks 200 pixels wide. The label text is aligned to the right, and the margin creates some space between the label and its control.

Listing 8-20. *A CSS Rule Aligning the Labels in a Form*

```
#info label {
  float: left;
  width: 200px;
  text-align: right;
  margin-right: 15px;
}
```

You can see the results in Figure 8-20, where the labels and text fields now align in two neat columns.

Your name
Your E-mail address
Your telephone number

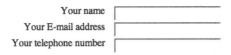

Figure 8-20. *The same form after the CSS is applied*

If that layout isn't to your liking and you'd prefer the labels above the controls, a simple `display: block`, as in Listing 8-21, does the trick. There's no need for floats or widths; simply treating the inline `label` element as if it were a block-level element will cause it to appear on its own line. The element itself remains inline in nature (it can still only contain text and inline elements), but a browser will render it otherwise.

Listing 8-21. *A CSS Rule Treating All label Elements As Block-Level*

```
label {
  display: block;
}
```

Figure 8-21 shows the result.

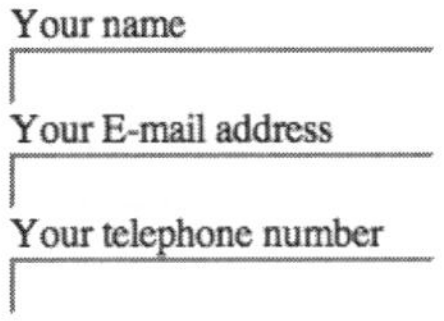
Your name
Your E-mail address
Your telephone number

Figure 8-21. *The labels are now treated as block-level, so each appears on its own line.*

Changing the Typeface in Form Controls

As you see in Figure 8-22, graphical browsers typically render text entered into a textarea element in a monospace typeface, while text in an input or select element is usually rendered in a variable-width, sans-serif typeface. This is in spite of any base font family declared for the rest of the document (as you learned to do in Chapter 4).

Figure 8-22. *The label text is rendered in Trebuchet, as inherited from the body element. Text in the text field, selection menu, and submit button is in another default typeface, and the contents of the textarea are in yet another typeface.*

To overcome the default typeface, the font-family property must be separately declared for input, select, and textarea elements. However, if you'd like those elements to share the same font family as the rest of your page, you needn't re-declare the same font family you applied to the body element. The key is the inherit value, as shown in Listing 8-22.

Listing 8-22. *A Simple CSS Rule to Inherit font-family in Form Controls*

```
input, select, textarea {
  font-family: inherit;
}
```

When the inherit keyword is used as the value of any property, it instructs the browser to use the same value that was applied to the element's parent. Because the value of font-family is automatically inherited by every other element except these form controls, the browser will follow the document tree all the way up to the body element to determine what value to apply, assuming no other ancestor along the way has been assigned a different value.

This CSS rule also combines all three elements into a single selector, separated by commas. Whenever the same set of declarations is meant to apply to several elements, they can be merged into a single CSS rule to minimize redundancy and keep your style sheet clean.

Figure 8-23 shows the same form, now with a consistent font family in all the form controls.

Figure 8-23. *The controls now inherit their font family—Trebuchet in this case—from their parent element.*

Summary

Forms are a vital and integral part of the World Wide Web. They open the flow of communication so information can move in both directions, from the website to the user and from the user back to the website. They're also the transit system that makes Internet commerce possible, which is essential to the success of many modern businesses. A form in XHTML consists of a `form` element that may contain a wide range of controls, each with a distinct purpose and function. The structure and utility of a form can and should be enhanced by grouping controls into field sets and giving each control a clear label.

Although the components of a form are few and simple, constructing an attractive, usable, accessible, and functional form can be challenging, especially if that form is long and complex. But by putting yourself into your visitors' shoes and thinking about the meaning and purpose of your forms, you can assemble forms that will meet all of these goals. Usable forms improve the interactive experience of using the web. Your visitors will appreciate it.

Different browsers running on different operating systems render form elements in very different styles. Even so, the structural markup around those form controls can be extensively styled with CSS. You can use CSS to influence the visual organization and arrangement of your forms, making them more attractive for most of your visitors without harming the underlying structure. You'll learn a lot more about using CSS to control and enhance the visual layout of your web pages in the next chapter.

■ ■ ■

CHAPTER 9

Adding Style to Your Documents: CSS

In Chapter 2 you were introduced to the basics of using CSS to style your documents. You saw how to use internal and inline styles as well as how to use selectors. Throughout the rest of the chapters you have seen some basic techniques on how to style the different elements covered. This chapter will give you additional background on using CSS and show you some additional styling techniques as well as how to handle the layout and positioning of your elements. It is meant to introduce you to the basics in order to style your own documents; to really dig into CSS and gain a thorough understanding of its features, we recommend *Beginning CSS Web Development* by Simon Collison (Berkeley, CA: Apress, 2006).

Using External Style Sheets

In Chapter 2 you saw how to add style sheets by using internal style sheets and inline styles. The other technique is to use external style sheets. *External style sheets* allow you to reuse the same style sheet for multiple documents or even multiple websites easily. You add an external style sheet to your document with the link element, covered briefly in Chapter 3. As you recall, the link element goes in the head section. The basic use of the link element is as follows:

```
<link href="mycssfile.css" type="text/css" rel="stylesheet" />
```

You place the link element within your document to point to a separate file that provides the style. You can then use the file in many different documents to provide a consistent look to a set of documents. Listing 9-1 shows the sample from Chapter 2 to introduce CSS, but this time it uses an external style sheet.

Listing 9-1. *Using the link Element to Add an External Style Sheet*

```
<!DOCTYPE html
PUBLIC "-//W3C//DTD XHTML 1.0 Strict//EN"
"http://www.w3.org/TR/xhtml1/DTD/xhtml1-strict.dtd">
<html xmlns="http://www.w3.org/1999/xhtml" xml:lang="en">
    <head>
        <title>Chapter Ten, External Style Sheets</title>
        <link href="mystyle.css" type="text/css" rel="stylesheet" />
    </head>
    <body>
        <p class="menu">It is easy to use XHTML</p>
        <p class="mainContent">It is easy to use XHTML</p>
        <p class="sideContent">It is easy to use XHTML</p>
    </body>
</html>
```

Listing 9-1 shows what the document will look like; notice that there are no style definitions in it. It contains the link element pointing to the external style sheet found in
Listing 9-2.

Listing 9-2. *The External Style Sheet*

```
p.menu {text-align:left;color:red;background-color:white;}
p.mainContent {text-align:center;color:black;background-color:white;}
p.sideContent {text-align:right;color:yellow;background-color:white;}
```

We saved the code in Listing 9-2 as a separate file in the same directory named myfile.css.
Figure 9-1 shows the document with the style sheet applied—wow, this looks the same as
Figure 2-2 shown in Chapter 2. The difference is we have removed the definitions of the
styles and placed them in an external file. This will allow us to easily change the styles of
many documents by simply changing the style sheet file.

■**Tip** You can also use external sheets within an inline style element by using the @import statement.
The @import statement instructs the browser to load an external style sheet and apply its styles. The @import
statement, as shown here, should be the first statement in the style element:

```
<style>
    @import "mystyle.css"

    ...
</style>
```

The style rules for an imported style sheet are applied before the internal style rules. You can also import more
than one style sheet, and the order matters in their precedence being applied.

Figure 9-1. *The XHTML document with the external style sheet applied*

Units of Measure

Before we jump into more features of CSS, we'll cover an important concept—unit of measure. CSS offers a variety of units of measure that you can use to specify the value of CSS properties. Table 9-1 lists the most common units used in CSS.

Table 9-1. *Units of Measure in CSS*

Unit	Description
%	Percent.
cm	Centimeter.
em	One em is the same as the font size of the current element.
ex	One ex is the x-height of a font.
in	Inch.
mm	Millimeter.
pc	One pica is the same as 12 points.
pt	One point is the same as 1/72 of an inch.
px	One pixel represents a single dot on a computer display.

You also have several ways to specify colors in CSS. Table 9-2 lists the various ways to specify color for those attributes that accept a color.

Table 9-2. *Specifying Color in CSS*

Unit	Description
Color name	A specific color name (blue).
#rrggBB	A hex number representing the color (#0000ff); as a shortcut, you can also use a three-digit version that will duplicate each digit. So for #0000ff, it would be #00f. Each pair for red, green, and blue is duplicated, as you can see.
rgb(r,g,b)	A value specifying a portion of red, green, and blue (such as rgb(0,0,255)).
rgb(r%,g%,b%)	A value specifying a portion of red, green, and blue as a percentage (such as rgb(0%,0%,255%)).

Layout

One of the key roles of CSS is to manage the layout of documents by providing the ability to position elements within a document precisely as needed. This in combination with using external style sheets provides the ability to create many different looks for the same document. This is often used when trying to display the same document on different devices.

Containers

As you have seen, many of the elements in XHTML are actually containers for other elements. This same concept of containers is also prevalent in the application of CSS. Take a look at the following code block:

```
<body>
    <p>
        Container #1
        <ul>
            <li>Pizza</li>
            <li>Spaghetti</li>
            <li>Cheese Sticks</li>
        </ul>
    </p>
    <p>
        Container #2
    </p>
</body>
```

Each indent in the code block represents an XHTML element, but it also is a container where CSS can be applied. The outermost container shown is the body element, and the innermost element is the li element. Using this sample block, you can also easily see the parent-child relationship; the li element is the child of the ul element, which is the child of the p element, and so on, until you get to the root body in this case. This concept plays a key role in understanding the application of styles to containers. When a style is applied to an element, most content that is contained within that element also inherits the style. Some styles, however, are not inherited; for example, you must specifically set background-image for each element. Also, if a style to make the text red was applied to the body element, every element contained within the body element would also have red text. Of course, you can always apply a style at a lower level that will supersede a style higher up the tree.

A container consists of several parts, as shown in Figure 9-2.

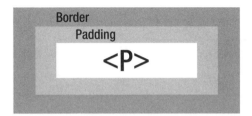

Figure 9-2. *Containers in CSS*

Margins

One of the more common elements of a container that is usually changed is the margin. The margin defines the space that exists around the container. It is similar to setting a margin in your favorite word processing program. You can set a different margin for each side of a container with the margin-left, margin-right, margin-top, and margin-bottom attributes. You can also use the shortcut margin attribute to set all the values with one attribute:

```
p {margin: 5cm 3cm 5cm 3cm}
```

The margin shortcut can be very complex since it allows you to pass a different number of values. If you specify a single value, all four sides will be set to that single value. If you specify two values, then the top and bottom will be set to the first value, and the second value applies to the left and right sides. If you specify three values, they are applied as top and left as the first and then the right and bottom as the second and third. If you specify all four, they are applied as top, right, bottom, and left. One point to remember is that the margin element is not considered when determining the overall size of the element.

■**Tip** Sometimes it is clearer to simply provide all four values when using the margin attribute.

Borders

A border is exactly what it sounds like—a visual border around the container that can be styled. You can apply several different attributes to a border: width, style, and color. As with the margin attribute, you can style each side of the border separately by adding the side you want to change to the attribute. For example, to change the border width of the top of the container, you can use the border-top-width attribute. (You can find a complete listing of the available attributes in Appendix B.) Here we will use the shortcut attributes border-width, border-style, and border-color to show their uses. The border-width attribute specifies the width of the border in one of the numerical units or from a predetermined set of values, as shown in Table 9-3. Unlike margin, the border-width attribute contributes to the overall size of the element.

Table 9-3. *border-width Values*

Value	Description
thin	Specifies a thin border
medium	Specifies a medium border
thick	Specifies a thick border
Numeric value	Allows you to specify a value

The border-style attribute allows you to make the border appear different visually. Table 9-4 lists the possible values for the border-style attribute.

Table 9-4. *border-style Values*

Value	Description
none	No border is set.
hidden	No border is set.
dashed	Specifies a dashed border.
dotted	Specifies a dotted border.
double	Specifies a border consisting of two borders where the width is set as the border width.
groove	Specifies a 3D grooved border.
inset	Specifies a 3D inset border.
outset	Specifies a 3D outset border.
ridge	Specifies a 3D ridged border.
solid	Specifies a solid border.

The border-color attribute allows you to specify the color of the border. You can use any of the formats shown in Table 9-2 to specify the color.

Padding

Padding affects the space between the border and the contents of the container. By adding padding, you allow space to be added between the actual content of the container and the border. Adding padding is key to making your documents not look crowded. The padding attribute works in the same way as the margin element.

```
p {padding: 5cm 3cm 5cm 3cm}
```

Listing 9-3 provides a sample of setting each of the attributes using the shortcuts. You can change the values in order to try different combinations. The padding elements does, however, contribute to the overall size of the element.

Listing 9-3. *Appling Styles to a Container*

```
<!DOCTYPE html
PUBLIC "-//W3C//DTD XHTML 1.0 Strict//EN"
"http://www.w3.org/TR/xhtml1/DTD/xhtml1-strict.dtd">
<html xmlns="http://www.w3.org/1999/xhtml" xml:lang="en">
  <head>
    <title>Using Container Attributes</title>
        <link href="sheet1.css" type="text/css" rel="stylesheet" />
  </head>
  <body>
    <p>
      We offer the following toppings on our pizzas:
    </p>
    <p>
      pepperoni, sausage,
      ham, bacon, hamburger, green pepper,
      onion, black olives, pineapple.
    </p>
  </body>
</html>
```

The file sheet1.css contains the following style:

```
p {border: thin outset gray;margin: 10px;padding: 1em;}
```

Figure 9-3 shows the results of applying the style.

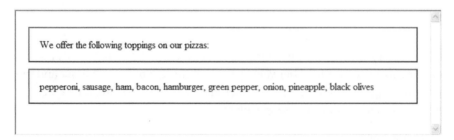

Figure 9-3. *Containers styled with CSS*

Container Sizing and Flow

In this section, we will cover how to set the size of a container. This is really the last piece that you need in order to start doing more complicated layouts. You can use the width and height attributes to set the dimension of a container. The width attribute is pretty self-explanatory. However, the height attribute can be a bit tricky. By default, containers are automatically created with the minimum height to contain all their data. If you specify a height value, it makes the size of the container fixed, and the data can spill over. This can generate some ugly results because the content can overwrite other content. You can control this spillover using the overflow and clip properties. The overflow property allows you to specify how you want any content that spills outside the container to be handled. The overflow property is not inherited by default. Table 9-5 displays the possible values for the overflow property.

Table 9-5. *Values for the overflow Property Available in CSS*

Value	Description
auto	Specifies that if the content spills over, the browser should display a scroll bar so the user can see the rest of the content; otherwise, it will not display the scroll bars.
hidden	Specifies that content will not be displayed outside the container; the browser will not display a scroll bar.
scroll	Specifies that content will not be displayed outside the container; the browser will display a scroll bar so the user can see the rest of the content.
visible	Specifies the content is allowed to spill over outside the element. This is the default value.

By default the clipping region is set to be the size of the container. Any content that goes outside this region will be treated based on the setting of the overflow property. You can use the `clip` property to change the size of the clipping region; this is often used to make the clipping region smaller.

```
p {clip: rect(top, right, bottom, left)}
```

You should not use the `clip` property for elements with an `overflow` property set to `visible`. By setting the `overflow` property to `visible`, you are telling the browser you always want the content to spill over. Listing 9-4 shows an example of setting the `overflow` property. In this example, the `width` and `height` properties are intentionally being set so that the content will exceed the size of the container. The `overflow` property has been set to `auto`, so the scroll bars will appear and allow the user to see all the content as needed.

Listing 9-4. *Using the width, height, and overflow Attributes*

```
<!DOCTYPE html
PUBLIC "-//W3C//DTD XHTML 1.0 Strict//EN"
"http://www.w3.org/TR/xhtml1/DTD/xhtml1-strict.dtd">
<html xmlns="http://www.w3.org/1999/xhtml" xml:lang="en">
  <head>
    <title>Using Container Attributes</title>
    <link href="sheet2.css" type="text/css" rel="stylesheet" />
  </head>
  <body>
    <p class="menu">
      We offer the following toppings on our pizzas:
    </p>
    <p class="top">
      pepperoni, sausage, ham, bacon, hamburger, green pepper, onion, pineapple,
      black olives
    </p>
  </body>
</html>
```

The file sheet2.css contains the following style:

```
p.menu {border: thin solid gray;margin: 10px;padding: 10px;}
p.top {width: 100px; height:100px;overflow: auto; border: thin solid gray;margin:
    10px;padding: 10px;}
```

As you can see in Figure 9-4, the height of the container is automatically adjusted as the width is decreased. The content is also adjusted and flows down automatically.

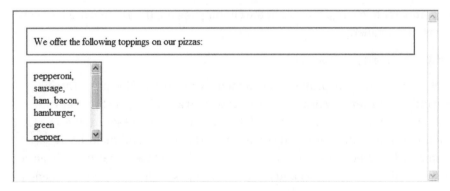

Figure 9-4. *The height is automatically adjusted when the width is changed.*

Positioning a Container

So far in this chapter we have spent a lot of time discussing containers, and this is where you will put all the concepts together. Now that you understand how containers work and how to style them, you need to learn how to position them in your document. CSS offers five ways to position your containers: static, relative, absolute, fixed, and float.

Static Positioning

Static is the default positioning and is what you are already familiar with. Basically, the elements within your document prior to the container are placed before the container, and elements that are after the container within the document are placed following the container.

Listing 9-5 shows an external style sheet that creates three boxes that are laid out using the default static positioning, as shown in Figure 9-5.

Listing 9-5. *The Default Positioning Is Static*

```
<!DOCTYPE html
PUBLIC "-//W3C//DTD XHTML 1.0 Strict//EN"
"http://www.w3.org/TR/xhtml1/DTD/xhtml1-strict.dtd">
<html xmlns="http://www.w3.org/1999/xhtml" xml:lang="en">
  <head>
    <title>Using Static Positioning</title>
    <link href="static.css" type="text/css" rel="stylesheet" />
  </head>
  <body>
    <p class="red">
      Container 1
    </p>
```

```
      <p class="white">
          Container 2
      </p>
      <p class="blue">
          Container 3
      </p>
   </body>
</html>
```

The file static.css contains the following style:

```
p {border-width: thin;border-style: solid; height: 100px; width: 100px;text-align:
    center}
p.red {background-color: red;}
p.white {background-color: white;}
p.blue {background-color: blue}
```

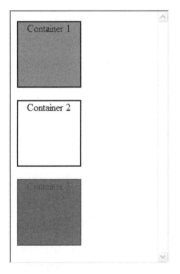

Figure 9-5. *Static positioning is the same as the default.*

Relative Positioning

Relative positioning is similar to static positioning, except that relatively positioned containers can be moved around from where they ordinarily would be. A relatively positioned container acts as part of the regular document flow. It takes up space and moves other neighboring containers as needed, just like all other statically positioned containers. The difference is that it is positioned in a different place than expected, shifted in one or more directions. Listing 9-6 uses relative positioning to stack the three boxes, as shown in Figure 9-6.

Listing 9-6. *Using Relative Positioning*

```
<!DOCTYPE html
PUBLIC "-//W3C//DTD XHTML 1.0 Strict//EN"
"http://www.w3.org/TR/xhtml1/DTD/xhtml1-strict.dtd">
<html>
  <head>
    <title>Using Relative Positioning</title>
    <link href="relative.css" type="text/css" rel="stylesheet" />
  </head>
  <body>
    <p class="red">
      Container 1
    </p>
    <p class="white">
        Container 2
    </p>
    <p class="blue">
        Container 3
    </p>
  </body>
</html>
```

The file relative.css contains the following style:

```
p {border-width: thin;border-style: solid; height: 100px; width: 100px;text-align:
    center}
p.red {background-color: red; position: relative; left: 0;}
p.white {background-color: white; position: relative; top: -100px;left: 50px;}
p.blue {background-color: blue; position: relative; top: -200px;left: 100px;}
```

In this sample, we have taken the same three boxes and layout that were in the static layout sample and used negative positions to stack them. The top property is a negative value in order to raise the boxes in the document. The left property is positive in order to spread them out across the document.

If you look closely, the only thing that changed in the actual XHTML markup was the style sheet that was in the link element. The point is by using external style sheets, you can keep the same markup in your document and present it in different ways by simply changing the style sheet.

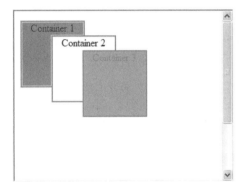

Figure 9-6. *The three boxes are now stacked by using relative positioning.*

Absolute Positioning

Absolute positioning allows complete control of the location. Instead of basing its location on another element, you specify its precise position. Each container that is absolute is independent of all the other containers. The element is located in the browser in a specified distance from the left side and from the top of the screen. Listing 9-7 shows an example of taking the same three boxes and lining them up across the document 50 pixels apart.

Listing 9-7. *Using Absolute Positioning*

```
<!DOCTYPE html
PUBLIC "-//W3C//DTD XHTML 1.0 Strict//EN"
"http://www.w3.org/TR/xhtml1/DTD/xhtml1-strict.dtd">
<html xmlns="http://www.w3.org/1999/xhtml" xml:lang="en">
  <head>
    <title>Using Absolute Positioning</title>
    <link href="absolute.css" type="text/css" rel="stylesheet" />
  </head>
  <body>
    <p style="background-color: red; position: absolute; top: 100px; left: 0;">
      Container 1
    </p>
    <p style="background-color: white; position: absolute; top: 100px;
      left: 150px;">
        Container 2
    </p>
    <p style="background-color: blue; position: absolute; top: 100px;
      left: 300px;">
        Container 3
    </p>
  </body>
</html>
```

The file absolute.css contains the following style:

```
p {border-width: thin;border-style: solid; height: 100px; width: 100px;text-align:
    center}
```

Notice that the top value is the same and only the left property is changing. Since the boxes are all the same size, this will align them across the page, and the various values of the left property will spread them out. The screen acts as a coordinate system, with the upper-left corner starting top 0 and left 0. As you move across to the right, the left value increases. As you move down, the top value increases. See Figure 9-7 for the sample in action.

You will also notice that we have mixed the use of external style sheets and inline styles to create this sample. This is perfectly legal and works, but whenever possible it is best to keep the styles in an external sheet.

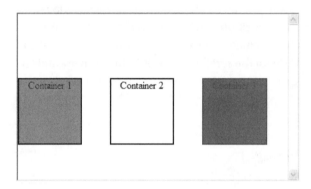

Figure 9-7. *The three boxes line up horizontally with absolute positioning.*

Fixed Positioning

Elements that use fixed positioning are locked into their position within a browser even if the user scrolls within the browser. Any other elements that are not fixed will scroll behind the fixed elements. You can use this property to make report headings that stick when a document is scrolled or to preserve a header in a table or a title at the top of a document. Listing 9-8 uses the three familiar boxes but locks them in place; any content that is not fixed will scroll behind them, as shown in Figure 9-8. Pretty cool!

Listing 9-8. *Using the Fixed CSS Attribute*

```
<!DOCTYPE html
PUBLIC "-//W3C//DTD XHTML 1.0 Strict//EN"
"http://www.w3.org/TR/xhtml1/DTD/xhtml1-strict.dtd">
<html>
```

```
<head>
  <title>Using Fixed Positioning</title>
  <link href="fixed.css" type="text/css" rel="stylesheet" />
</head>
<body>
  <p class="red">
    Container 1
  </p>
  <p class="white">
      Container 2
  </p>
  <p class="blue">
      Container 3
  </p>
.
. Add lots of content here
.
  </body>
</html>
```

The file fixed.css contains the following style:

```
p {border-width: thin;border-style: solid; height: 100px; width: 100px;text-align:
    center}
p.red {background-color: red; position: fixed; top: 0; left: 0}
p.white {background-color: white; position: fixed; top: 0; left: 150px}
p.blue {background-color: blue; position: fixed; top: 0; left: 300px}
```

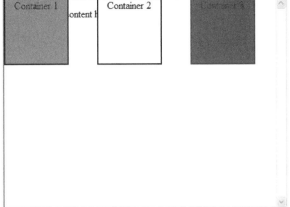

Figure 9-8. *Using fixed positioning locks the container onto its location.*

■**Tip** Although using fixed positioning sounds great, you should consider that fixed positioning has just been recently supported in Internet Explorer 7. Therefore, fixed positioning will not work properly in previous versions of Internet Explorer.

Float Positioning

The use of float positioning seems to be increasing. When you float an element, it becomes a box that can be can be shifted to the left or right on the current line. The available values for the float attribute are left, right, and none. A box that has been floated will shift in the specified direction until its outer edge touches the containing block's edge or the outer edge of another float. The remaining content will flow down the opposite side of the box that was floated and wrap around the floated element. However, the border, background image, and background color will extend underneath the floated box.

■**Tip** You should almost always set the width of a floated item. Failing to do so can have unpredictable results. However, when working with images, you do not have to set a width since it is provided by the image itself.

Sometimes you might not want elements that are below a floated element to wrap around it; you can use the clear property on the element following the floated element.

Listing 9-9 uses the familiar boxes and floats them to the right, as shown in Figure 9-9.

Listing 9-9. *Using the CSS Float Attribute*

```
<!DOCTYPE html
PUBLIC "-//W3C//DTD XHTML 1.0 Strict//EN"
"http://www.w3.org/TR/xhtml1/DTD/xhtml1-strict.dtd">
<html>
  <head>
    <title>Using Float Positioning</title>
    <link href="float.css" type="text/css" rel="stylesheet" />
  </head>
  <body>
    <p class="red">
      Container 1
    </p>
    <p class="white">
        Container 2
    </p>
```

```
    <p class="blue">
        Container 3
    </p>
  </body>
</html>
```

The file float.css contains the following style:

```
p {border-width: thin;border-style: solid; height: 100px; width: 100px;text-align:
    center;float: right;}
p.red {background-color: red;}
p.white {background-color: white;}
p.blue {background-color: blue;}
```

Figure 9-9. *Using float positioning puts all the boxes on the right side of the document.*

If you want to learn more about using a float layout, you can visit `http://webdesign.about.com/od/advancedcss/a/aa010107.htm`, which has a tutorial on using floats for layout. We will visit floats again briefly in Chapter 11 where we will be using float positioning to build the sample website.

Setting the Order of Containers

In the relative positioning sample, we stacked the three boxes. However, in what order should the browser stack them? By default when containers overlap, the browser always puts the last box coded on top of the previous. That explains why the boxes were stacked with each new box on top of the previous. This may not always be what you want. Using the `z-index` property, you can completely control the order in which the containers are displayed. The `z-index` property determines the stacking order of an element. A container with a higher `z-index` property will always be displayed in front of another container with a lower `z-index`. Listing 9-10 will once again use the three squares, but the squares will be stacked in the opposite order with the first one on top.

Listing 9-10. *Using the z-index Property*

```
<!DOCTYPE html
PUBLIC "-//W3C//DTD XHTML 1.0 Strict//EN"
"http://www.w3.org/TR/xhtml1/DTD/xhtml1-strict.dtd">
<html xmlns="http://www.w3.org/1999/xhtml" xml:lang="en">
  <head>
    <title>Using z-index</title>
    <link href="z-order.css" type="text/css" rel="stylesheet" />
  </head>
  <body>
    <p style="background-color: red; position: relative; left: 0;z-index: 10">
      Container 1
    </p>
    <p style="background-color: white; position: relative; top: -100px;
      left: 50px;z-index: 5">
        Container 2
    </p>
    <p style="background-color: blue; position: relative; top: -200px;
      left: 100px;z-index: 0">
        Container 3
    </p>
  </body>
</html>
```

The file z-order.css contains the following style:

```
p {border-width: thin;border-style: solid; height: 100px; width: 100px;text-align:
    center}
```

Figure 9-10 shows the result we wanted. By making the first container have the largest z-index, it appears to be on the top of the stack. You can use any numeric values including negatives to specify the z-index value.

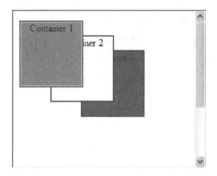

Figure 9-10. *Using z-index to set the order in which the boxes should appear*

Backgrounds

Adding a background to style your document can really dress it up and make it look professional. Table 9-6 lists the available properties when applying a background to a container.

Table 9-6. *Background Properties Available in CSS*

Property	Description
background	A shortcut property that allows the setting of all background properties at once
background-attachment	Specifies whether a background image is fixed or should scroll with the rest of the document
background-color	Specifies the background color of an element
background-image	Specifies an image to be used as the background
background-position	Specifies the starting position of a background image
background-repeat	Specifies whether/how a background image will be repeated

If you simply want to add a background color to a container, you can use the background-color property along with a color in one of the formats listed in Table 9-2.

```
p {background-color: #F5F5DC;
```

Sometimes you might want to add an image as a background. You can specify an image to use with the background-image property. The background-image property accepts a URL to the image you want to use:

```
body
{
    background-image: url(pizza.jpg);
}
```

Here I am specifying that I want to use an image called pizza.jpg as my background for my entire document since it is specified in the body element. If the image you are using is small in size, you may want to repeat the image with the background-repeat property. Table 9-7 lists the options available for the background-repeat property.

Table 9-7. *Values for the background-repeat Available in CSS*

Value	Description
no-repeat	Specifies that the background image will be displayed only once
repeat	Specifies that the background image will be repeated horizontally and vertically
repeat-x	Specifies that the background image will be repeated horizontally
repeat-y	Specifies that the background image will be repeated vertically

If we wanted to have the background displayed only one time, we merely need to add the boldfaced code shown here:

```
body
{
    background-image: url(pizza.jpg);
    background-repeat: no-repeat;
}
```

The background-position property is pretty self-explanatory; it basically allows you to provide the specific location of a background image. The last property, background-attachment, provides an interesting effect. When set to the value fixed, any background image will scroll with the document when the user scrolls. However, if it is set to scroll, the image will remain constant in the background, and the document will scroll over it.

■**Tip** It is a good idea to set a background color even when you set a background image. If for some reason an image is not found or not allowed, the document will still have some type of style that matches the rest of the document.

Styling Text

Chapter 4 discussed some of the ways you can style text, and this section will expand on some of the commonly used styles. Oftentimes you may want to underline text in your document or provide some type of editing markup, and you can use the text-decoration property for this:

```
p {text-decoration: underline}
```

This will take the text in each p element and underline the text. Table 9-8 provides a list of the values for the text-decoration property.

Table 9-8. *Values for the text-decoration Available in CSS*

Value	Description
blink	Specifies text as blinking on and off
line-through	Specifies that a line be drawn through the text
none	Specifies normal text with no decoration
overline	Specifies that a line be over the text
underline	Specifies that a line be under the text

Another common property is the text-align property; as its name suggests, it allows you to define how the text will be aligned within the container. Table 9-9 lists the possible values.

Table 9-9. *Values for the text-align Available in CSS*

Value	Description
center	Specifies the text as being centered within the container
justify	Specifies the text as being justified within the container
left	Specifies the text as being left aligned within the container
right	Specifies the text as being right aligned within the container

For example, if you wanted to center the text for all your top-level headings, you could use the following style:

```
body {text-align: left}
h1 {text-align: center}
```

This code will left align all the content in the body and center all the top-level headings. Pretty simple! Using the text-indent property, you can specify how much you want the first line of text to be indented. Using this property you can provide a common look to your document. You can specify how much you want the text to be indented with either a specific value or as a percentage of the parent.

If you wanted to make sure all the paragraphs describing the entrees on the menu were indented 12 pixels, you could use the style shown here:

```
p {text-indent: 12px}
```

Chapter 4 talked a bit about trying to avoid using the b (bold) element within your documents. This is really a presentation request and should therefore be done using CSS and not be part of the document. The font-weight property provides several weights you can apply to a container. Table 9-10 lists the possible values.

Table 9-10. *Values for the font-weight Available in CSS*

Value	Description
bold	Specifies thick characters for text
bolder	Specifies thicker characters for text
lighter	Specifies lighter characters for text
normal	Specifies normal characters for text
100–900	Specifies from thinner to thicker in increments of 100

You can use four standard weights as well as specifying a specific weight from 100–900 in increments of 100. Normal text has the value of 400, and boldfaced text is around 700, which gives you an idea of what setting the other possible weights will do. To use font-weight, simply apply the value to the property as follows:

```
p {font-weight: bold}
```

Along the same lines, if you wanted to style your text, you can use the font-style property. Table 9-11 lists its values; the italic and normal values are the most commonly used, while the oblique value is rarely used.

Table 9-11. *Values for the font-style Available in CSS*

Value	Description
italic	Specifies text to be displayed as italic
normal	Specifies text to be displayed as a normal font
oblique	Specifies text to be displayed as oblique (leaning slightly to the right)

The last text style we will cover, and probably the most commonly used, is the color style. This one is really easy to use; you simply specify the color using one of the formats found in Table 9-2:

```
p {color: red}
```

Media Types

Some CSS properties make sense only for specific media types. The `volume` property found in the aural CSS implementation does not make sense to use when presenting a document on the screen or in print. Other times a property might make sense for different media types, but you might want to use different values for each media type. You can use the `@media` rule or the `media` attribute to specify different styles for different media types. Table 9-12 lists all the media types for which you can create specific styles.

Table 9-12. *Media Types Available in CSS*

Media Type	Description
all	Specifies all media type devices
aural	Specifies media for speech systems
braille	Specifies media for Braille-enabled devices
embossed	Specifies media for Braille printers
handheld	Specifies media for small or handheld devices
print	Specifies media for printers
projection	Specifies media for projected images and presentations
screen	Specifies media for computer screens
tty	Specifies media for fixed-pitch devices such as Teletypes and terminals
tv	Specifies media for television devices

One common use for the `@media` rule is to specify different fonts between a screen presentation and a printed document. Sometimes you may want to have specific elements display on the screen and not on a printed version. An invoice application may display an invoice on the screen along with different actionable buttons or links. When you print this screen, you might not want to display these actionable buttons or links since the user cannot use them on a printed page. You can achieve hiding these actionable items by using a style sheet as well:

```
@media screen
{
p {font-family:verdana,sans-serif; font-size:14px}
}
```

```
@media print
{
p {font-family:times,serif; font-size:10px}
.hideprint {display:none}
}
```

In this style sheet we have selected a different font size for all text contained in a p element within the document. We have also created a `hideprint` class; when this is applied to any actionable button or link, the button/link will not be printed on the physical printed page but yet will appear on the computer screen.

Compatibility

In this chapter we have treated CSS as a single entity. In reality, like all the other technologies presented in this book, there are several versions of CSS with varying degrees of support among browsers. HTML and XHTML have gone through several versions and many years of change, thus allowing the browsers to get pretty consistent in their implementations. CSS, on the other hand, is a bit more in the wild. There are several versions of CSS that have varying degrees of adoption amongst the major browsers.

Appendix B lists the CSS attributes that are supported amongst the major browsers. This is where things can get a little tricky—make sure that whatever attributes you are using are supported by your target browser, or the user will not get the intended visual representation. In addition, always test your documents on several of the major browsers that are available. Although this might seem like a lot of work, it is the only way to be sure that your document is presented exactly how you wanted.

Summary

Each chapter in this book has not only shown you a new topic in XHTML but has also shown you some of the basic CSS styles that can be applied to it. This chapter has expanded on some of the styles presented throughout the book; it also detailed how containers work and how they can be used to handle layouts. This chapter has really only scratched the surface of what CSS can do. To truly make a professional-looking document, we recommend picking up *Pro CSS and HTML Design Patterns* by Michael Bowers (Berkeley, CA: Apress, 2007) as well as visiting many of the great websites on the Internet. The next chapter will cover the basics of client-side scripting. Client-side scripting will allow you to make your documents more interactive.

■ ■ ■

CHAPTER 10

Client-Side Scripting Basics

In this chapter, you'll learn the basics of using JavaScript with your documents. Scripting provides a way to make your documents dynamic and respond to users' actions.

What Is Scripting?

Scripting comes in several flavors when working with XHTML documents. You can use scripting within the browser itself or on the hosting server. Scripting on the server generates XHTML documents, sends e-mails, uploads files, and more. You typically use different technologies such as Java, ASP.NET, PHP, ColdFusion, and Perl, to mention a few. This chapter concentrates on scripting on the client within the browser itself. Only one technology for client-side scripting works across all major browsers: JavaScript.

JavaScript is actually a programming language that allows you to create mini programs within your documents. These programs are interpreted at specific points within your browsing session in order to react to selections, validate input, or make your document more dynamic by changing colors or backgrounds of specific elements. One of the really cool things you can do is combine JavaScript with CSS to produce some stunning visual effects. Using JavaScript, you can validate the forms you created back in Chapter 8. By using edits, you verify the validity of the data entered by users. The Internet offers a wealth of information on JavaScript and freely available scripts that let you do just about anything you need.

▉Note Remember, JavaScript is not Java. Java is a full-fledged programming language that you can use in a variety of ways. JavaScript is a scripting (not compiled) language you can use within a browser. The name JavaScript takes advantage of the popularity of the programming language Java. This has caused some confusion over the years with newbie programmers, to say the least.

Placement of JavaScript

Back in Chapter 3, you learned about the script element. In Listing 10-1, you can see the script element within the head section.

Listing 10-1. *Placement of JavaScript in the head Section*

```
<head>
    <title>JavaScript Basics</title>
    <script ype="text/javascript">
        alert("This is a sample of inline Javascript");
    </script>
</head>
```

You place most of your JavaScript between the script tags. In the "Handling Events" section, you'll see where you must use small bits of JavaScript code outside of the script element in order to hook into events. As with CSS, you can either place the code inline between the <script> tags or in an external file, as shown in Listing 10-2.

Listing 10-2. *Using an External File for JavaScript*

```
<head>
    <title>JavaScript Basics</title>
    <script src="myscript.js" type="text/javascript">
    </script>
</head>
```

The src attribute directs the browser where to look for the JavaScript file. You can use both relative and absolute links in the src attribute, which allow you to reference scripts within other directories. Oftentimes, you will have multiple files you want to include, which you can do by using multiple <script> tag sets. You can also mix the use of external and inline JavaScript by simply using multiple sets of <script> tags. However, external files keep your document cleaner and make it easier to reuse your code in other documents. The external file is simply a text file that contains any JavaScript you want to use in your document. The common convention is to use the .js extension in the file name so that it's clear what type of file it is. Some authors also tend to place all their JavaScript files together in a single directory on the web server.

■**Tip** Using external JavaScript files is a good practice for several reasons. First, it allows you to keep your document more pure by separating the document content from scripting. Second, it allows you to reuse a script across multiple pages without having to repeat it within the document. Finally, it allows you to make updates within the script file, which will be applied across all the documents that use the JavaScript file.

When using JavaScript, you must consider what will happen if a user's browser doesn't support JavaScript or if the user has disabled JavaScript. XHTML provides the `<noscript>` tag for this purpose. When a browser doesn't support scripting and has a noscript element, it will display whatever content is in the noscript element. If the browser does support scripting, then it will disregard the content within the noscript element. You can place the content of your scripts within an XHTML comment element, as shown in Listing 10-3.

Listing 10-3. *Using Comments to Hide JavaScript*

```
<body>
...
<script type="text/javascript">
<!--
    alert('Your browser does support JavaScript');
 //-->
</script>
<noscript>Your browser does not support JavaScript</noscript>
...
</body>
```

Placing JavaScript within an XHTML comment element allows older browsers that don't support JavaScript to ignore the JavaScript code. Those that do support JavaScript will run the JavaScript as expected. If you don't place your JavaScript code within an XHTML comment, older browsers (or browsers with JavaScript disabled) will show the JavaScript code when displaying the document. In reality, the developers don't use the `<noscript>` tag often. Today, most web developers ensure their content is properly available even when JavaScript is not available.

JavaScript, the Language

JavaScript is a full-fledged computer programming language. JavaScript can be broken down into several smaller topics, which the following sections cover:

- JavaScript syntax rules

- Variables

- Operators and expressions

- Statements

- Looping

- Functions

- Arrays

- Objects

■**Note** Entire books have been written about how to program in JavaScript. This chapter provides you with the basics, but if you want to see more advanced uses of JavaScript, the Internet provides a wealth of JavaScript samples and explanations. We also recommend picking up the book *Beginning JavaScript with DOM Scripting and Ajax*,[1] which provides an in-depth look at programming with JavaScript.

JavaScript Syntax Rules

JavaScript, like any other computer-programming language or spoken language, has specific rules that must be followed so that everyone, including computers, can understand it. This section describes some of the basic rules for JavaScript.

Comments

Just as in an XHTML document, you can add comments to your JavaScript code. The browser completely ignores comments, so they have no effect on the code itself. Comments are useful to document what a specific section of JavaScript does. Comments come in two flavors: single-line and multiline. A single-line comment looks like this:

```
// This is a comment line
```

The browser ignores any text following (and including) the double slash (//) on that line. You can also use the single-line comment multiple times in a row:

```
// This is comment line 1
// This is comment line 2
// This is comment line 3
```

If you have a multiline comment, it is often easier to use this alternative syntax:

```
/* This is comment line 1
   This is comment line 2
   This is comment line 3 */
```

---

1. Christian Heilmann, *Beginning JavaScript with DOM Scripting and Ajax* (Berkeley, CA: Apress, 2006).

A multiline comment starts with a /* and ends with a */. Everything in between these sets of characters is considered a comment. You can use comments when trying to debug a problem with a script by using them to temporarily remove code to find a problem.

Capitalization

JavaScript is a case-sensitive language, meaning that case matters. Not only must you spell all script correctly, but you also must make sure it's in the correct case. As you'll see, many built-in functions are available for your use. For example, JavaScript provides a function named alert, which accepts a string as a parameter that places a dialog box on the screen with the string parameter as a message. If you were to type Alert("My message here"), the browser would not understand and would produce an error, since the function actually begins with a lowercase as follows: alert("My message here").

Statements and White Space

Statements are at the core of JavaScript. Statements are instructions written in JavaScript that tell the browser to take an action or to perform an instruction. This chapter explores assignment and conditional statements. Just like XHTML, JavaScript ignores extra white space, which allows you the freedom to add space as needed in order to make your code more readable. It is also a good practice to finish each statement with a semicolon, as Listing 10-4 shows.

Listing 10-4. *Completing Each JavaScript Statement with a Semicolon*

```
if(iAge == "")
    alert("Please enter your age");
else
    alert("Thank you for entering your age!");

//Add more code below
```

Notice the semicolons after each statement and the blank line before the comment. Often when writing JavaScript code, it's good to leave some white space between different code blocks so that you and others can more easily make sense of it when you come back to it at a later date.

Variables

In JavaScript, variables are containers that hold data. Oftentimes, you'll find that you need to calculate a value or use a variable to store a piece of data. Variables are identified by name. You must follow several rules when naming a variable:

- Variable names are case-sensitive.

- Variable names can only use letters, numbers, and underscores.

- Variable names can contain numbers, but not in the first position.

- Variable names cannot be the same as a reserved word (see `http://javascript.about.com/library/blreserved.htm` for a complete list).

Listing 10-5 shows a few examples of setting the value of a variable.

Listing 10-5. *Using Variables*

```
iAge=37;
sLanguage1 = "JavaScript";
_bDone = true;
```

When setting a variable, you always place the variable name on the left and the variable value to the right. In the previous code, you can see that the value of iAge is set to the value 37. In the second sample, the "JavaScript" is considered a literal value because it is a string of characters in between a set of quotation marks. When you work with variables, you can categorize them as one of a number of data types (see Table 10-1).

Table 10-1. *Data Types in JavaScript*

Data Type	Description	Example
Boolean	Can only contain a true or false value	true
Number	A numeric value	29
Null	No value	null
Object	Any of the built-in JavaScript objects or ones you create	Date
String	Any characters within quotes	"This is a test!"

Operators and Expressions

Listing 10-5 shows you how to assign a specific value or a literal value to a variable. Often, you want to compute a value or create a string that is made up of several other variables added together. You can do this using operators. These operators are arranged in different categories, and do different things to the values they're applied to. For example, you can use operators to set a value to a variable or do mathematical functions:

```
iTotal += 20;
sForeName = "Bob";
sSurName = "Smith";
sFullName = sForeName + " " + sSurName;
```

Arithmetic operators—probably the easiest to understand—represent the normal math you use in day-to-day life (see Table 10-2).

Table 10-2. *Arithmetic Operators*

Operator	Example	Description
+	a + b	Adds a and b together
-	a - b	Subtracts b from a
*	a * b	Multiplies a and b together
/	a / b	Divides a by b

You use assignment operators to assign a value to a variable (see Table 10-3). Notice that several assignment operators are simply shortcuts so you can write less code.

Table 10-3. *Assignment Operators*

Operator	Example	Description
=	a = b	Sets a equal to b
+=	a += b	Shortcut for a = a + b
-=	a -= b	Shortcut for a = a - b
*=	a *= b	Shortcut for a = a * b
/=	a /= b	Shortcut for a = a / b

Comparison operators are used widely in JavaScript code when comparing values in conditional statements (covered in the "Conditional Statements" section). A comparison operator tells you whether the values on both sides of the operator are the same. A comparison operator always returns a boolean value of true or false, as Table 10-4 shows.

Table 10-4. *Comparison Operators*

Operator	Example	Description
==	a == b	true if a and b are the same value. This operator also changes data types to do comparisons.
===	a === b	true if a and b are the same value without changing data types.
!=	a != b	true if a and b are not the same value. This operator also changes data types to do comparisons.
!==	a !== b	true if a and b are not the same value without changing data types.
>	a > b	true if a is greater than b.

Table 10-4. *Comparison Operators (Continued)*

Operator	Example	Description
<	a < b	true if a is less than b.
>=	a >= b	true if a is greater than or equal to b.
<=	a <= b	true if a is less than or equal to b.
||	a || b	true if either a or b is true.
&&	a && b	true if both a and b are true.

JavaScript provides several operators you can use for counting while using special processes such as loops, which are covered in the "Looping" section. These operators tend to cause a lot of confusion amongst JavaScript newbies. When the operator occurs before the variable (e.g., ++b or --b), this is referred to as pre-increment/decrement and means that the value in the variable will be incremented (++b) or decremented (--b) before the rest of the statement is completed. A post-increment/decrement (e.g., b++ or b--) means that the value in the variable will be incremented (b++) or decremented (b--) after the statement completes. Table 10-5 shows the increment and decrement operators.

Table 10-5. *Increment/Decrement Operators*

Operator	Description
b++	Increments b by 1 after the statement is executed
++b	Increments b by 1 before the statement is executed
b--	Decrements b by 1 after the statement is executed
--b	Decrements b by 1 before the statement is executed

Statements

JavaScript statements are the heart and soul of JavaScript. Everything you've learned up to this point has been the groundwork for the rest of this chapter.

Expressions

An expression statement returns a value. You've seen several of them so far in this chapter. Using an expression with numeric data results in a normal arithmetic function:

```
itotal = 100 + 29;
```

As expected, the total variable contains the result of adding 100 and 29. However, the answer is not necessarily as clear when using alphanumeric data:

```
address = streetNumber + " " + streetName;
```

This statement takes the text in the streetNumber variable, adds a space, and adds the text from the streetName variable. It then stores the result in the address variable. Notice the use of the + operator. Even though you're dealing with text, this operator concatenates the text together. When using JavaScript, you'll often want to treat data as a different type than what it is stored as. For example, you would want to treat an age entered into a web document as a numeric value instead of the string that is normally returned in a form. Many different built-in functions do data-type conversions. Some of the more common functions include parseInt(), parseFloat(), and ToInt32(). You can find a great resource on JavaScript data-type conversion at http://www.jibbering.com/faq/faq_notes/type_convert.html.

Conditional Statements

Conditional statements are common and used extensively in JavaScript. Oftentimes, you'll want to see if a variable is equal to another value. Conditional statements provide you with this information. A conditional statement does a comparison between two values and always returns a boolean value. The first conditional statement we'll cover is the basic if statement. An if statement allows you to check if a value is true and perform other statements if it is. This example shows the basic syntax of the if statement:

```
if(iAge > 20)
    alert("You are over 20 years of age");
```

Listing 10-6 demonstrates how to use JavaScript to determine if a user is 21 years of age or older. The value of the iAge variable is tested to see if it is greater than 20. If the value is greater than 20 (as seen in Figure 10-1), then the result is true and a dialog displays on the screen. If the value of the iAge variable is less than 21, then the result is false and the dialog box doesn't display. When a value tests true, you may want to perform multiple statements, which you can do using a code block. You define a code block using the opening curly brace ({) at the start of the block and the closing curly brace (}) at the end of the block.

Listing 10-6. *Using a Conditional if Statement*

```
<!DOCTYPE html
PUBLIC "-//W3C//DTD XHTML 1.0 Strict//EN"
"http://www.w3.org/TR/xhtml1/DTD/xhtml1-strict.dtd">
```

```
<html>
  <head>
    <title>JavaScript Basic If</title>
    <script type="text/javascript">
      var iAge;

      iAge = prompt("Please enter your age in years.",0);
      if(iAge > 20)
        {
          //The value tested true
          alert("You are over 20 years of age");
          //more statements can follow here
        }
    </script>
  </head>
  <body>
  </body>
</html>
```

In Figure 10-1, you can see that the age test uses an `if` statement. First, the user enters an age into the prompt, then an appropriate message is returned.

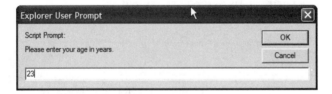

Figure 10-1. *Displaying a conditional message*

An extension of the `if` statement is the `if/else` statement, which provides the ability to run statements when a statement is `false`, as Listing 10-7 shows.

Listing 10-7. *Using an if/else Statement*

```
if(iAge > 20) {
    alert("You are over 20 years of age");
}
else {
    alert("You are under the age of 21");
}
```

When the iAge variable is greater than 20, then a message appears indicating this is so. When the condition tests false, the code block after the else statement runs and produces a message stating that the age is less than 21.

You can also place an if/else statement within another if/else statement. This concept, referred to as nesting, is shown in Listing 10-8.

Listing 10-8. *Nesting Conditional Statements*

```
<!DOCTYPE html
PUBLIC "-//W3C//DTD XHTML 1.0 Strict//EN"
"http://www.w3.org/TR/xhtml1/DTD/xhtml1-strict.dtd">
<html>
  <head>
    <title>JavaScript Nested Ifs</title>
    <script type="text/javascript">
      var iAge;
      var sMF;

      iAge = prompt("Please enter your age in years.",0);
      sMF = prompt("Are you a (M)ale or (F)emale?","M");

      if(iAge > 20) {
        if(sMF == "M") {
          alert("You are a male over 20 years of age");
        }
        else {
          alert("You are a female over 20 years of age");
        }
      }
      else {
        if(sMF == "M") {
          alert("You are a male under the age of 21");
        }
        else {
          alert("You are a female under the age of 21");
        }
      }
    </script>
  </head>
  <body>
  </body>
</html>
```

Figure 10-2 shows the script being run. The script first prompts for the user's age, then asks whether the user is male or female. The last dialog box is the result of JavaScript interpreting the values the user entered.

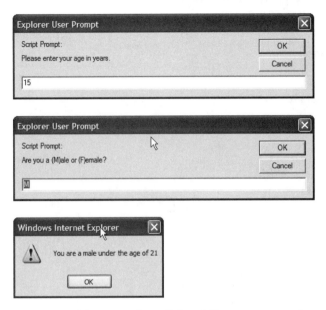

Figure 10-2. *Using nested conditional if statements to determine the message*

Notice that the code in Listing 10-8 places the curly braces a little differently. Remember, JavaScript doesn't care about white space, so this is perfectly legal. Actually, many people prefer to place the opening curly brace at the end of the conditional statement. In this case, the outside if statement is evaluated first, which determines the age. Next, the inside if statement is evaluated, which determines if the user is a male or female. It then displays the proper message.

There is one last if statement to cover: the if/else/if statement, as shown in Listing 10-9. This one may seem a little tricky to follow, but it's actually very similar to the nested if statement.

Listing 10-9. *Using the if/else/if Conditional Statement*

```
<!DOCTYPE html
PUBLIC "-//W3C//DTD XHTML 1.0 Strict//EN"
"http://www.w3.org/TR/xhtml1/DTD/xhtml1-strict.dtd">
```

```html
<html>
  <head>
    <title>JavaScript if/else/if statement</title>
    <script type="text/javascript">
      var iAge;

      iAge = prompt("Please enter your age in years.",0);

      if(iAge > 50) {
        alert("You are over 50 years of age");
      }
      else if(iAge > 30) {
        alert("You are between the ages of 30 and 40");
      }
      else {
        alert("You are under the age of 31");
      }
    </script>
  </head>
  <body>
  </body>
</html>
```

In Figure 10-3, you can see the age test using an if/else/if statement. First, the user enters the age into the prompt, then a series of if/else/if statements determines the appropriate message to display.

Figure 10-3. *Using if/else/if statements to determine the message*

The code in Listing 10-9 can be tricky to follow. The rule is to start at the top and work your way down. Once you match a true condition to any one of the if statements, the code under it executes and then jumps out of the if/else/if statement.

The last conditional statement we cover is the switch statement, which you can use to evaluate a single expression for multiple values. This can really save on creating a lot of if statements sometimes (see Listing 10-10).

Listing 10-10. *Using the switch Statement*

```
<!DOCTYPE html
PUBLIC "-//W3C//DTD XHTML 1.0 Strict//EN"
"http://www.w3.org/TR/xhtml1/DTD/xhtml1-strict.dtd">
<html>
  <head>
    <title>JavaScript Switch Statement</title>
    <script type="text/javascript">
      var sDrink;

      sDrink = prompt("Please enter your favorite drink (C)offee, (S)oda,
        (W)ater or (O)ther"," ");
      switch(sDrink)
      {
        case "C":
          alert("You chose coffee as your favorite drink.");
          break;
        case "S":
          alert("You chose soda as your favorite drink.");
          break;
        case "W":
          alert("You chose water as your favorite drink.");
          break;
        default:
          alert("I am not sure what your favorite drink is.");
      }
    </script>
  </head>
  <body>
  </body>
</html>
```

Figure 10-4 is the result of Listing 10-10. First, the script prompts for the user's favorite drink. Next, a dialog box is returned confirming what the user chose by using the `switch` statement.

Figure 10-4. *Using a switch statement to determine the message*

The switch statement begins with the keyword switch and is followed by an expression (or variable) you wish to evaluate. This expression is then matched against the value following each case. If a match is found, the code contained inside that case executes. If no match is found, the JavaScript interpreter executes the default statement at the end of the switch statement. You use the break statement to break out of a switch statement. The next label or the selected construct's closing curly brace denotes the end of a particular case. Each case label acts as the entry point. The only time the break statement is required is when you need to break out of the switch statement. In Listing 10-10, the variable sDrink is checked against various drinks, and a message is displayed when a match is found. If no match is found, a message is displayed stating, "I am not sure what your favorite drink is."

Looping

Often when you write code, you may want the same block of code to run over and over again in a row. Instead of adding several almost-identical lines in a script, you can use loops to perform this task. Loops come in two different varieties: for and do. Using these two constructs, you can create three different types of loops: a counted loop (for), a precondition loop (while), and a postcondition loop (do).

The for Loop

You use the for loop when you know in advance how many times you'd like the statements that are to be iterated to run. The basic syntax of the for loop is as follows:

```
for (loop init;test condition;increment loop counter)
{
    code to be executed
}
```

This is a little different than anything you've seen so far. The for loop starts by initializing any variables to be used in the loop (typically, this is a single variable). Next, the for loop sets a condition that needs to be checked each time to see if the condition should continue. Lastly, the variables controlling the loop are incremented or decremented. Listing 10-11 shows a quick example so you can see how the for loop works.

Listing 10-11. *Using the for Loop*

```
<!DOCTYPE html
PUBLIC "-//W3C//DTD XHTML 1.0 Strict//EN"
"http://www.w3.org/TR/xhtml1/DTD/xhtml1-strict.dtd">
<html>
  <head>
    <title>JavaScript for loop</title>
    <script type="text/javascript">
    <!--
      var sNewLine = "<br />";
      document.write("for loop is starting" + sNewLine);
      for (var iCount=0;iCount<=10;iCount++)
      {
        document.write("iCount = " + iCount);
        document.write(sNewLine);
      }
      document.write("for loop completed");
    //-->
    </script>
  </head>
  <body>
  </body>
</html>
```

Figure 10-5 shows the use of the for loop. Notice that it goes from 0 to 10. This shows how important it is to understand how many times a loop will execute.

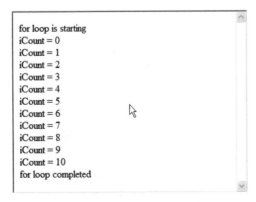

Figure 10-5. *Results of using the for loop to count from 0 to 10*

In Listing 10-11, the keyword for is followed by the parameters for the loop. The first parameter is the loop variable; in this case, it is iCount, which is initialized to 0. Next, the test condition is set: iCount <= 10. The loop continues to run while this statement evaluates to true. A statement that manipulates the loop variable is then either incremented or decremented. This sample executes a total of 11 times, once for each value from 0 to 10. It starts by going through the loop once and executing any code in the code block. The value of the variable iCount is then incremented based on the third parameter. Lastly, the condition is tested to see if the code should go through the loop again.

You need to remember a couple of things when working with loops. First, you can use the pre- or post-incrementors to determine when the loop count is advanced. Second, you can also make a loop that decrements and goes backwards if the need arises. You would start the initial value at the maximum level and decrement the counter. Be sure to set up the condition correctly as well.

The while Loop

The while loop has two different varieties: the regular while loop and the do . . . while loop. You use the regular while loop when you want a loop to execute while a specific condition is true (see Listing 10-12).

Listing 10-12. *Using the while Loop*

```
<!DOCTYPE html
PUBLIC "-//W3C//DTD XHTML 1.0 Strict//EN"
"http://www.w3.org/TR/xhtml1/DTD/xhtml1-strict.dtd">
<html>
  <head>
    <title>JavaScript while statement</title>
    <script type="text/javascript">
    <!--
      var iCount = 0;
      var sNewLine = "<br />";
      document.write("While loop is starting");
      document.write(sNewLine);

      while(iCount < 10){
        document.write("iCount = " + iCount);
        document.write(sNewLine);
        iCount++;
      }
      document.write("While loop completed");
    //-->
```

```
    </script>
  </head>
  <body>
  </body>
</html>
```

Figure 10-6 shows a while loop that starts at zero and goes through 9, since the test is done prior to executing the loop.

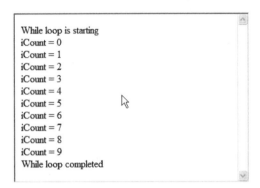

Figure 10-6. *Results of running while to execute a loop*

The while loops require you to define the variable to be tested outside the loop, as Listing 10-12 does with the variable iCount. Next, you code the while statement along with the condition to be tested in parentheses. Lastly, in the code block, you insert the statements you wish to execute within the loop. Remember to be sure to manipulate the variable that you're testing for within the loop. In Listing 10-12, you increment the value of iCount by one each time. If you don't manipulate the control variable, the code could get stuck in the loop, and the page will appear to be stuck. One thing to consider with a while loop as shown here is that it does the condition test first. There is no guarantee that the loop will ever execute at all if the condition fails the first time.

If you're in a situation where you need to guarantee that a loop executes at least one time, you can use the do . . . while loop (see Listing 10-13).

Listing 10-13. *Using the do . . . while Loop*

```
<!DOCTYPE html
PUBLIC "-//W3C//DTD XHTML 1.0 Strict//EN"
"http://www.w3.org/TR/xhtml1/DTD/xhtml1-strict.dtd">
```

```
<html>
  <head>
    <title>JavaScript do statement</title>
    <script type="text/javascript">
    <!--
      var sNewLine = "<br />";
      var iCount = 0;
      document.write("do loop is starting" + sNewLine);
      do
      {
        document.write("iCount = " + iCount);
        document.write(sNewLine);
        iCount++;
      } while (iCount < 10);
      document.write("do loop completed");
    //-->
    </script>
  </head>
  <body>
  </body>
</html>
```

Figure 10-7 shows the use of a do . . . while loop. Notice that the condition check in Listing 10-13 is at the end of the loop.

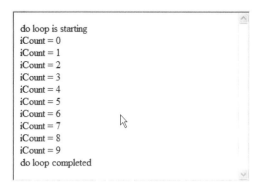

Figure 10-7. *Using the do . . . while loop to make sure the loop executes at least once*

This time, you place the while condition after the code block, and you place a do statement up front. The condition check is done after the code block, ensuring that the loop executes at least one time. Notice that in this case, the loop count variable iCount is initialized to 0, and the while statement runs only when iCount is less than 0. Since this is a do . . . while loop, the check is done after the first time through the loop, and the message "The number is 0" is produced.

Tip Each loop has a specific use. You should use the `for` loop when you know exactly how many iterations of a loop you need to do. The `while` loop is best used when you need to execute a loop until a specific condition occurs. Lastly, the `do` loop is almost the same as the `while` loop, except the condition check occurs after the first iteration, thus guaranteeing at least one iteration through the loop.

Functions

A function is used to group together a group of statements that need to be executed in sequence. Functions are often used to organize and reuse code across different documents. When you create a function, you give it a specific name that is used to call it specifically. The basic structure of a function is as follows:

```
function name(arguments) {
    one or more statements go here
}
```

The keyword `function` is followed by the name you've given the function. You use the name later in your code to execute the function. The name is followed by parentheses that contain zero or more variables that can be passed into the function. For example, if you want to create a function that adds two values together and returns the result, it would look like this:

```
function addTwoNumbers(value1,value2) {
    return value1 + value2;
}
```

You can use this function anywhere in your JavaScript code to add two numbers together. You specify which two numbers you'd like added together when making the function call. For example, if you want to add 25 and 51, you would call the function as follows:

```
var total = addTwoNumbers(25,51);
```

When the function is called, JavaScript takes the first number in parentheses and maps it to the first variable name in the function. In other words, value1 is set to 25. Next, it sets the value 51 to the second variable in the function definition: value2. This happens for each parameter defined in the function. You must match the number of parameters in your function call to the number when you actually use the function; otherwise, an error will occur. You can also create a function that doesn't have any parameters by simply creating an empty parameter list:

```
function noParams() {
    // Statements to execute
    return true;
}
```

You need to get used to coding and calling functions in JavaScript, where they are commonly used. JavaScript itself provides a wealth of built-in functions such as the alert() function you saw earlier.

Arrays

An array is a special type of variable that holds a collection of values. Arrays allow you to group many values together in a single variable. A single array can hold many values, so you may wonder how you can access the individual values within the array. As you'll see, you can do this by using an index in brackets next to the number. Let's start by first creating an array and seeing how to use it, as Listing 10-14 shows.

Listing 10-14. *Creating an Array in JavaScript*

```
var myBeverages = new Array();
var allBeverages;

myBeverages[0] = "Coffee";
myBeverages[1] = "Tea";
myBeverages[2] = "Soda Pop";
myBeverages[3] = "Lemonade";
allBeverages = "";
for (i=0;i< myBeverages.length;i++)
{
  allBeverages = allBeverages  + myBeverages[i] + ", ";
}
alert("Here are the choice of beverages " + allBeverages);
```

An array is actually considered an object in JavaScript. Most people have heard of the term *object* in regards to computer programming. An object is simply a bunch of functions and attributes that together provide a common theme. An array object groups together the functionalities of arrays. Objects are the basis of object-oriented programming (OOP).

In Listing 10-14, you start by creating a new array named myBeverages and filling it with four values. Notice the index number after the array name; this is how you differentiate each value in the array. Also, take note that the index value starts at 0 and not 1, as many developers may assume. In order to access or set a value in an array, you simply use the array name followed by the index you want. The sample uses a built-in function for arrays— the length function—to return the number of elements in the array. It then uses a loop to retrieve all the values one at a time. The length function returns the number of elements in the array.

Advanced Topics

Up until this point, we've covered the essential basics of JavaScript. The rest of this chapter will concentrate on practical uses of this knowledge while adding some new material.

Handling Events

Using events is one of the main areas where JavaScript can really shine. An event is an action that either the browser takes or the users invoke based on something they do in your document. For example, one of the most common scripting events is the load event. Each time a web browser loads your document, it invokes the load event. The submit event is a good example of an event that is invoked by user action. When a user submits a form (as discussed in Chapter 8), the submit event validates form values prior to submitting them to the web server. Table 10-6 provides a list of events that you can attach to your JavaScript code.

Table 10-6. *JavaScript Events*

Event	Description
abort	Occurs when the user has canceled the page load
blur	Occurs when a control is losing the cursor focus to move to another control
change	Occurs when the user selects a different value in a select box
click	Occurs when the user single-clicks on an element
dblclick	Occurs when the user double-clicks on an element
error	Occurs when the browser encounters an error in the script
focus	Occurs when a control receives the cursor focus
keydown	Occurs when the user holds down a key on the keyboard
keypress	Occurs when the user presses a key and releases it
keyup	Occurs after an onkeydown event when the user releases the key
load	Occurs when the browser loads your document
mousedown	Occurs when the user user depresses the mouse button
mousemove	Occurs when the user moves the mouse around the document on the screen
mouseout	Occurs when the user moves the mouse off an element in the document
mouseover	Occurs when the user moves the mouse over an element

Table 10-6. *JavaScript Events*

Event	Description
mouseup	Occurs when the user releases the mouse button after holding it down
reset	Occurs when the user presses a button that resets or clears the program
resize	Occurs when the user changes the size of the browser window
select	Occurs when the user clicks on a radio button or checkbox
submit	Occurs when the user submits a form

To use these events, you need to add code within your document to call functions that will execute when the event occurs. You can use one of three techniques to link JavaScript code to an event. First, you can use the onload event. In order to add code for the onload event, you need to specify what to do when the onload event occurs. Listing 10-15 shows you how to use the simplest technique, referred to as the *inline model*.

Listing 10-15. *Hooking Events with the Inline Model*

```
<!DOCTYPE html
PUBLIC "-//W3C//DTD XHTML 1.0 Strict//EN"
"http://www.w3.org/TR/xhtml1/DTD/xhtml1-strict.dtd">
<html>
  <head>
    <title>JavaScript inline Events</title>
    <script type="text/javascript">
        function fn_load()
        {
            alert("Page has been loaded!");
        }
    </script>
  </head>
  <body onload="fn_load()">
  </body>
</html>
```

You create a function in the <script> block, then you hook into the load event in the body section of your document. All you need to do is tell the browser what function you want to execute when the event occurs. Figure 10-8 shows how a message is displayed when the load event occurs.

Figure 10-8. *A message box displayed once the load event occurs*

The second technique you can use to link JavaScript code to an event is known as the *traditional model*. This model allows you to use scripting to add or remove events, as Listing 10-16 shows.

Listing 10-16. *Hooking Events with the Traditional Model*

```
<!DOCTYPE html
PUBLIC "-//W3C//DTD XHTML 1.0 Strict//EN"
"http://www.w3.org/TR/xhtml1/DTD/xhtml1-strict.dtd">
<html>
  <head>
    <title>JavaScript traditional model</title>
    <script type="text/javascript">
        window.onload = fn_load;
        function fn_load()
        {
            alert("Page has been loaded!");
        }
    </script>
  </head>
  <body>
  </body>
</html>
```

If you want to remove an event, you simply set its method to null:

```
window.onload = null;
```

The third technique you can use to link JavaScript code to an event is the most complex yet flexible method: the Document Object Model (DOM). See Listing 10-17.

Listing 10-17. *Hooking Events with the DOM*

```
<!DOCTYPE html
PUBLIC "-//W3C//DTD XHTML 1.0 Strict//EN"
"http://www.w3.org/TR/xhtml1/DTD/xhtml1-strict.dtd">
<html>
  <head>
    <title>JavaScript do statement</title>
    <script type="text/javascript">
        document.addEventListener( "load", fn_load, true );

        function fn_load()
        {
            alert("Page has been loaded!");
        }
    </script>
  </head>
  <body>
  </body>
</html>
```

The DOM model lets you add what is called a listener for a specific event that will be called when the event occurs. You can also register multiple handlers for the same event. In order to remove a listener, you can use the removeEventListener() function.

■**Tip** Windows Internet Explorer doesn't follow the W3C event DOM model, because Microsoft created its event model prior to the ratification of the W3C standard. Microsoft has two functions, attachEvent() and detachEvent(), that it uses in place of the ones described in the DOM model.

Responding to events is one of the main uses of JavaScript, so you really need to understand how to use them.

The DOM

The DOM is the means by which JavaScript can access and manipulate the content of an XHTML document as well as any style sheets at run time dynamically. The DOM is actually the standard way of traversing an XML document. Since you're using XHTML in this book, you might want to use the DOM because it understands the documents you've created. All XHTML elements, including their text and attributes, can be modified or deleted through the DOM. The DOM provides an intuitive way for you to navigate through your documents. The DOM, much like CSS, uses a hierarchical tree structure to represent your document. Each element within the tree has relationships (such as child, parent, and sibling) with other nodes within the tree. You can navigate the tree and delete, change, or add nodes and attributes. Using the DOM is an advanced topic that is beyond the scope of this book, but you can surf over to `http://www.howtocreate.co.uk/tutorials/javascript/dombasics` to get the basics of using the DOM.

Form Validation

Back in Chapter 8, you saw how to create your own forms using several different available controls. Forms allow users of your website to input information. What if a user places an order but forgets to leave a credit card number? Or a name? This can wreak havoc on your site. Fortunately, JavaScript can help. You can use JavaScript to validate user input.

■**Tip** It is always good practice to validate the user input on the client within the browser and also when processing the form on the server. On the client, you should use JavaScript. On the server, though, it depends on the platform you're using to publish your documents. Failing to validate can lead to problems in security and data validity. If users don't allow JavaScript or their browser doesn't support JavaScript and you don't validate the form data on the server, there is no telling what the client will pass through your server-side programs.

To show a sample of JavaScript form validation in action, we'll use the Contact Us form you'll be creating in Chapter 11. This basic form allows users of your website to contact the restaurant and provide several pieces of information; see Figure 10-9.

As you can see, the user must enter his or her name and e-mail address, select the type of inquiry, and type a message. You can use JavaScript to make sure the user puts a valid value in each of these controls. If the user doesn't put a value in each of the controls, the JavaScript will display a message describing what the user needs to do (see Figure 10-10).

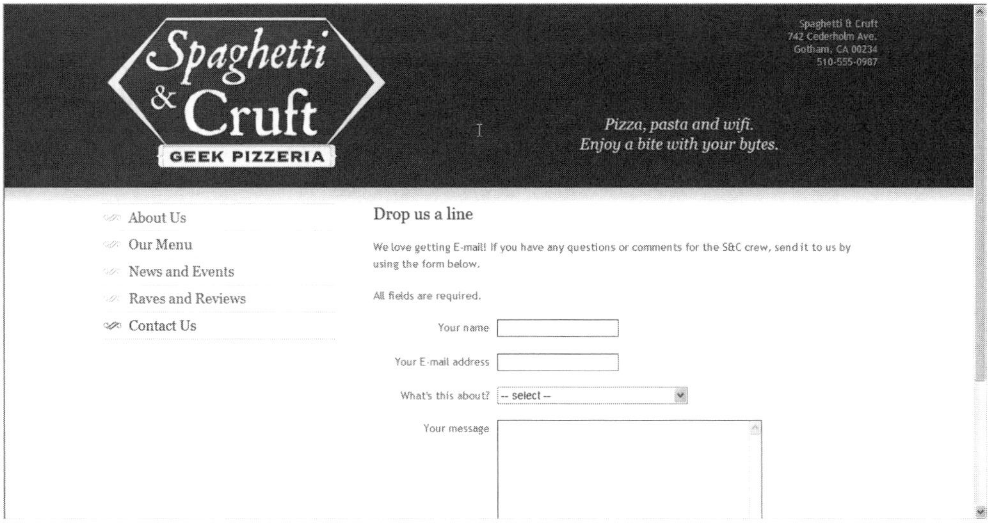

Figure 10-9. *The Contact Us form waiting for user input*

Figure 10-10. *The Contact Us form with validation errors*

If the form doesn't pass validation, it won't be sent on to the server for processing. In this case, the user didn't enter any text for any of the controls and instead simply clicked the Send button. This in turn produced an error for each field. Listing 10-18 shows the JavaScript code used to validate the form.

Listing 10-18. *JavaScript Code Used to Validate the Contact Us Form*

```
<script type="text/javascript">
    function fn_ValForm()
    {
      var sMsg = "";
      if(document.getElementById("name").value == ""){
        sMsg += ("\n* Name not entered");
      }
```

```
        if(document.getElementById("email").value == ""){
          sMsg += ("\n* Email not entered");
        }
        else{
        if(!fn_valEmail(document.getElementById("email").value)){
            sMsg += ("\n* Invalid Email address entered");
          }
        }
        if(document.getElementById("message").value == ""){
          sMsg += ("\n* Message not entered");
        }
        if(document.getElementById("subject").value == ""){
          sMsg += ("\n* Subject not entered");
        }
        if(sMsg != ""){
          alert("Please correct the following errors:\n" + sMsg);
          return false;
        }
        else
          return true;
        }


        function fn_valEmail(src) {
          var emailReg = "^[a-z0-9][a-z0-9_\.-]{0,}[a-z0-9]@[a-z0-9]"
          emailReg += "[a-z0-9_\.-]{0,}[a-z0-9][\.][a-z0-9]{2,4}$";

          var regex = new RegExp(emailReg);
          return regex.test(src);
        }
</script>
```

The code is invoked when the event handler fn_ValForm() is called when the user clicks
on the Send button. This function for the most part uses many of the JavaScript techniques
you've already seen in this chapter. The function starts by defining a variable used to hold
any messages for validation errors. Next, the code tests each control to see if the user
placed a value into it. If the user entered a value, the next control is checked. If the user
didn't enter a value, a message is added to the sMsg variable. At the end of the function, the
code checks the sMsg variable to see if any messages need to be sent to the client. If no
messages need to be returned to the client, the value true is returned, indicating the form
can be sent for processing on the server. If sMsg has any messages in it, a message box is
displayed, indicating to the user what needs to be corrected. The value false is also returned,
indicating to the browser that the form should not be submitted for processing on the server.

You can make validation as easy or as complex as you'd like. For example, in the Contact Us form validation function, you can check to make sure that the user has entered a valid e-mail address. You call the function `fn_valEmail()`, which uses something new—a regular expression. Regular expressions are great for validating data. A regular expression uses pattern matching to validate whether a string or number is made up of specific data types or a pattern of numbers (e.g., an e-mail address or phone number). You can use a regular expression by creating a regular expression object and passing into it a string that contains the pattern you want to match your data against. Next, you call the `test()` function, passing in the value you want to test against the pattern. If the value matches the pattern, `true` is returned; otherwise, `false` is returned. You can find a detailed explanation of regular expressions at `http://www.regular-expressions.info/javascript.html`. Many regular expression patterns are readily available; you can find a large library of common ones at `http://regexlib.com/`.

Summary

This chapter covered a lot of territory. In fact, you've learned an entire new computer programming language in a single chapter. This chapter has shown you the basics of adding JavaScript to your documents. You've learned how to validate form values, change CSS dynamically, and produce some really cool effects. Keep in mind that these effects only work in visual web browsers; other devices may not implement JavaScript. This chapter has really only scratched the surface of using JavaScript. Many functions prebuilt into JavaScript weren't covered here. We recommend that you search the Internet or pick up one of the titles mentioned in this chapter to expand your JavaScript skills. In Chapter 11, you'll take everything you've learned throughout the book and put it together. You'll learn how to produce a full, working website from start to finish.

CHAPTER 11

■■■

Putting It All Together

You've learned a lot about modern, standards-compliant markup over the past ten chapters, along with a healthy dose of CSS and just a dash of JavaScript mixed in. But don't worry, nobody expects you to memorize everything at once. Although XHTML and CSS are rich and nuanced languages, the fundamentals are still quite simple, and there are just a few important rules to follow. In time, as you gain experience putting together your own websites, you'll become intimately familiar with the primary languages the web is built on until it all becomes instinctive.

Of course, knowing the technical ins and outs of XHTML and CSS is only half the battle. Assembling a well-formed, accessible, and flexible document requires a bit of thought and planning. Consider the meaning of your content, and choose the elements that best align with that meaning, validating your markup to ensure that you've adhered to the specifications. Once you've built a solid foundation of valid, meaningful markup, you can move on to styling your document's presentation with CSS and adding behavioral enhancements with JavaScript.

This chapter will cover the process of planning, designing, and constructing a simple website from start to finish, from concept to code. We'll talk you through the tactical procedure we followed to design and build the Spaghetti & Cruft website, offering an example of one workflow that tends to work well for most projects. You'll see how the site was put together from the ground up, exploring the blend of markup and style that makes the site a reality (or at least as real as a site for a fictional pizzeria can be).

Introducing Our Case Study: Spaghetti & Cruft

Imagine a vibrant and progressive metropolis called Gotham, California. This city—which doesn't exist—has attracted, for some reason or another, a large number of computer software companies and Internet-based enterprises. Many of their offices are concentrated in the city's trendy and equally nonexistent Riverbend district, drawn perhaps to the neighborhood's plethora of empty warehouses and decrepit lofts that have since been remodeled into hip and nearly affordable office spaces. These companies employ a great many smart and talented people, and those people need to eat.

Recognizing the demand for good food at fair prices in this booming part of town, two brothers, Mario and Luigi, opened a neighborhood pizzeria. Business was good and their reputation grew, but things really took off when the brothers had the brilliant notion of catering to the neighborhood geeks—the designers and developers busily building new pieces of the World Wide Web. The brothers brought in comfy couches to complement the red-checkered tablecloths, installed an array of wireless routers to provide free broadband connectivity for their customers, and even tracked down a vintage Asteroids arcade machine. They changed the name of their eatery from Mario and Luigi's Pizza to Spaghetti & Cruft Geek Pizzeria. Naturally, they'll need a new website to go with the new name.

EXPLAINING THE NAME

If you're wondering about the name Spaghetti & Cruft, we've got our tongues planted firmly in cheek on this one. In the past, many web designers produced overcomplicated markup loaded with messy, presentational tags and attributes (and far too many designers still do it that way). This is called *spaghetti code* because the markup is an unwieldy tangle, extremely difficult to sort out and maintain. The word *cruft* is programmer jargon for any excess, outdated code that is no longer necessary, if it was ever needed to begin with.

So, spaghetti and cruft are two things we've spent ten chapters advising you strongly against—markup sins you'll never commit because you've read this book and learned to do it the right way. Go ahead and smirk knowingly at our cleverness.

The Design Process

There is no single, one-size-fits-all, written-in-stone procedure for designing and constructing a website, and the process demonstrated in this chapter is by no means the only approach you can take. With that said, it's important to establish *some* kind of process and to follow a rational series of steps to keep your work—and your thoughts—organized and on track. Developing a website without a plan of attack will only lead to frustration and chaos.

Every site you build and every project you undertake will be just a little bit different, but all will share a few common guiding principles. With experience, you'll find a process that works best for you, and you'll also find ways to make your process adaptable enough to handle the curve balls every new project throws at you. The Spaghetti & Cruft website followed this general outline, and something similar may work well for you.

Step 1: Defining Goals

Any good plan actually begins at the end: take aim at a specific, desired outcome. Defining goals early on will help you stay on target in every decision you make along the way, always moving toward that end result. Deciding just what those goals will be demands some consideration, some research, and some important questions. What is the site meant to accomplish, and what sort of information should it include to that end? Who are the people using the site, what do *they* hope to accomplish during their visit, and what sort of information will they need to achieve that? Are there other websites that perform similar tasks or that appeal to the same audience? If so, what do those sites do right? How could they be improved? The answers to these and other questions form a list of goals and requirements to guide the entire project.

Step 2: Contemplating Architecture

With goals in hand, we turn our attention to mapping out the site's structure, beginning with the content. Determine what types of content you'll need to present in order to meet the site's goals, and then organize that content into logical sections. This kind of *information architecture* is often one of the more challenging steps in any design process, depending on the size and complexity of the website.

Think about organizing a bookstore; all the art books logically belong together, separate from the fiction, poetry, and astronomy books. Within the art section, books about painting might belong together in one area, and the sculpture books might belong in another area. If you have quite a few painting books, they might be split into even smaller groups, with one shelf devoted to impressionism, another to abstract expressionism, and yet another to books about realism. This practice of sorting information into broad categories first and then sorting it further into increasingly specific subcategories is sometimes referred to as *chunking* in the field of information architecture—the content is broken down into manageable chunks, which are then grouped according to their purpose and subject matter.

You can visualize a site's architecture as a flowchart with connections drawn between the sections to represent the path a user might take to reach them. Figure 11-1 shows a flowchart mapping the navigation and structure for the Spaghetti & Cruft site. The home page acts as a central hub—the gateway to the entire site—though any of the major pages can also be reached from any other page.

This site is rather simple and offers a relatively a small amount of content. A larger site would probably call for a more complex architecture, with more tiers of information sorted into more granular categories.

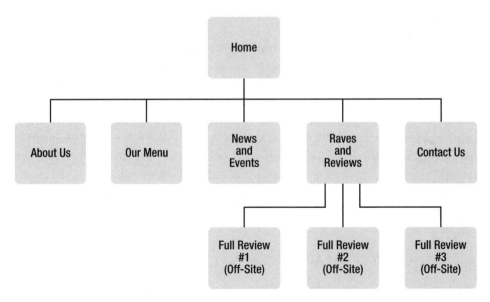

Figure 11-1. *The architecture of the Spaghetti & Cruft website, drawn out in a flowchart*

Step 3: Arranging the Template

Now that we understand what the site needs to do and have worked out how the content will be organized and the pages interconnected, it's time to start thinking about the pages themselves. Almost any website you see will have a consistent, overall layout for each of its pages. There may be a sitewide header displaying the site's title, a primary set of navigation links, and a large area housing the main content of each page. Establishing some visual and structural consistency throughout a site makes every page look like it belongs to part of the greater whole. We'll call this surrounding framework the *page template*, for lack of a better term.

This is also the point in the design process where we begin to seriously think about markup, deciding which elements will form the framework that upholds every page like the beams and columns that support a building. Some sites have several different templates—one for each type of page when those pages hold different types of content. The Spaghetti & Cruft site is simple and straightforward, so it needs only one general template for all of its pages.

When you're planning a page template, it's useful to list all the bits and pieces that will become part of it. Most importantly, each page in the Spaghetti & Cruft site will require a large space for the main content, including a page title. Additionally, we also know there will be a branded masthead featuring the pizzeria's logo, street address, and company tag line. Each page of the site will need to include a navigation menu, which is simply a collection of links leading to the other sections of the site. Every page on this site will also display a small copyright statement.

Reorganized and listed in approximate order of importance, the Spaghetti & Cruft template needs to include the following:

- The main content area
  - A page title leading the content
- The main navigation menu
- A masthead
  - The Spaghetti & Cruft logo
  - The street address
  - The tag line
- A copyright statement

This list will become our guide for both the structural XHTML and the design of the site's visual presentation. We're not really thinking about the site's appearance just yet, we've been focusing entirely on content and organization. Not all web designers arrange their process in this sequence, beginning instead with the graphic design—deciding just how they want the finished site to look—and then building markup and CSS to achieve that presentation. But that places presentation ahead of content and structure, and presentational thinking often leads to presentational markup. When you move from design to construction, you might find yourself choosing XHTML elements for their visual effect rather than their inherent meaning.

Take the time to understand your content first and then build outward. When you separate content from presentation in your markup, you can also separate them in your workflow. Prioritizing structured content first and visual design second will ultimately make your design better informed when the time comes, helping you avoid the pitfalls of nonstructural, presentational markup.

In the real world, you may not always have the luxury of constructing your document before considering its surface appearance. If you do choose to create the visual design first, you should at least be *thinking* about how you're going to assemble the document as you work on its eventual presentation. As you're visually arranging content on the page, think about the markup that will eventually support it. Drawing a picture of an attractive page is one thing; actually building it with accessible, meaningful XHTML and clean CSS is something quite different. Setting up your document's underlying structure early in the process can be extremely helpful later.

Step 4: Creating the Design

With all the planning settled and a document template constructed, next comes the really cool part: deciding what the site will look like. As with every other phase in the process, there isn't any one definitive approach to creating a visual design. You might start with sketches, color swatches, and scrapbooks of design motifs to grasp the general mood before focusing your efforts on the real thing. It's common to produce multiple design variations before finally choosing the one you like best (or at least the one your client or boss likes best). You might work through numerous iterations of a single design, gradually homing in on something approaching perfection.

Whatever approach you take, your finished visual design will be more enlightened and practical because you took the time to understand your content and give it a solid, meaningful structure. If someone else is responsible for the site's visual design (as is often the case in larger teams), providing them with the guidelines you've worked so hard to gather will help them produce a better design that is aligned with the project goals and the site's structure.

For the Spaghetti & Cruft site, we started with some sketches—shown in Figure 11-2—to quickly work through a few different layout options. Once we found something we liked, we moved on to Adobe Photoshop to produce a more polished mock-up of our chosen layout.

Figure 11-2. *A few rough sketches for the Spaghetti & Cruft website, trying out several different layouts before picking one to proceed with*

In web design parlance, a *mock-up* (also called a *composite*, or *comp* for short) is a full-scale image of a page design, essentially a picture of the finished site. It allows the designer (and other project stakeholders) to get a sense of what the real site will look like without yet committing the design to markup and CSS; you can adjust the mock-up without rebuilding any pages.

Mario and Luigi asked for a design that's simple, clean, and sleek but with classical influences and a distinctly Italian flair. We chose a red and white color scheme with green accents—the colors of the Italian flag. A few Renaissance-style flourishes give it that old-world touch, but the overall look and feel remains decidedly modern. You can see the finished mock-up in Figure 11-3.

Figure 11-3. *The final mock-up for the new Spaghetti & Cruft website. This will be our guide as we work on the CSS.*

We showed this to Mario and Luigi, and they loved it (of course they did, we made them up). With our client's approval, we can proceed to author the CSS that will make this design a reality, converting our "picture of a website" into an actual website.

Step 5: Assembling the Website

With the CSS initially written and integrated with the template, the next obvious step is to continue constructing the rest of the site. Each page begins with a blank template, and the content is inserted, always considering the meaning of the content and supporting it with valid, semantically appropriate markup. The site's style sheet will continue to expand during this stage, inserting new presentation rules for different types of content as needed. We'll cover the construction of a few pages in the Spaghetti & Cruft website in detail later in this chapter.

Step 6: Testing

Even though this step appears last, it's an ongoing process throughout the site's production. When the template is constructed, it should be tested and the markup validated. While you're working on the CSS, you should frequently test the site in a browser as you add new style rules. Validate your style sheets as well to make sure they're correct and well formed.

View the site in multiple browsers—as many as you can get your hands on. Each browser may treat your CSS in slightly different ways. However, don't be misled into believing that a website should look exactly the same in every browser. Trying to achieve pixel-perfect, identical presentation across different browsers and operating systems is a recipe for distress. Rather, try to treat each browser as an entity unto itself; real users don't open two browsers side by side for precise comparison.

Instead of striving to achieve an identical appearance in every browser, concentrate on offering the most common browsers an *equivalent experience*. Is the site functional, and does it look presentable? Are any elements the wrong size, completely misaligned, or in the wrong position? Some small variations are to be expected, but as long as those variations don't harm the design or make the site more difficult to use, they might not be worth worrying about. As you make adjustments and corrections, retest the site in multiple browsers to ensure that fixing a problem in one browser doesn't break something in another.

Building Spaghetti & Cruft

Now that we've described the design process, the rest of this chapter goes into a bit more detail on the actual construction of the Spaghetti & Cruft website, beginning with the page template markup. This template lays the groundwork and establishes the common page elements that will persist throughout the site.

Setting Up the Document

You saw the standard document skeleton way back in Chapter 2, but here it is again in Listing 11-1 to refresh your memory. It includes all the essential pieces, as well as a link to an external style sheet in the document's head element. We haven't actually authored that style sheet yet, but adding a link to it now will establish it in the template markup for all the pages to come.

Listing 11-1. *A Blank XHTML Document*

```
<!DOCTYPE html PUBLIC "-//W3C//DTD XHTML 1.0 Strict//EN"
  "http://www.w3.org/TR/xhtml1/DTD/xhtml1-strict.dtd">
<html xmlns="http://www.w3.org/1999/xhtml" xml:lang="en" lang="en">
  <head>
    <meta http-equiv="Content-Type" content="text/html; charset=utf-8" />
    <title>Spaghetti &#38; Cruft: Geek Pizzeria</title>
    <link rel="stylesheet" type="text/css" href="styles.css" />
  </head>
  <body>

  </body>
</html>
```

You might have spotted the addition of a meta element in the document's head, declaring this document's content type as text/html and its character set encoding as UTF-8 (a widely supported standard). This declaration isn't strictly necessary because a web server is usually configured to transmit the information automatically. However, it's still recommended that you include it in the document's head element. Declaring the character encoding is especially important because it will assist user-agents in processing the document's text. The W3C's online validation service (http://validator.w3.org) will default to UTF-8 if no character encoding is declared in the document, so including it here saves us a bit of trouble when we validate the site's markup.

Marking Up the Masthead

The first essential content to appear in the body element will be the site's branded masthead (also called a *header*; the terms are pretty much interchangeable), which will help a viewer instantly identify the website. We've already determined that the masthead will feature Spaghetti & Cruft's logo (which also serves as the name of the website), its street address (so a visitor to the website can easily find out where the restaurant is located), and its company tag line (which is part of the pizzeria's marketing), so the entire section can be contained in an element that will group those other elements together: a div.

However, thinking it through, we realize the tag line isn't really "essential content"; it's supplemental to the rest of the page, and removing the tag line entirely wouldn't hinder a reader's understanding of the other content. So rather than include the tag line alongside the company name and street address, we'll place it near the end of the document and position it at the top of the page with CSS. The masthead markup will comprise only the logo and address, collected in a div.

Assigning a unique id attribute to that containing div element will distinguish it from other portions of the document and provide a useful "hook" for styling its contents with a CSS ID selector. We could identify the element as the "masthead" or "header," which would work perfectly well as a CSS selector. But the words "masthead" and "header" both imply that the element is located at the head of the page, which might be a reference to the element's presentation (even though it actually is at the head of the page in this particular design). We're calling it a masthead to describe its purpose as a vehicle for site branding, not to describe its placement on the page. A masthead could just as easily run down one side of the page, or even appear at the bottom. Instead of identifying an element according to its presentation, you should identify it based on its meaning and purpose. The Spaghetti & Cruft masthead is a major part of the site's visual branding, so an id value of branding accurately describes why the element exists.

When identifying or classifying an element (with an id or class attribute, respectively), consider the element's purpose and choose a name to describe it. An ID of "leftcolumn" or a class of "blue" becomes rather meaningless if the element is colored red and positioned on the right. Treat an id attribute as a declaration that "this is the element that serves this specific purpose" and a class attribute as a statement that "this element belongs in the same category as other elements in its class."

The Spaghetti & Cruft logo will be an image (embedded with the inline img element, covered in Chapter 5), but it's more than that: the logo also acts as the title of the entire website. Placing that inline image in an h1 element solidifies its meaning as the most important title in the document. Alternatively, the title of an individual page might be considered more important than the site's title. If that's your preference, you could surround the page title in an h1 element and the site's title in some other element befitting of its relative importance. For this site, we're using an h1 element for the site title and we'll use an h2 element to designate page titles.

You might be tempted to mark up a company's street address in an address element, especially when that address pertains to the company responsible for the site. But generally speaking, an address element should contain contact information for the document's author, not just the company that owns the site. We've chosen a more general element and marked up the address as a paragraph with id="address" to identify it. We've inserted line breaks (<br />) to enforce some visual formatting, breaking the address onto four separate lines. It's a minor presentational compromise, but this formatting improves the readability of the address; those line breaks enhance the content more than they harm it.

After all this semantic pontification, you can at last see the markup for the site's masthead in Listing 11-2.

Listing 11-2. *The Spaghetti & Cruft Masthead Markup*

```
<div id="branding">

  <h1><img src="images/logo.gif" width="375" height="200" ➥
    alt="Spaghetti and Cruft: Geek Pizzeria" /></h1>

  <p id="address">
    Spaghetti &#38; Cruft<br />
    742 Cederholm Ave.<br />
    Gotham, CA 00234<br />
    510-555-0987
  </p>

</div>
```

Marking Up the Main Content Area

After the company name and address, the next most important part of the page is the main content—the reason for the page's very existence. Arguably, the content could be considered *the most* important part and could appear in the document even before the masthead. Because this case study is a site for a fictional brick-and-mortar business, we decided that the company name and address were the most important pieces and placed them ahead of the main content to emphasize them. A different type of website might lead to a different decision.

As you construct any XHTML document, be mindful of the sequence in which the elements occur (known as their *source order*). If the page's presentation layer is removed from the equation—by a screen reader or a nongraphical web browser, for instance—the content will be read from top to bottom in the same order as the document's source markup. Try to order elements according to the importance of their contents, not their spatial arrangement on the rendered page. You can use CSS to reposition elements for display in graphical browsers without altering their underlying structure.

For the time being, we're just building the template that will surround the content and aren't yet ready to add any real content to the page. Once again, we'll use a div element to act as a container for the other elements that will eventually populate it. Giving the div an ID of main-content describes exactly what that div contains. As you can see in Listing 11-3, we've included a heading and a paragraph as temporary placeholders. They'll be replaced with actual content as the site's assembly progresses.

Listing 11-3. *The Main Content Section*

```
<div id="main-content">
  <h2>The page title will go here</h2>
  <p>The page content will go here.</p>
</div>
```

Marking Up the Navigation

The site's primary navigation is a list of links, so it should be marked up as a list of links—it's as simple as that. The list doesn't need to follow a specific sequence because a user can click through to any page they please, so we'll make it an unordered list (ul). However, there's a certain hierarchy we want to imply so the list items will still occur in a deliberate order, according to the importance of the section to which each link leads. Listing 11-4 shows the completed navigation list. The files these links lead to don't exist yet, but now is as good a time as any to decide what they'll be named.

Listing 11-4. *The Navigation Menu*

```
<ul id="navigation">
  <li><a href="menu.html">Our Menu</a></li>
  <li><a href="about.html">About Us</a></li>
  <li><a href="reviews.html">Raves and Reviews</a></li>
  <li><a href="news.html">News and Events</a></li>
  <li><a href="contact.html">Contact Us</a></li>
</ul>
```

The navigation comes *after* the main content, which might seem to defy logic. Once a lengthy helping of content is added, you'd have to scroll all the way to the bottom to find a link to another page. But we're arranging the elements from the top down in order of each one's importance, and content is usually more important than navigation. We'll use CSS to position this menu at the top of the page when a graphical browser renders it.

Marking Up the Tag Line and Footer

The final components of the template are the branded tag line and a footer to display the copyright statement. The company tag line—"Pizza, pasta, and WiFi. Enjoy a bite with your bytes"—could be held in a paragraph, but in this case we've decided to treat it as two separate statements in two paragraphs (they're two distinct thoughts) and collect them in a div element (because the two thoughts are related to each other and separate from the rest of the content). We'll position the tag line over the site's masthead with CSS.

The site's footer is simply a paragraph containing a copyright statement. Some websites include a lot more supplemental information in their footers, such as contact details or a list of links to administrative pages (terms of use, privacy policies, job openings, and so on). If a site's footer will hold more than just text, it's sensible to use a div to contain all the footer elements. The Spaghetti & Cruft site's footer is nothing more than a copyright statement, so a solitary paragraph is sufficient.

As with other parts of the template, we'll give these components unique IDs, but we're not going to identify the footer as "the footer." This part of a web page is called a *footer* only because it typically appears at the very bottom of a page. But you know by now that it's not wise to identify an element based on its presentation, so the paragraph will be dubbed "copyright," as you can see in Listing 11-5. This ID describes the element's true purpose, not its placement in the visual layout. If the footer contained other information in addition to a copyright, a different ID—"site-info," for example—would be appropriate. The numeric character reference © will be rendered as the international copyright symbol (©), though we could also use the character entity ©.

Listing 11-5. *The Tag Line and Copyright Statements*

```
<div id="tagline">
  <p>Pizza, pasta, and WiFi.</p>
  <p>Enjoy a bite with your bytes.</p>
</div>


<p id="copyright">&#169; 2007 Spaghetti &#38; Cruft: Geek Pizzeria</p>
```

The Completed Template

That's really all there is to it. We've added all the vital portions that will surround and support each page of the site, giving each one a sensible identifier that states the purpose of each element and provides us with the necessary apparatus to style the site with CSS. Listing 11-6 is the full template markup—lean, clean, and valid.

Listing 11-6. *The Completed Markup Template for the Spaghetti & Cruft Site*

```
<!DOCTYPE html PUBLIC "-//W3C//DTD XHTML 1.0 Strict//EN"
  "http://www.w3.org/TR/xhtml1/DTD/xhtml1-strict.dtd">
<html xmlns="http://www.w3.org/1999/xhtml" xml:lang="en" lang="en">
<head>
  <meta http-equiv="Content-Type" content="text/html; charset=utf-8" />
  <title>Spaghetti &#38; Cruft: Geek Pizzeria</title>
  <link rel="stylesheet" type="text/css" href="styles.css" />
</head>
```

```
<body>
<div id="branding">
  <h1><img src="images/logo.gif" width="375" height="200" ➥
      alt="Spaghetti and Cruft: Geek Pizzeria" /></h1>

  <p id="address">
    Spaghetti &#38; Cruft<br />
    742 Cederholm Ave.<br />
    Gotham, CA 00234<br />
    510-555-0987
  </p>
</div>

<div id="main-content">
  <h2>The page title will go here</h2>
  <p>The page content will go here.</p>
</div>

<ul id="navigation">
  <li><a href="menu.html">Our Menu</a></li>
  <li><a href="about.html">About Us</a></li>
  <li><a href="reviews.html">Raves and Reviews</a></li>
  <li><a href="news.html">News and Events</a></li>
  <li><a href="contact.html">Contact Us</a></li>
</ul>

<div id="tagline">
  <p>Pizza, pasta, and WiFi.</p>
  <p>Enjoy a bite with your bytes.</p>
</div>

<p id="copyright">&#169; 2007 Spaghetti &#38; Cruft: Geek Pizzeria</p>
</body>
</html>
```

From this point on, every new page we create for the site will begin its life as a copy of this blank template document. We can begin to construct the style sheet using the template as a framework before building the entire site. It might be necessary to make changes to the markup during the CSS development phase, and it'll be much easier to do that in the master template instead of altering every document in the site.

Designing Spaghetti & Cruft with CSS

With the template built and the design mock-up suitably polished, the next step is writing the style sheet that will bring the two into harmony. From the very first stages of visual design—when you first lay pen to paper or mouse to pad—you should be thinking about the content and markup you'll eventually be styling. This is the very reason we chose to construct the site template before plunging into graphic design; an understanding of the document's structure is invaluable when deciding how that document should be presented.

Figure 11-4 shows our template document as seen with a browser's default style sheet. We've added a few paragraphs to the content area to offer a better sense of how the different parts of the page relate to each other.

Spaghetti & Cruft
742 Cederholm Ave.
Gotham, CA 00234
510-555-0987

Hot food at a cool joint

Spaghetti & Cruft opened our doors in 1999, bringing great pizza and pasta to the heart of the city's trendy Riverbend district. We handcraft our pizzas on the spot using only the best ingredients, and then we bake them to perfection in our rustic wood-fired brick oven. We sell pizza by the slice or by the pie and even offer catering for any occasion all around the neighborhood.

Our broad menu of pasta dishes puts a modern twist on Old Italia, served in heaping bowlfuls sure to satisfy any appetite (though we bet you'll want seconds anyway). But it's not all noodles and crust at Spaghetti & Cruft; we also have fresh veggie sides, an all-you-can-eat salad bar, and the best cannolis in town!

- Our Menu
- About Us
- Raves and Reviews
- News and Events
- Contact Us

Pizza, pasta, and WiFi.

Enjoy a bite with your bytes.

© 2007 Spaghetti & Cruft : Geek Pizzeria

Figure 11-4. *The Spaghetti & Cruft template viewed with a web browser's default styling*

Throughout the rest of this chapter, you'll see how the Spaghetti & Cruft style sheet came together bit by bit, making this drab, unstyled document come to life using many of the CSS techniques you've seen elsewhere in this book, as well as a few new ones. We won't go into detail on every part of the site, but you can download all the markup, CSS, and images from the Apress website (http://www.apress.com). You can also see the finished Spaghetti & Cruft website online at http://www.beginninghtmlbook.com.

Styling the Page Body

If you flip back to our design mock-up in Figure 11-3, one of the first things you'll notice is the large, red banner across the top of the page (it really is red, take our word for it) that becomes the backdrop for the masthead. The banner isn't a solid color—it graduates from a lighter color to a darker color, and there's a subtle shadow that descends into the white content area.

CSS doesn't offer a method of transitioning from one color to another (not in current versions of the language, at least), so we'll need to use a background image to achieve this effect. If the background image is applied to the masthead container, the image will end where the masthead's content ends. Instead of styling the branding div, let's not overlook the ever-present (and required) html element, which is equally susceptible to styling with CSS. Applying a background to the html element allows the image to tile across the entire browser portal and extend downward into the content area; all the content will overlay the image. Listing 11-7 shows the CSS rule styling the html element.

Listing 11-7. *Applying a Background to the html Element*

```
html { background: #ffffff url(images/background.gif) repeat-x; }
```

The background property is CSS *shorthand*, condensing several values into one declaration. This single declaration takes the place of separate declarations for background-color, background-image, and background-repeat, saving a bit of space in our style sheet. Any undeclared values will be filled in by the browser's default styles, so there's no need to specify a value for background-position here; the image begins tiling from the top-left corner automatically.

As you can see in Figure 11-5, attaching the background image to the html element works like a charm. The image is only 4 pixels wide and 280 pixels high, so the file size is quite small and should download quickly, even over a slow Internet connection. The image doesn't need to be any wider because it repeats infinitely along the x-axis.

Figure 11-5. *The background image tiles across the top of the html element and hence across the entire browser portal.*

Fixed or Liquid?

An important decision must be made now: will the site's layout have a *fixed* width that is always the same no matter how wide the browser window is, or will its width be *liquid* and adjust dynamically to the window's width? This has been a topic of much lively debate among web designers. Many prefer to design sites with a fixed width because it allows for precise alignment of the page elements in a rigid grid. Other designers prefer liquid widths that flex automatically, letting viewers set their browsers as wide or narrow as they like while the page layout adjusts to their preferences.

Fixed and liquid layouts both have their own clear benefits, as well as a few potential drawbacks. Opting for a fixed-width layout is often the easier choice because it eliminates one more variable from the complicated task of designing a website with CSS, but fixed widths don't allow for a browser window that's narrower than the design, causing the dreaded horizontal scroll. Narrow fixed layouts can waste a lot of screen real estate in wider windows. A liquid width gives first priority to the user's preferred window width, but it can cause text to stretch out to very long lines in wide windows, making the content more difficult to read. If the window is very narrow, the content gets compressed into narrow columns, and some elements might overlap each other.

Neither side of the debate is completely right or completely wrong, which is probably why the debate still rages on. It's a decision that must be made on a case-by-case basis, and it's just one of those factors that makes every project a new and exciting challenge. Whichever layout you choose—fixed or liquid—always be conscious of both the content and the people using it; that's what should ultimately influence your decision. In the end, you'll just have to use your own best judgment.

We've decided on a liquid layout for the Spaghetti & Cruft site. Given the simplicity of this design—with only a few major page elements to worry about—we can achieve it with minimal fuss. First we'll give the body element a width of 80%. An element's percentage width is calculated as a percentage of its parent element's width. The body element's parent is the root html element, which has no width in this case, so the body will naturally occupy 80% of the browser portal, however wide that may be. Listing 11-8 shows the beginnings of a CSS rule styling the body element, and we'll expand this rule as we add more style properties.

Listing 11-8. *Declaring a Width for the body Element*

```
body { width: 80%; }
```

Centering the Page with Margins

With the body element successfully narrowed, it will be pressed against the left side of the window by default, with space on the right side taking up the remaining 20%. Our design shows the page body horizontally centered in the window, and we'll accomplish this with the margin-left and margin-right properties, both with a value of auto. The browser will automatically calculate auto as half the available space on either side of the element. This translates to a 10% space on the left side of the window, the body filling 80%, and another 10% space on the right. Those proportions will always be consistent, regardless of how wide or narrow the window might be, giving us the centered, liquid layout we want. Listing 11-9 shows this revision to our body rule.

Listing 11-9. *Centering the body Element*

```
body {
  width: 80%;
  margin-left: auto;
  margin-right: auto; }
```

To simplify this, you can combine the margin-left and margin-right properties into one declaration with the shorthand margin property (there are similar padding and border shorthand properties as well). For lack of a better term, we'll refer to these as *box model properties* because they relate to the size and spacing of rendered boxes.

You can format the value of a box model shorthand property in a few different ways. You can style each side of the box individually using any combination of units, for example, margin: 2px 4.2em 3% .5in, where each value applies to each side in clockwise order: top, right, bottom, and left. If the top and bottom sides have the same value and the left and right sides have the same value, you can shorten the declaration like so: margin: 4px 5%, with the first value applying to both the top and bottom, and the second value applying to the left and right. If the top and bottom values are different but the left and right values are the same, you can arrange the declaration like so: margin: .5em 0 1em, where the first value is the top margin, the second applies to both the left and right sides, and the third value is the bottom margin. Lastly, if all four sides of the box will carry the same value, the shorthand property needs only a single value, as in margin: 15px.

Our body element will have no top and bottom margins (a value of 0), so we can rewrite its margin value as 0 auto, shown in Listing 11-10. Many graphical browsers automatically apply a small amount of padding to the body element, which we can neutralize with the declaration padding: 0, affecting all four sides with a single declaration.

Listing 11-10. *The Shorthand margin and padding Properties*

```
body {
  width: 80%;
  margin: 0 auto;
  padding: 0; }
```

You can see the combined effect in Figure 11-6; the body has been narrowed and centered with 10% margins on both sides. The width and margins will automatically adjust to fit the width of the browser window.

Spaghetti & Cruft
742 Cederholm Ave.
Gotham, CA 00234
510-555-0987

Hot food at a cool joint

Spaghetti & Cruft opened our doors in 1999, bringing great pizza and pasta to the heart of the city's trendy Riverbend district.
We handcraft our pizzas on the spot using only the best ingredients, and then we bake them to perfection in our rustic
wood-fired brick oven. We sell pizza by the slice or by the pie and even offer catering for any occasion all around the
neighborhood.

Figure 11-6. *The body element now occupies 80% of the window's width and is horizontally centered.*

■Caution Versions of Internet Explorer for Windows prior to version 6 didn't support this method of centering elements with automatic margins. Version 6 and newer support the `auto` value, but only in compliance mode, invoked by a complete doctype (which you must always include anyway). Internet Explorer 6 and 7 don't automatically calculate margins in quirks mode for the sake of backward compatibility with outdated websites that were designed before the value was properly supported.

Shorthand for Fonts

As you learned in Chapter 4, most font styles declared for the body element will be inherited by all the elements that descend from it. Body copy on the Spaghetti & Cruft site will be set in Trebuchet MS at 90% of the browser's designated size (about 14 pixels, assuming a default size of 16 pixels) with a `line-height` value of 1.7 ems (1.7 times the text size). By declaring the font size as a percentage of the default, we can accommodate any user's size preference; all the text on the site can freely scale larger or smaller. We've added these declarations to our body rule in Listing 11-11.

Listing 11-11. *Adding Font Properties to the body Rule*

```
body {
  width: 80%;
  margin: 0 auto;
  padding: 0;
  font-family: "Trebuchet MS", Helvetica, Verdana, sans-serif;
  font-size: 90%;
  line-height: 1.7em; }
```

We can condense this using the shorthand font property. This single property can carry values for most font styles in a space-separated list, and those values must occur in a specific sequence to be recognized: font-style, font-variant, font-weight, font-size/line-height, and font-family. A slash (/), not a space, separates the values for font-size and line-height, binding the two values together. Any values not declared with font will be inherited from an ancestral element, or else the browser will fall back to its default value for that property. Listing 11-12 shows the updated rule.

Listing 11-12. *The Shorthand font Property*

```
body {
  width: 80%;
  margin: 0 auto;
  padding: 0;
  font: 90%/1.7 "Trebuchet MS", Helvetica, Verdana, sans-serif; }
```

Notice that the line-height value suddenly lacks a unit of measure. For the line-height property, a numeric value without a unit is interpreted as a multiplier of the font size. Therefore, line-height: 1.7 achieves the same result as line-height: 1.7em or line-height: 170%; all three are proportional to the font size. This is the preferred way to declare line heights, since that multiplier will be inherited by any descendant elements and automatically scaled according to the element's font size (whether that size is inherited or declared).

■**Tip** Eric Meyer offers a much more detailed explanation of unitless line-height values in his weblog entry "Unitless line-heights" (http://meyerweb.com/eric/thoughts/2006/02/08/unitless-line-heights/).

Shorthand for Colors

Colors are frequently expressed in CSS using *hexadecimal notation,* which is a six-digit number that indicates a specific color as a combination of red, green, and blue—the primary colors of light that make up every color the human eye can perceive. Each two-digit pair in the six-digit hex number represents a value of one primary color. When the hex number consists of three matched pairs (such as #ffcc99 or #3355ee), you can compress the number to only three digits in CSS (#fc9 or #35e). The savings may seem minor, but sometimes every last byte counts.

Body copy for the Spaghetti & Cruft site will appear in a dark, neutral gray, the hex color #555555, which we can shorten to #555. This becomes the base foreground text color for the entire site by adding a color property to our body rule, as you see in Listing 11-13. Although most visual browsers default to black text, a slightly lighter color causes less eyestrain and will be more readable against a bright white background.

Listing 11-13. *Declaring a Foreground Color with Shorthand Hex Notation*

```
body {
  width: 80%;
  margin: 0 auto;
  padding: 0;
  font: 90%/1.7 "Trebuchet MS", Helvetica, Verdana, sans-serif;
  color: #555; }
```

You can see the result of our new font styles and text color in Figure 11-7. The website is gradually taking shape, and just a little bit of typographic style has made a remarkable impact on the design.

Spaghetti & Cruft
742 Cederholm Ave.
Gotham, CA 00234
510-555-0987

Hot food at a cool joint

Spaghetti & Cruft opened our doors in 1999, bringing great pizza and pasta to the heart of the city's trendy Riverbend district. We handcraft our pizzas on the spot using only the best ingredients, and then we bake them to perfection in our rustic wood-fired brick oven. We sell pizza by the slice or by the pie and even offer catering for any occasion all around the neighborhood.

Figure 11-7. *Reloading the template page in a web browser shows the newly styled font and foreground color (compare this to Figure 11-6).*

Styling Links

Most graphical browsers present a text anchor as underlined, blue text by default, and its color will change to purple after you've visited the link's destination. These default styles date back to the earliest web browsers in the mid-90s, but today we're not limited to the defaults. Even so, web users have grown accustomed to text links appearing in a different style than normal text, and some kind of visual differentiation is critical; your readers won't be able to locate links that don't look like links.

To fit into the overall look and feel of the Spaghetti & Cruft site, we're going to change the color of text links from blue to green, and visited links will appear in a slightly paler grayish-green, as if using the link has depleted its original color. The link's color will change to red when a user's pointer passes over it to call attention to the link as if it's shouting, "Click me!" Our new CSS rules are shown in Listing 11-14.

Listing 11-14. *Styling Links with Pseudo Classes*

```
a:link { color: #006d14; }
a:visited { color: #48a95a; }
a:hover { color: #ab0000; }
a:focus, a:active { color: #c50000; background-color: #ddd; }
```

These rules must appear in this sequence in the style sheet so the cascade can work properly—the style for an active link takes precedence over a hovered link, which takes precedence over a visited link, which takes precedence over an unvisited link. We've grouped the styling of focused and active links under a single rule—giving links in both states a slightly brighter red color as well as a light gray background—to offer keyboard users some visual indication as to which link has focus when they use their Tab key to cycle through links on the page. Internet Explorer doesn't support the :focus pseudo class, but it treats the :active pseudo class as :focus for links. You learned about these pseudo class selectors in Chapter 2. Combining them with the a element selector means these styles won't be applied to any other elements, only anchors.

We're changing the coloring of text links but leaving the default underline style intact. Even if links are displayed in a different color from surrounding text, people with low vision or some types of colorblindness may not be able to detect that contrast. Links should always be visually indicated by some decoration apart from their color, and that usually means an underline. Similarly, regular text that is *not* a link should never be underlined. Web users over the years have become so familiar with the convention of underlined text indicating a link that *any* underlined text is assumed to be one; if something is underlined but isn't a link, you'll only confuse your readers.

■**Caution** Older versions of HTML included a presentational u element to define underlined text. Because it was so often confused with linked text, the element was formally deprecated years ago and should never be used.

Styling the Masthead

The masthead is held in a div element with a unique ID of "branding," so we can target that specific element with an ID selector in our style sheet. The elements inside the branding division can be specifically targeted by using the ID selector as part of a descendant selector, eliminating the need to give each element within the masthead an ID of its own (though some of them do bear IDs, both for semantic reasons and to offer more specific CSS selectors, as you'll see later).

Absolutely Relative

Referring to our design mock-up, the Spaghetti & Cruft address belongs in the upper-right corner of the masthead, but the paragraph that contains it is naturally positioned after the logo because that's where it occurs in the document's source. We'll move the address using the position property with a value of absolute and providing a specific location where the element should appear, shown in Listing 11-15 (we've also made it a lighter color to show up against the dark background).

Listing 11-15. *Positioning the Address*

```
#address {
  color: #eee;
  position: absolute;
  top: 15px;
  right: 10px; }
```

However, as you can see in Figure 11-8, this isn't quite what we're after—the address is against the right edge of the browser portal. But we know the body element is 80% of that width, so shouldn't the address line up with the invisible edge of the body?

Figure 11-8. *The template page after the address has been positioned. We've drawn borders around the address and the body element for this illustration.*

When an element is absolutely positioned, its placement is determined in relation to its *nearest positioned ancestor*—the first ancestral element in the document tree bearing a position value of absolute, relative, or fixed. If no positioned ancestor is found, the element is positioned in relation to the root html element, which fills the browser portal because it lacks a width. Our address paragraph has no positioned ancestor, so the result shown in Figure 11-9 is utterly correct and rendered according to the CSS we've written. To solve this, we must position one of the address's ancestors to provide a new frame of reference.

Applying position: relative to the masthead container (the div with the ID "branding") while leaving out any values for top, left, bottom, or right will position the container exactly where it would normally be by default, but now elements within it can be absolutely positioned in relation to the container; the branding div becomes the address's nearest positioned ancestor.

While we're at it, we can give the entire masthead a height of 250 pixels and a 15-pixel bottom margin, reserving 265 pixels of vertical space and preventing the other page content from moving upward into the masthead. It's usually inadvisable to declare a fixed height for any elements because it can wreak havoc when text is resized or content is added. But in the case of this branded header, which holds so little content and already has a height implied by the background image, declaring a fixed height shouldn't cause any problems. The address text can still expand significantly before it overflows the masthead.

Listing 11-16 shows the new CSS rule.

Listing 11-16. *Giving the Masthead Container a Position, Height, and Margin*

```
#branding {
  position: relative;
  height: 250px;
  margin-bottom: 15px; }
```

You can see the results in Figure 11-9; the address is correctly positioned within the masthead area thanks to its positioned container.

Figure 11-9. *With a positioned ancestor to refer to, the address is now placed against the right edge of the masthead.*

The address is now just where we want it . . . almost. We specified a top value of 15px, but the address is more than 15 pixels from the top of the page. A graphical web browser will give all paragraphs default top and bottom margins to create the blank lines we expect as visual separation between two paragraphs. That default margin is creating extra space above the address paragraph, pushing the element down from the top. We can counteract that by supplying a new margin value of 0, applied to all four sides simultaneously with the shorthand margin property. We've also added some more declarations to align the text to the right, slightly reduce the font size, and compress the line height a bit.

The h1 element that encloses the logo also receives some default margins, and neutralizing them will bump the logo to the top of the page. A bit of top padding places the logo just where we want it to be. Listing 11-17 shows the updated CSS.

Listing 11-17. *The Finished Rules That Style the Address and Logo*

```
#address {
  color: #eee;
  position: absolute;
  top: 15px;
  right: 10px;
  margin: 0;
  text-align: right;
  font-size: 90%;
  line-height: 1.3; }


#branding h1 { margin: 0; padding: 10px 0 0; }
```

With our CSS rules complete, the address and logo should now appear just as they did in the mock-up (or at least a very close match). Figure 11-10 shows our progress so far.

Figure 11-10. *The updated page with the address fully styled and the logo's placement adjusted*

Compensating for Missing Images

A new problem has become evident at this point: the masthead relies on a background image to define its area, but the entire page reverts to a solid white background color if the image isn't available. The address would be nearly impossible to read without a dark background to provide sufficient contrast, yet applying a solid background color to either the address itself or the branding div would cover the gradient background image.

We can solve this dilemma by applying a solid background color to the masthead container but also applying the same background image we used for the html element. Background images are rendered on top of background colors, so the two images will overlay each other and merge seamlessly. The masthead's background color becomes visible if images are disabled while the rest of the page keeps its white background.

Listing 11-18 shows the changes to the style sheet. We've added a background property to the masthead container, filling it with a dark red color behind the image. We've also applied a white foreground color to the h1 element. Most graphical browsers display the value of alt attributes when images are disabled, so this will help to make even the logo's alternative text readable against the dark background.

Listing 11-18. *Ensuring Color Contrast When Images Are Absent*

```
#branding {
  position: relative;
  height: 250px;
  margin-bottom: 15px;
  background: #900 url(images/background.gif) repeat-x; }

#branding h1 {
  margin: 0;
  padding: 10px 0 0;
  color: #fff; }
```

Figure 11-11 shows the page with images disabled. The solid color doesn't extend to the full window width, but the masthead remains readable and the design's general color scheme survives, in keeping with the principle of graceful degradation. This "CSS on, images off" scenario is fairly uncommon, but some people—especially those using slow Internet connections—choose to disable images in order to speed up their browsing. Spending a few extra minutes to ensure sufficient background/foreground color contrast will benefit those visitors.

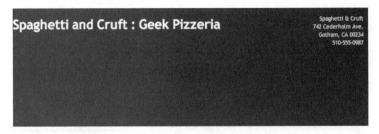

Figure 11-11. *The masthead as it appears when images are disabled*

Laying Out the Page

With the masthead looking good, we can move down to the real meat of the page. The content area and navigation menu form two columns in our design mock-up. We can easily achieve this effect by declaring a width for each element and floating them in opposite directions, as in Listing 11-19. (We've also neutralized the default presentation of the navigation list.) The main content section will move as far to the right as possible, the navigation menu will move all the way to the left, and both will be held in check by the body element. Choosing percentages for the width values maintains the fluidity of our liquid layout.

Listing 11-19. *Floating Elements in Opposite Directions*

```
#main-content {
  width: 65%;
  float: right; }

#navigation {
  width: 30%;
  float: left;
  list-style: none;
  margin: 0;
  padding: 0; }
```

Using floats for page layout can be tricky at times. If two elements are floating adjacent to each other and one of them becomes too wide for the containing element to accommodate them both, the two floating boxes will collide, and whichever element comes later in the source order will wrap *under* the previous element.

A visual web browser converts percentage dimensions into a number of pixels in order to render the elements on the screen. Imagine two adjacent, floated elements in a box, each with a width of 50%. If their container is 800 pixels wide, both elements will be exactly 400 pixels wide and can float side by side in harmony. Now resize your imaginary container to 799 pixels wide—the two floating boxes need to be 399.5 pixels wide each. There's really no such thing as half a pixel, so browsers are forced to round to the nearest whole pixel. The two floating boxes remain 400 pixels wide in a box that is too narrow to contain them, so the second element gets pushed below the first.

You can prevent this disastrous scenario by ensuring that the two elements' combined widths never exceed 100% of their container's width, making allowances for rounding to whole pixels. Our floating content and navigation boxes total 95%, allowing a 5% space between them (the space between columns is called a *gutter*, another term borrowed from traditional graphic design).

Clearing Floats

Another potential quagmire that comes packaged with float-based layouts is the matter of *clearing* floated elements. A floated element is partially removed from the natural flow of content, allowing subsequent content to flow upward and wrap around the floating box. However, when two adjacent boxes are both floating, there is nothing to tell the browser where their lower boundary should be drawn. Content can flow upward around those boxes, squeezing into whatever space is available. You can see an example of this phenomenon in Figure 11-12; because the content and navigation are floating, the tag line and copyright statement flow up into whatever space they can find, even squeezing into the gutter. We've drawn borders around the boxes for this illustration.

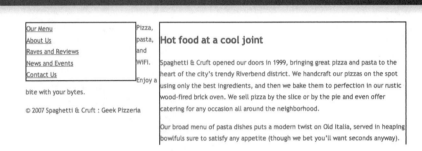

Figure 11-12. *A demonstration of what can happen when floating elements aren't cleared*

To remedy the situation, we must clear the floats by drawing an invisible line across their lower border beyond which no content will flow. In other cases and with other layouts, this can sometimes be difficult without resorting to extra, presentational markup. But on the Spaghetti & Cruft site, the only elements that come after the two floating boxes are the tag line and copyright statement. The tag line will be styled and positioned at the top of the page, so it won't be in danger of flowing around the content and navigation. However, the copyright statement will form a footer at the bottom of the page, so that element can also serve as a clearing line by styling it with the declaration `clear: both`. We've done just that in Listing 11-20.

Listing 11-20. *The Copyright Paragraph Clears the Floats Above It*

```
#copyright { clear: both; }
```

Assigning the `clear` property to the copyright statement with a value of `both` instructs the browser to not allow any floats to descend below that line or any content to flow above it. Figure 11-13 shows the result; the copyright statement now rests at the bottom of the page in spite of the floating boxes above it. Once again, the borders are just for illustration.

Figure 11-13. *The copyright statement now clears the floats above it rather than flowing upward around them. The tag line isn't shown here because we've positioned it over the masthead.*

Tip For much more detailed information on clearing and containing floats, see Eric Meyer's article "Containing Floats" (http://www.complexspiral.com/publications/containing-floats/). You can find a few alternative clearing methods at the "Clearing Space" page of the CSS-Discuss wiki (http://css-discuss.incutio.com/?page=ClearingSpace). CSS-Discuss is a popular mailing list for—you guessed it—discussing CSS.

Styling the Navigation

The site's navigation menu is nothing more than an unordered list containing ordinary text links. It's fully functional as is, and we've already placed it roughly where we want it by floating the element to the left. But it's still not a very attractive menu and is just begging for a touch of style.

We'll target the navigation list items with a descendant selector and specify a different font family, as well as enlarging the text and padding each list item at its top and bottom to add some more white space between the links. The design mock-up calls for thin, gray lines between each list item, easily accomplished with the shorthand `border-bottom` property. This one property takes the place of the longhand properties `border-bottom-width`, `border-bottom-style`, and `border-bottom-color`, accepting all three values in a single declaration to apply a border to the bottom of each list item (the values can occur in any order).

We'll also apply an equivalent `border-top` declaration to the navigation `ul` element, and we'll add another rule that removes underlines from the navigation links. Usability and accessibility guidelines have long discouraged removing underlines from links (we even discouraged it earlier in this chapter). However, the links in this menu are already visually distinct and separate from other text content, so removing the underlines here is a small compromise to make in the name of aesthetics. Listing 11-21 shows the CSS rules styling the menu.

Listing 11-21. *Styling the Navigation Menu*

```
#navigation {
  float: left;
  width: 30%;
  margin: 0;
  padding: 0;
  list-style: none;
  border-top: 1px solid #b5b5b5; }

#navigation li {
  padding: 6px 0;
  font: 130% Georgia, "Times New Roman", Times, serif;
  border-bottom: 1px solid #b5b5b5; }

#navigation a { text-decoration: none; }
```

You can see the menu nearing completion in Figure 11-14.

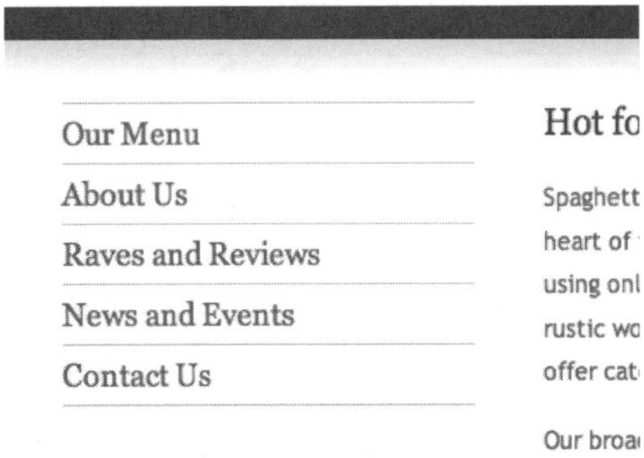

Figure 11-14. *The navigation menu is now rendered in a different typeface with lines drawn between the list items and underlines removed from the links.*

Background Bullets

In Chapter 4, you learned how to replace the default bullet character with a graphic using the list-style-image property. But there's another method to achieve a similar visual effect using a background image and a bit of padding. With the bullets removed entirely (with list-style: none), a background image is applied to the li element, and some padding on the element's left side indents the text to make space (otherwise, the text would overlap the image). Many designers prefer this technique because it grants them more precise control over the positioning of the bullet image. You can see how it's done in Listing 11-22.

Listing 11-22. *Adding a Bullet-Style Background to Menu Items*

```
#navigation li {
  font: 130% Georgia, "Times New Roman", Times, serif;
  border-bottom: 1px solid #e4e4e4;
  padding: 6px 0 6px 35px;
  background: transparent url(images/ornament.gif) 0 50% no-repeat; }
```

We're using the shorthand background property again, this time including values for background-position to place the image at the element's left side, vertically centered. A vertical position of 50% will be half the element's height, whatever that height may be, so the image stays properly aligned when text is resized (you learned about positioning background images in Chapter 5). Figure 11-15 shows the finished menu.

Figure 11-15. *The finished menu, now with fancy bullet background images*

Styling the Footer

In our mock-up, the copyright notice has a red top border, but it's not quite as simple as border-top: 1px solid red. There's a small flourish at one end of the line, something that can be accomplished only with an image. Alas, CSS as it exists today doesn't provide the means to specify an image as an element's border, but maybe that will be added in a future version of the language (are you listening, W3C?). Until then, we can use a background image to achieve the effect.

As you saw in the navigation menu, you can apply padding to an element to wedge in some space where a background image will appear. We can create our decorative border with a bit of top padding and a background image spreading across the width of the element, something a bit more interesting than a plain line. Listing 11-23 is the final CSS rule that styles the copyright paragraph. You'll recognize all of these properties by now.

Listing 11-23. *Styling the Footer*

```
#copyright {
  clear: both;
  text-align: right;
  font-size: 80%;
  color: #888;
  padding-top: 15px;
  background: transparent url(images/footerline.gif) 100% 0 no-repeat; }
```

Figure 11-16 shows the result.

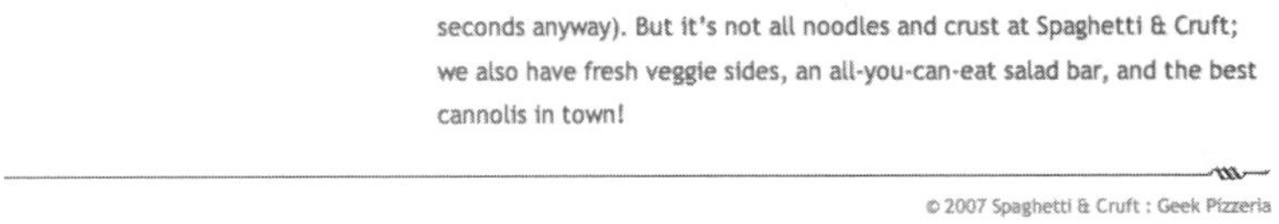

seconds anyway). But it's not all noodles and crust at Spaghetti & Cruft;
we also have fresh veggie sides, an all-you-can-eat salad bar, and the best
cannolis in town!

© 2007 Spaghetti & Cruft : Geek Pizzeria

Figure 11-16. *Our restyled copyright statement. Compare this to how it appeared in Figure 11-13.*

The curly twist that decorates the border image appears at only one end of the line, so the background image needs to be extremely wide if it's going to span the entire liquid page at any size. This graphic is 2000 pixels wide, but it's only 14 pixels tall and has been reduced to just a few colors, resulting in a very small file that should download quickly. The background stretches all the way to the left end of the element because it's positioned at the far right.

There's just one problem with this technique: visual web browsers that honor the CSS but don't display images—if the user has disabled downloading images, for example—won't display any border at all. In the case of this footer, the border is purely decorative and isn't really essential to understanding the content, so using an image here does no harm.

Assembling the Pages

With our page template completed and styled, we can finally start fleshing out the rest of the site. We'll create all the pages and fill them with content, which we'll always structure with semantically appropriate markup. We'll inevitably need to return to our style sheet to enhance the content's presentation as it's added along the way.

The Menu Page

The Spaghetti & Cruft menu is split into three categories—Pizza, Pasta, and Desserts— listing dishes and their prices within each category (if this were a real pizzeria, it would probably serve more options than we're listing, but this is enough for our demonstration). Although a menu might lend itself to a list format—a menu is a list of choices, after all—we're choosing tables to draw an emphatic connection between each item and its different prices, sorted into rows and columns.

The page title, "Good eats for hungry geeks," is marked up as an h2 element, and each menu category has an h3 subheading. The tables themselves use table headers to mark both the price columns (with scope="col") and the rows for individual dishes (with scope="row"). Where these rows and columns intersect, the price contained in that table cell is clearly associated with both the name of the dish and the price category. You can see an example of our menu table markup in Listing 11-24, shortened here for the sake of brevity (we're showing only one row plus the header row). Each of the three tables follows a similar pattern. You learned about all of these elements and attributes in Chapter 7.

Listing 11-24. *A Truncated Example of a Menu Table*

```
<table class="menu" summary="Pizzas and their prices, ➥
in five rows of five columns">
  <thead>
    <tr>
      <td></td>
      <th scope="col">Slice</th>
      <th scope="col">Small</th>
      <th scope="col">Medium</th>
      <th scope="col">Large</th>
    </tr>
  </thead>
  <tbody>
    <tr>
      <th scope="row">Pizza Napoli <em>Vegetarian</em></th>
      <td>$2.50</td>
      <td>$9.00</td>
      <td>$11.00</td>
      <td>$15.75</td>
    </tr>
  </tbody>
</table>
```

Figure 11-17 shows two tables from the menu page in their current state, rendered with only inherited CSS (we've already styled the h3 headings in another typeface). Because the tables lack presentational width attributes, each is only as wide as its contents. But we had the foresight to give each table a class attribute, classifying them as "menu" tables so that we can easily style them later with CSS.

Pizzas

	Slice	Small	Medium	Large
Pizza Napoli *Vegetarian*	$2.50	$9.00	$11.00	$15.75
Pizza Roma	$2.25	$8.50	$10.50	$14.00
Pizza Sicilia	$2.25	$8.50	$10.50	$14.00
Pizza Classico *any two toppings*	$2.75	$9.50	$11.50	$15.00
Pizza Vegetario *Vegetarian*	$1.75	$7.50	$9.75	$12.80

Pasta

	Half	Full
Classic Spaghetti	$4.50	$8.00
Fettuccine Alfredo *Vegetarian*	$5.25	$9.50
Linguini Bolognese	$5.25	$9.50
Fusilli Marinara *Vegetarian*	$2.75	$9.50

Figure 11-17. *A portion of the menu page, showing the tables as they appear with their inherited styles*

Styling the Menu Tables

We've given ourselves the menu class as a useful hook from which to hang our style rules. In addition to offering a handy CSS selector, this classification differentiates menu tables from any other tables that may appear on the site, uniting them and establishing their relationship in a meaningful way. Because these tables belong to the same class, they can also share aspects of their presentation.

To begin, we can address the width issue with a simple width property and a value of 100%; these tables will now occupy the full available width, which will be the same width as the main content div that surrounds them, adjusting fluidly with the window size. A bottom margin will create a bit of vertical spacing between the end of each table and the heading that follows it.

Although each menu table has a width of 100%, the cells within them have no declared width at all. The browser will automatically calculate their widths to be at least as wide as their contents and then expand them further to occupy the full width of the table (the calculated widths of each cell in a row will add up to 100%). Each of our three tables has a different number of columns, so the column widths are calculated differently in each table. Declaring a width for th elements within the table bodies brings the price columns in line while each price column itself is still sized automatically.

Many graphical browsers display the contents of table headers in a boldfaced font horizontally centered. This styling is important to distinguish header cells from data cells, but we can use CSS to alter that default presentation and still make them visually distinct.

Because th elements appear in both the thead and tbody elements, we can rely on their ancestors to differentiate the two kinds of table headers with descendant CSS selectors.

Some menu items include a note of extra information contained in an em element. Those notes inherit their size, weight, and color from the th elements that contain them, but we'll use a descendant selector to declare that those specific em elements should appear slightly smaller, in a normal weight, and in a different color. The notes are still semantically emphasized by the em elements—we're altering only their presentation.

Lastly, we'll add a light gray border to the bottom of th and td elements, drawing a horizontal line between each row to help our readers visually scan across the table. Most graphical browsers render tables with a small amount of spacing between cells (usually about 2 pixels), causing tiny gaps in the line. Adding a border-collapse: collapse declaration to the .menu rule instructs the browser to close those default gaps and draw a continuous border.

Listing 11-25 shows the complete set of CSS rules to style the menu tables.

Listing 11-25. *Styling the Menu Tables*

```
.menu {
  width: 100%;
  margin-bottom: 3em;
  border-collapse: collapse; }

.menu td { border-bottom: 1px solid #ddd; }

.menu th {
  color: #ab0000;
  text-align: left;
  border-bottom: 1px solid #ddd; }

.menu thead th { font-size: 85%; }

.menu tbody th { width: 50%; }

.menu tbody th em {
  font-size: 90%;
  font-weight: normal;
  color: #555; }
```

Figure 11-18 shows an updated example of the menu tables, which have improved much since you last saw them in Figure 11-17.

Pizzas

	Slice	Small	Medium	Large
Pizza Napoli *Vegetarian*	$2.50	$9.00	$11.00	$15.75
Pizza Roma	$2.25	$8.50	$10.50	$14.00
Pizza Sicilia	$2.25	$8.50	$10.50	$14.00
Pizza Classico *any two toppings*	$2.75	$9.50	$11.50	$15.00
Pizza Vegetario *Vegetarian*	$1.75	$7.50	$9.75	$12.80

Pasta

	Half	Full
Classic Spaghetti	$4.50	$8.00
Fettuccine Alfredo *Vegetarian*	$5.25	$9.50
Linguini Bolognese	$5.25	$9.50
Fusilli Marinara *Vegetarian*	$2.75	$9.50

Figure 11-18. *The finished Spaghetti & Cruft menu*

Updating the Navigation

The Spaghetti & Cruft site features *persistent navigation*; the same list of links appears on every page of the site so a user to can easily reach any other page from whichever page they happen to be reading. When a user follows a navigation link to arrive at a new page on the site, that original link is no longer needed in the navigation. Your visitors might not remember which link they clicked to land on a new page, so if that link is still present, they could become confused when clicking it doesn't seem to lead anywhere (the link would still work; they would just end up exactly where they already were).

Yet we wouldn't want to remove the item from the navigation list entirely; we only want to make it so that it's no longer a link. Removing the anchor but leaving the original text lets the list item act as a signpost, telling the user, "You are here." That signpost can also be styled differently from the other items in the navigation menu to make it stand out and provide an additional hint that it's no longer a clickable link. Listing 11-26 shows the updated navigation list as it appears in the menu page markup.

Listing 11-26. *Indicating the Current Page in the Navigation Menu*

```
<ul id="navigation">
  <li class="current">Our Menu</li>
  <li><a href="about.html">About Us</a></li>
  <li><a href="reviews.html">Raves and Reviews</a></li>
  <li><a href="news.html">News and Events</a></li>
```

```
<li><a href="contact.html">Contact Us</a></li>
</ul>
```

We've added `class="current"` to the list item that corresponds to the current page. We'll use this primarily as a selector to apply CSS, but it also has some additional meaning: it classifies this item as the currently active item in the list. To visually distinguish that item, we can change the color and style of its text contents as well as swap in a different background image. Listing 11-27 shows the CSS rule. The new background image will be used because this rule has a more specific selector, but the `background-position` value carries through from the less specific rule that appears elsewhere in the style sheet.

Listing 11-27. *Styling the Current Menu Item*

```
#navigation li.current {
  color: #ab0000;
  font-style: italic;
  background-image: url(images/ornament-current.gif); }
```

Figure 11-19 shows the result, clearly indicating the current page in the navigation list.

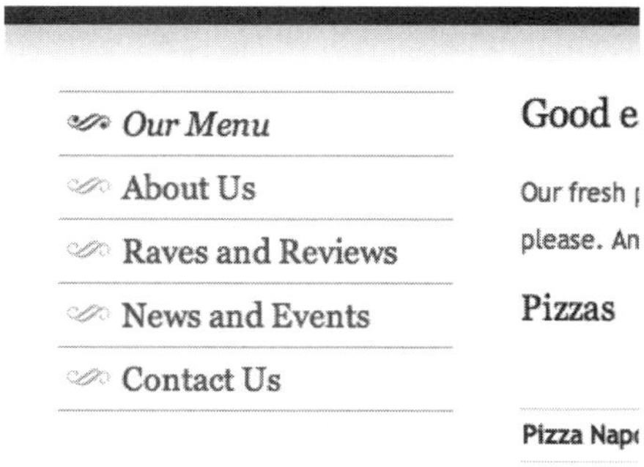

Figure 11-19. *The navigation menu as it now appears, with the current page highlighted*

Every subsequent page we create will receive this alteration to its navigation list, removing the corresponding link and indicating the current page with the addition of a simple `class` attribute.

The Reviews Page

Spaghetti & Cruft has been written up favorably in local newspapers and on community websites, so Mario and Luigi have asked for a place to showcase reviews on their website. Instead of publishing the reviews in their entirety, we're going to include only a short excerpt of each review paired with a link leading to the full review at the original website (if possible). Each excerpt will be marked up in a `blockquote` element, followed by a `cite` element featuring a link to the original source. Both are grouped in a div that's classified as a "blurb." Listing 11-28 shows an example.

Listing 11-28. *An Example of a Quoted Passage from a Review*

```
<div class="blurb">
  <blockquote cite="http://example.com/SpaghettiCruft/">
    <p>Spaghetti &#38; Cruft offers tasty, wood-fired pizzas at affordable
    prices, served in a hip, relaxed atmosphere. Comfortable seats, free
    WiFi, and abundant power outlets make this a popular spot for the
    neighborhood technophiles to linger with their laptops.</p>
  </blockquote>

  <p class="source"><cite><a href="http://example.com/SpaghettiCruft/"➥
    title="Read this full review at example.com">
    Gotham Examiner, November 22, 2006</a></cite></p>
</div>
```

The link to the original article is nested within the cite element and class="source" is added to its parent paragraph to set it apart both semantically and stylistically once we author the CSS. The link's title attribute offers a hint at where the link will lead so a reader won't be too surprised when they're whisked away to another website. You can see this quotation in Figure 11-20 before any further styling has been applied.

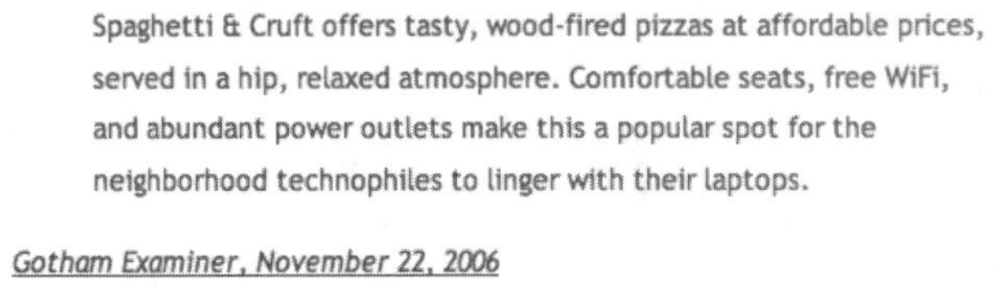

> Spaghetti & Cruft offers tasty, wood-fired pizzas at affordable prices,
> served in a hip, relaxed atmosphere. Comfortable seats, free WiFi,
> and abundant power outlets make this a popular spot for the
> neighborhood technophiles to linger with their laptops.
>
> *Gotham Examiner, November 22, 2006*

Figure 11-20. *The review blurb as it appears in a graphical browser with its inherited styling*

Block quotations appear as indented blocks with margins on the left and right sides by default. We'll adjust those margins with the CSS margin property, giving each review quote a left and right margin of 20 pixels and a top and bottom margin of 1 em space, using the blurb class as our style hook (only block quotations descended from that class will be granted these style properties, rather than all blockquote elements sitewide).

To visually separate each review blurb (the term *blurb* refers to any short quote taken from a longer review, such as you've seen on movie posters or on the back cover of a book), each one will have a small decorative graphic beneath it. It's applied to the containing div the same way we added decorative background images to the navigation items and the copyright statement, using the `background` shorthand property and some padding to create adequate space.

Just to make them a bit more interesting to look at and to further distinguish them from regular, nonquoted text elsewhere on the page, we'll italicize these blurbs with the declaration `font-style: italic`. However, because the `cite` element is italicized by default in most browsers, citations might tend to blend in with the quotation. We can override that default style with the declaration `font-style: normal`, using a descendant selector so `cite` elements elsewhere won't be affected. We'll also align the citation to the right and reduce its font size, using the class we added to its containing paragraph in our selector.

Listing 11-29 shows the full set of CSS rules that style the review excerpts.

Listing 11-29. *Styling Review Excerpts*

```
.blurb {
  margin-bottom: 1em;
  padding-bottom: 30px;
  background: transparent url(images/blurb.gif) 50% 95% no-repeat; }

.blurb blockquote {
  margin: 1em 20px;
  font-style: italic; }

.blurb cite { font-style: normal; }

.blurb p.source {
  text-align: right;
  font-size: 90%; }
```

Figure 11-21 shows a portion of the Spaghetti & Cruft reviews page, illustrating the effects of the previous CSS.

Figure 11-21. *Two styled blurbs from the Spaghetti & Cruft reviews page*

The Contact Page

The Spaghetti & Cruft contact page will allow site visitors to reach Mario and Luigi by filling in a simple form. A form handler on the server processes the entered data, automatically sending the message to both brothers via e-mail.

The form includes text fields in which a visitor can enter his or her name and e-mail address, a selection menu to choose one of a few possible message subjects, a larger text area for the message, and a button to submit the whole thing. Because each of these controls represents a discrete action on the user's part, they can be semantically separated any number of ways. Each could be contained in a div element, logically grouping the control with its text label. They could also be wrapped in paragraphs, with each label/control pair representing a distinct thought or idea. But for this site, we're choosing to mark up the form as an ordered list, with each control and its label playing the role of one step in a sequence.

Listing 11-30 presents the contact form markup in its entirety. All of the XHTML elements used here should be familiar to you by now (you can turn back to Chapter 8 for a refresher on form markup).

Listing 11-30. *The Spaghetti & Cruft Contact Form*

```
<form method="post" action="/path/to/formhandler/">
<fieldset id="contact">

<legend>Contact us</legend>

<ol>
  <li>
    <label for="name">Your name</label>
    <input type="text" id="name" name="name" />
  </li>

  <li>
    <label for="email">Your E-mail address</label>
    <input type="text" id="email" name="email" />
  </li>

  <li>
    <label for="subject">What's this about?</label>
    <select id="subject" name="subject">
      <option value="" selected="selected">-- select --</option>
      <option value="Hello">I'm just saying "hello"</option>
      <option value="Menu Question">I have a question about your menu</option>
      <option value="Catering">I have a question about catering</option>
```

```
      <option value="Complaint">I'd like to lodge a complaint</option>
    </select>
  </li>

  <li>
    <label for="message">Your message</label>
    <textarea id="message" name="message" cols="40" rows="10"></textarea>
  </li>

  <li>
    <input type="submit" id="submit" name="submit" value="Send" />
  </li>
</ol>

</fieldset>
</form>
```

As you learned in Chapter 8, form controls tend to look very different from one browser to the next. We're going to leave these controls alone for the most part, allowing each browser to display them in its native style rather than risk any usability snags brought on by overstyling interactive input widgets. On the other hand, the structural elements surrounding those controls are wide open for styling. Figure 11-22 shows what this form looks like in Firefox 2.0 for Mac OS X, displayed with only the style properties it inherits from elsewhere in the style sheet along with the browser defaults.

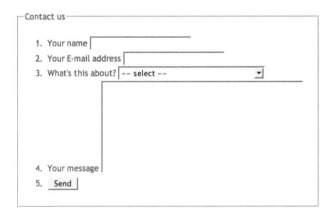

Figure 11-22. *The contact form as rendered by Firefox for Mac OS X before we've applied any further styling*

To begin sprucing up this form with a touch of CSS, we'll remove the default border and padding from the surrounding field set (as you learned to do in Chapter 8) and the default numbering from the ordered list (as you learned to do in Chapter 4). The `fieldset` element has been identified as `contact`, so we can use that ID as a hook in all our subsequent CSS rules. We'll also neutralize the default margins and padding on the ordered list while we're at it.

We'll align the controls in a neat column by converting their labels to floating blocks with a declared width; this technique was also covered in Chapter 8. This time, we'll make the `label` elements 30% of the main content area's width and they'll adjust automatically with the liquid layout.

To combat any problems with the floating labels bumping into each other, we can also float the list items that contain them; a floated element will automatically contain another floated element, so each floating `li` element effectively clears the floating `label` inside it. Declaring a width of 100% for those list items prevents them from collapsing around their contents—floated elements are reduced to the width of their content, so declaring a width counteracts this so-called shrink-wrapped effect. A bit of top and bottom margins on the list items and a right margin on the labels spaces everything out nicely.

We'll bring the submit button in line with the form controls above it with the addition of a 32% left margin (the width of the labels plus their right margins). We can target the button specifically by its unique ID, differentiating it from other `input` elements. The button is rather small because of its short text label, so we'll increase its width to present a larger target for easier clicking, using ems once again to keep the button's width proportional to the text size.

As you learned in Chapter 8, form controls won't always inherit their font styles from their `parent` element, easily remedied with `font-family: inherit` and `font-size: 100%`.

Lastly, the form's legend could use some attention. Even though the `legend` element is difficult to style in some browsers, it's not entirely immune to CSS. We can make it look just like one of our `h3` headings by applying the same style declarations to the `legend` element. Many browsers apply some default padding or margins to the left and right sides of form legends, so removing those will help it align flush to the left as if it were a regular heading. Why not simply use an `h3` element to begin with? Remember, `legend` is a required element for field sets, and it brings improved form accessibility along with it. We want it to only *look* like a level-three heading without losing the benefits of a proper `legend` element.

Listing 11-31 shows these new additions to the style sheet, making the contact form more attractive and more in line with the overall look of the site.

Listing 11-31. *Styling the Contact Form*

```
#contact {
  border: none;
  margin: 0;
  padding: 0; }

#contact ol {
  list-style: none;
  margin: 0;
  padding: 0; }

#contact li {
  margin: .2em 0;
  float: left;
  width: 100%; }

#contact label {
  width: 30%;
  float: left;
  text-align: right;
  margin-right: 2%; }

#contact input#submit {
  margin-left: 32%;
  width: 10em; }

#contact input, #contact select, #contact textarea {
  font-family: inherit;
  font-size: 100%; }

#contact legend {
  color: #ab0000;
  font: 135% Georgia, "Times New Roman", Times, serif;
  margin: auto 0;
  padding: 0; }
```

Figure 11-23 shows the result: the finished Spaghetti & Cruft contact page.

Figure 11-23. *The finished Spaghetti & Cruft contact page*

Summary

This has been one of the longest chapters in this book, but we hope it has also been one of the most enlightening. You've learned about just one approach to the web design process and seen it put into action, following the design and construction of our fictional site for Spaghetti & Cruft. We didn't cover every last corner of the site, but we walked you through some of the more interesting parts in enough detail to give you a feel for how it all came together. All of the markup and CSS examples you've seen in this book—including this entire case study site—are available at the Apress website (http://www.apress.com) to download and dissect at your leisure. You can also visit this book's companion site (http://www.beginninghtmlbook.com) to see the completed Spaghetti & Cruft website along with some other useful information about how it was made.

HyperText Markup Language is the very foundation of the World Wide Web. It's the common root language without which this vast frontier of cross-referenced information at our fingertips wouldn't be possible. This language and the web it weaves allows us to stay abreast of current affairs in our communities, delve into the histories of distant cultures, study the latest breakthroughs in particle physics, and giggle at adorable pictures of cats with poor grammar. HTML is truly a marvelous thing—powerful yet approachable.

Now that you've grasped the fundamentals of modern, semantic markup and CSS, you might be wondering, what's the next step? Keep learning, of course. This book has offered only a glimpse of what it's possible to create with these core web languages. Go online and explore some of the many and varied resources available to you. Graduate to the next level and further hone your skills with CSS and JavaScript. We highly recommend *Beginning CSS Web Development*, by Simon Collison (Berkeley, CA: Apress, 2006), and *Beginning JavaScript with DOM Scripting and Ajax*, by Christian Heilmann (Berkeley, CA: Apress, 2006), as helpful guides on your path from novice to professional.

But above all, experiment. Open a text editor, grab your favorite web browser, and just dive in. We've shown you that it doesn't require any expensive tools or arcane knowledge to create innovative websites. The web was built by enthusiastic tinkerers, so get out there and tinker.

■ ■ ■

XHTML 1.0 Strict Reference

This appendix provides a reference to the elements described throughout the text. The elements listed are from the XHTML 1.0 Strict specification, which you can find at http://www.w3.org/TR/xhtml1/. You can also check out the actual Document Type Definition (DTD) at http://www.w3.org/TR/xhtml1/dtds.html.

Core Attributes

The core attributes are common attributes found in most XHTML elements. The following elements only support some of the attributes: base, html, meta, param, script, style, and title.

Attribute	Description
class	Indicates the class or classes that a particular element belongs to
id	Specifies a unique identifier to be associated with an element
style	Specifies an inline style for the element
title	Supplies text that is often rendered as a tooltip when the mouse is over the element

Internationalization Attributes

Internationalization attributes are valid in all elements except base, br, param, and script.

Attribute	Description
dir	Sets the text direction.
xml:lang	Specifies the language being used for the enclosed content; see http://www.w3.org/XML/1998/namespace for more details. This replaces the deprecated lang attribute.

Keyboard Attributes

Keyboard attributes are valid in most elements and pertain to using the keyboard.

Attribute	Description
accesskey	Sets a keyboard shortcut to access an element
tabindex	Sets the tab order for an element

<!DOCTYPE>

The <!DOCTYPE> declaration is at the top of the XHTML document and specifies which XHTML specification the document uses. The possible values for this are the DTDs representing the XHTML Strict DTD, the XHTML Transitional DTD, and the XHTML Frameset DTD.

Required attributes: None

Optional attributes: None

Core attributes: None

Event attributes: None

See Chapter 3 for usage.

<a>

The a element is used to specify an anchor within your document. You can use an anchor to link to another document or to a shortcut within the same document.

Required attributes: None

Optional attributes:

- charset: Specifies a character set used in the encoding of the target URL.

- coords: Specifies coordinates that are used to define a shape used in a client-side image map.

- `href`: This the URL that you wish the browser to open when the user clicks on the link. This is the most commonly used attribute for the anchor tag.

- `hreflang`: Specifies the base language used in the URL specified by the `href` attribute.

- `rel`: Specifies the relationship between the current document and the target URL. Possible values include `alternate`, `stylesheet`, `start`, `next`, `prev`, `contents`, `index`, `glossary`, `copyright`, `chapter`, `section`, `subsection`, `appendix`, `help`, and `bookmark`.

- `rev`: Specifies the relationship between the target URL and the current document. Possible values include `alternate`, `stylesheet`, `start`, `next`, `prev`, `contents`, `index`, `glossary`, `copyright`, `chapter`, `section`, `subsection`, `appendix`, `help`, and `bookmark`.

- `shape`: Defines the type of region for mapping in the current area element in an image map. Possible values include `rect`, `circle`, `default`, and `poly`.

- `type`: Specifies the MIME type of the target URL. Refer to Chapter 1 for details on the MIME types.

Core attributes: `accesskey`, `class`, `id`, `dir`, `lang`, `style`, `tabindex`, `title`, `xml:lang`

Event attributes: `onblur`, `onclick`, `ondblclick`, `onfocus`, `onkeypress`, `onkeydown`, `onkeyup`, `onmousedown`, `onmouseup`, `onmouseover`, `onmousemove`, `onmouseout`

See Chapter 6 for usage.

`<abbr>`

The `abbr` element specifies an abbreviation, such as "Co." and "Mr." By marking up abbreviations, you can provide useful information to other applications that may be interpreting your document.

Required attributes: None

Optional attributes: None

Core attributes: `class`, `dir`, `id`, `lang`, `style`, `title`, `xml:lang`

Event attributes: `onclick`, `ondblclick`, `onkeydown`, `onkeypress`, `onkeyup`, `onmousedown`, `onmousemove`, `onmouseover`, `onmouseout`, `onmouseup`

See Chapter 4 for usage.

<acronym>

The acronym element specifies that the content is an acronym, such as *RAM* for *random access memory*. By marking up acronyms, you can provide useful information to other applications that may be interpreting your document.

Required attributes: None

Optional attributes: None

Core attributes: class, dir, id, lang, style, title, xml:lang

Event attributes: onclick, ondblclick, onkeydown, onkeypress, onkeyup, onmousedown, onmousemove, onmouseover, onmouseout, onmouseup

See Chapter 4 for usage.

<address>

The address element specifies an address. You should use this element to specify an address or signature of a document.

Required attributes: None

Optional attributes: None

Core attributes: class, dir, id, lang, style, title, xml:lang

Event attributes: onclick, ondblclick, onkeydown, onkeypress, onkeyup, onmousedown, onmousemove, onmouseover, onmouseout, onmouseup

See Chapter 4 for usage.

<area>

The area element is used to specify a region in a client-side image map.

Required attributes:

- alt: Specifies text to be used as an alternative for the area

Optional attributes:

- coords: This attribute defines the position and shape within a map. The area is clickable using a mouse, but it's also selectable with a keyboard. When the shape attribute equals rect, then the format is left, top, right, and bottom. If the shape attribute equals circ, then the format is center x, center y, and radius. If the shape attribute equals poly, then the format is x1, y1, x2, y2, . . . xn, yn.

- href: A URL that specifies the link to another resource for the area.

- nohref: Used to exclude an area from an image map.

- shape: Specifies the shape of an area. Valid values are circle, default, poly, and rect.

Core attributes: accesskey, class, id, dir, lang, style, tabindex, title, xml:lang

Event attributes: onblur, onclick, ondblclick, onfocus, onkeypress, onkeydown, onkeyup, onmousedown, onmouseup, onmouseover, onmousemove, onmouseout

See Chapter 6 for usage.

<b>

The b element is used to specify text as being rendered as bold. Using CSS is the preferred method instead of using this element.

Required attributes: None

Optional attributes: None

Core attributes: class, dir, id, lang, style, title

Event attributes: onclick, ondblclick, onkeydown, onkeypress, onkeyup, onmousedown, onmousemove, onmouseover, onmouseout, onmouseup

See Chapter 4 for usage.

<base>

The base element specifies a base URL for all the relative URLs in a document. This element appears in the head section of the document.

Required attributes:

- href: Specifies a URL to use as the base URL for all links in the document

Optional attributes: None

Core attributes: None

Event attributes: None

See Chapter 3 for usage.

<bdo>

The bdo element is used to override the default text direction.

Required attributes:

- dir: Specifies the direction of the text. Valid values are ltr (right to left) and rtl (right to left).

Optional attributes: None

Core attributes: class, id, lang, style, title, xml:lang

Event attributes: None

See Chapter 4 for usage.

\<big>

The big element is used to specify text as being rendered larger than normal. Using CSS is the preferred method instead of using this element.

Required attributes: None

Optional attributes: None

Core attributes: class, dir, id, lang, style, title

Event attributes: onclick, ondblclick, onkeydown, onkeypress, onkeyup, onmousedown, onmousemove, onmouseover, onmouseout, onmouseup

See Chapter 4 for usage.

\<blockquote>

The blockquote element specifies a long quotation. Typically, a blockquote renders in a browser by placing white space on both sides of the text.

Required attributes: None

Optional attributes:

- cite: If the quote is from an Internet source, a URL will point to where the quote is from.

Core attributes: class, dir, id, lang, style, title, xml:lang

Event attributes: onclick, ondblclick, onkeydown, onkeypress, onkeyup, onmousedown, onmousemove, onmouseover, onmouseout, onmouseup

See Chapter 4 for usage.

\<body>

The body element defines the document's body. It contains all the content for the document.

Required attributes: None

Optional attributes: None

Core attributes: class, dir, id, lang, style, title, xml:lang

Event attributes: onclick, ondblclick, onkeydown, onkeypress, onkeyup, onload, onunload, onmousedown, onmousemove, onmouseover, onmouseout, onmouseup

See Chapter 2 for usage.

\

The br element inserts a single line break. The br element doesn't have a closing element; therefore, it should be used as \
. However, due to compatibility, a space is often placed prior to the closing tag: \
.

Required attributes: None

Optional attributes: None

Core attributes: class, id, style, title

Event attributes: None

See Chapter 4 for usage.

\<button>

The button element specifies a push button within your document. A button element can contain text or images.

Required attributes: None

Optional attributes:

- disabled: Makes the button disabled and removes the control from tab navigation. The control's value won't be submitted when the form is submitted.

- name: Specifies the unique name for the button.

- type: Specifies the type of button. Valid values include button, reset, and submit. If no type is specified, the default value is submit.

- value: Removes the control from tab navigation and won't submit the control's value when the form is submitted.

Core attributes: accesskey, class, id, dir, lang, style, tabindex, title, xml:lang

Event attributes: onblur, onclick, ondblclick, onfocus, onkeypress, onkeydown, onkeyup, onmousedown, onmouseup, onmouseover, onmousemove, onmouseout

See Chapter 8 for usage.

<caption>

The caption element is used to place a caption above the table; it is not contained within a row or cell. The caption element is placed immediately after the start tag for the table. You can specify a single caption per table.

Required attributes: None

Optional attributes: None

Core attributes: class, id, dir, lang, style, title, xml:lang

Event attributes: onclick, ondblclick, onkeydown, onkeypress, onkeyup, onmousedown, onmousemove, onmouseout, onmouseover, onmouseup

See Chapter 7 for usage.

<cite>

A citation is a reference to another resource.

Required attributes: None

Optional attributes: None

Core attributes: class, dir, id, lang, style, title, xml:lang

Event attributes: onclick, ondblclick, onkeydown, onkeypress, onkeyup, onmousedown, onmousemove, onmouseover, onmouseout, onmouseup

See Chapter 4 for usage.

<code>

The code element is used to define text as computer code.

> *Required attributes*: None
>
> *Optional attributes*: None
>
> *Core attributes*: class, dir, id, lang, style, title, xml:lang
>
> *Event attributes*: onclick, ondblclick, onkeydown, onkeypress, onkeyup, onmousedown, onmousemove, onmouseover, onmouseout, onmouseup

See Chapter 4 for usage.

<col>

The col element is used to define the attribute values for one or more columns in a table. You can use the col element to specify whatever attributes you want to be in common for each column.

> *Required attributes*: None
>
> *Optional attributes*:

- align: Specifies the alignment of the text within a cell. Possible values include center, char, justify, left, and right.

- char: Specifies which character the text should be aligned on. This requires the use of the align attribute with the value set as char.

- charoff: Specifies in pixels or as a percentage how far the alignment should be adjusted to the first character to align on. This requires the use of the align attribute with the value set as char.

- span: Specifies the number of columns the col should occupy as a number.

- valign: Specifies the vertical alignment of cell content. Possible values include baseline, bottom, middle, and top.

- `width`: Specifies the width of the table in pixels or as a percent.

Core attributes: class, dir, id, lang, style, title, xml:lang

Event attributes: onclick, ondblclick, onkeydown, onkeypress, onkeyup, onmousedown, onmousemove, onmouseout, onmouseover, onmouseup

See Chapter 7 for usage.

\<colgroup\>

The colgroup element is used to define a group of col elements. You should use this element only within a table element. Use this element to group columns for formatting.

Required attributes: None

Optional attributes:

- `align`: Specifies the alignment of the text within a cell. Possible values are center, char, justify, left, and right.

- `char`: Specifies which character the text should be aligned on. This requires the use of the align attribute with the value set as char.

- `charoff`: Specifies in pixels or as a percentage how far the alignment should be adjusted to the first character to align on. This requires the use of the align attribute with the value set as char.

- `span`: Specifies the number of columns the colgroup should occupy as a number.

- `valign`: Specifies the vertical alignment of cell content. Possible values are baseline, bottom, middle, and top.

- `width`: Specifies the width of the table in pixels or as a percent.

Core attributes: class, dir, id, lang, style, title, xml:lang

Event attributes: onclick, ondblclick, onfocus, onkeydown, onkeypress, onkeyup, onmousedown, onmousemove, onmouseout, onmouseover, onmouseup

See Chapter 7 for usage.

<dd>

The dd element marks the start of a definition for a term within the definition list. A definition term must be within a set of definition list (dl) elements.

Required attributes: None

Optional attributes: None

Core attributes: class, dir, id, lang, style, title, xml:lang

Event attributes: onclick, ondblclick, onkeydown, onkeypress, onkeyup, onmousedown, onmousemove, onmouseover, onmouseout, onmouseup

See Chapter 4 for usage.

<del>

The del element can be used to specify text that has been deleted in a document. It is often used when you're editing a document and trying to keep track of all the original content. Most web browsers display the text with a line through it.

Required attributes: None

Optional attributes:

- cite: If the quote is from an Internet source, the citation will point to the URL where the quote is from.

- datetime: Specifies the date and time that the text was marked as deleted.

Core attributes: class, dir, id, lang, style, title, xml:lang

Event attributes: onclick, ondblclick, onkeydown, onkeypress, onkeyup, onmousedown, onmousemove, onmouseover, onmouseout, onmouseup

See Chapter 4 for usage.

<div>

The div element specifies a division or section within a document.

Required attributes: None

Optional attributes: None

Core attributes: class, dir, id, lang, style, title, xml:lang

Event attributes: onclick, ondblclick, onkeydown, onkeypress, onkeyup, onmousedown, onmousemove, onmouseover, onmouseout, onmouseup

See Chapter 4 for usage.

<dfn>

The dfn element is used to define a definition within text.

Required attributes: None

Optional attributes: None

Core attributes: class, dir, id, lang, style, title, xml:lang

Event attributes: onclick, ondblclick, onkeydown, onkeypress, onkeyup, onmousedown, onmousemove, onmouseover, onmouseout, onmouseup

See Chapter 4 for usage.

<dl>

The dl element marks the start of a definition list. A definition list must be in the body of the document.

Required attributes: None

Optional attributes: None

Core attributes: class, dir, id, lang, style, title, xml:lang

Event attributes: onclick, ondblclick, onkeydown, onkeypress, onkeyup, onmousedown, onmousemove, onmouseover, onmouseout, onmouseup

See Chapter 4 for usage.

<dt>

The dt element marks the start of a term within the definition list. A definition term must be within a set of dl elements.

Required attributes: None

Optional attributes: None

Core attributes: class, dir, id, lang, style, title, xml:lang

Event attributes: onclick, ondblclick, onkeydown, onkeypress, onkeyup, onmousedown, onmousemove, onmouseover, onmouseout, onmouseup

See Chapter 4 for usage.

<em>

The em element is used to define text that will be emphasized when rendered.

Required attributes: None

Optional attributes: None

Core attributes: class, dir, id, lang, style, title, xml:lang

Event attributes: onclick, ondblclick, onkeydown, onkeypress, onkeyup, onmousedown, onmousemove, onmouseover, onmouseout, onmouseup

See Chapter 4 for usage.

<fieldset>

A fieldset element is used to draw a box around the element within it. It is often used when grouping elements within a form to help nonvisual browsers.

Required attributes: None

Optional attributes: None

Core attributes: class, dir, id, lang, style, title, xml:lang

Event attributes: onclick, ondblclick, onkeydown, onkeypress, onkeyup, onmousedown, onmousemove, onmouseover, onmouseout, onmouseup

See Chapter 8 for usage.

<form>

The form element is used to contain other elements that make up a form used for user input. Forms are used to pass data from controls to a specified URL.

Required attributes:

- action: Specifies a URL where to send the data when the user clicks the Submit button on the form. It is also possible that the form was submitted using script, in which case it will act as if the Submit button was clicked.

Optional attributes:

- accept: A comma-separated list of MIME types that the server accepts and processes correctly as files.

- accept-charset: A comma-separated list of possible character sets for the form data.

- enctype: The MIME type used to encode the data within the form when the method attribute is set to post.

- method: The HTTP method for sending data to the URL specified by the action attribute. Possible values are get and post. Specifying get appends the data after the URL itself in the URL. Specifying post places the data within the request itself.

Core attributes: class, dir, id, lang, style, title, xml:lang

Event attributes: onclick, ondblclick, onkeydown, onkeypress, onkeyup, onmousedown, onmousemove, onmouseover, onmouseout, onmouseup, onreset, onsubmit

See Chapter 8 for usage.

<h1> - <h6>

The h1 - h6 elements define headers within the document. h1 specifies the largest header, while h6 specifies the smallest header.

Required attributes: None

Optional attributes: None

Core attributes: class, dir, id, lang, style, title, xml:lang

Event attributes: onclick, ondblclick, onkeydown, onkeypress, onkeyup, onmousedown, onmousemove, onmouseover, onmouseout, onmouseup

See Chapter 4 for usage.

<head>

The head element contains information about the XHTML document. Typically, nothing in the head section is displayed to the user in a browser.

Required attributes: None

Optional attributes:

- profile: A space-separated list of URLs that point to metadata profiles about the page

Core attributes: dir, lang, xml:lang

Event attributes: None

See Chapter 3 for usage.

<hr>

The hr element is used to display a horizontal line when rendering the document.

Required attributes: None

Optional attributes: None

Core attributes: class, dir, id, lang, style, title, xml:lang

Event attributes: onclick, ondblclick, onkeydown, onkeypress, onkeyup, onmousedown, onmousemove, onmouseover, onmouseout, onmouseup

See Chapter 4 for usage.

<html>

This element tells a browser that the document is an HTML document and is the parent of all the other major sections within the document.

Required attributes:

- `xmlns`: Used to define the XML namespace attribute. However, most validators assume the value `"http://www.w3.org/1999/xhtml"` since it is a fixed value.

Optional attributes: None

Core attributes: `dir`, `id`, `lang`, `xml:lang`

Event attributes: None

See Chapter 2 for usage.

<i>

The `i` element is used to specify text as being rendered in italics. Using CSS is the preferred method instead of using this element.

Required attributes: None

Optional attributes: None

Core attributes: `class`, `dir`, `id`, `lang`, `style`, `title`

Event attributes: `onclick`, `ondblclick`, `onkeydown`, `onkeypress`, `onkeyup`, `onmousedown`, `onmousemove`, `onmouseover`, `onmouseout`, `onmouseup`

See Chapter 4 for usage.

<img>

The img element specifies an image within a document.

Required attributes:

- alt: Specifies a brief description of the image

- src: Specifies the URL of the image to be displayed

Optional attributes:

- height: Specifies the height of an image.

- ismap: Specifies that the image should be used as a server-side image map.

- longdesc: Specifies a URL to a document that contains a long description of the image.

- usemap: Specifies the image as a client-side image map. The browser should look for the map and area elements for the specifics.

- width: Specifies the width of an image.

Core attributes: class, dir, id, lang, style, title, xml:lang

Event attributes: onclick, ondblclick, onkeydown, onkeypress, onkeyup, onmousedown, onmousemove, onmouseover, onmouseout, onmouseup

See Chapter 5 for usage.

<input>

The input element specifies the start of an input field where the user can enter data.

Required attributes: None

Optional attributes:

- accept: A comma-separated list of MIME types that indicate the type used for a file transfer when using the file value for the type attribute.

- alt: Specifies a brief description of the image.

- checked: Indicates that the input element should be checked (selected). This is valid with the checkbox and radio types.

- disabled: If set to the value disabled, it will make the <input> control disabled and not respond to user interaction.

- ismap: Specifies that the image should be used as a server-side image map.

- maxlength: Specifies the maximum number of characters allowed in a text field when using the text value in the type attribute.

- name: Specifies the unique name for the input element.

- readonly: Specifies the value readonly. It indicates that the value of the field cannot be modified when using the text value in the type attribute.

- size: Specifies the size of the input element in characters.

- src: Specifies the URL of an image to be displayed when using the value image with the type attribute.

- type: Specifies the type of the input element. Valid values are button, checkbox, file, hidden, image, password, radio, reset, submit, and text (default).

- usemap: Specifies the image as a client-side image map. The browser should look for the map and area elements for the specifics.

- value: The value attribute has different meaning based on the type attribute's value. For button, reset, and submit types, it specifies the text that appears on the button. For the image type, it specifies the symbolic result of the field passed to a script. For the checkbox and radio types, it specifies the result of the input element when clicked.

Core attributes: class, dir, id, lang, style, tabindex, title, xml:lang

Event attributes: onblur, onchange, onclick, ondblclick, onfocus, onkeydown, onkeypress, onkeyup, onmousedown, onmousemove, onmouseover, onmouseout, onmouseup, onselect, tabindex

See Chapter 8 for usage.

<ins>

The ins element can be used to specify text that has been inserted into a document. It is often used when editing a document and trying to keep track of all the content. In most web browsers, the displayed text is underlined.

Required attributes: None

Optional attributes:

- cite: If the quote is from an Internet source, a URL will point to where the quote is from.

- datetime: Specifies the date and time that the text was marked as deleted.

Core attributes: class, dir, id, lang, style, title

Event attributes: onclick, ondblclick, onkeydown, onkeypress, onkeyup, onmousedown, onmousemove, onmouseover, onmouseout, onmouseup

See Chapter 4 for usage.

<kbd>

The kbd element is used to define text as being keyboard text.

Required attributes: None

Optional attributes: None

Core attributes: class, dir, id, lang, style, title, xml:lang

Event attributes: onclick, ondblclick, onkeydown, onkeypress, onkeyup, onmousedown, onmousemove, onmouseover, onmouseout, onmouseup

See Chapter 4 for usage.

<label>

The label element provides a programmatic association between the prompt and the form control, so that assistive technology can interact with the element effectively. In visual browsers, if the user clicks the text within the label element, the element will manipulate the control as if the user clicked on the control itself.

Required attributes: None

Optional attributes:

- for: Specifies which element within a form the label is attached to and will manipulate. This attribute should be set to the ID of another form element.

Core attributes: class, dir, id, lang, style, title, xml:lang

Event attributes: accesskey, onfocus, onblur, onclick, ondblclick, onmousedown, onmouseup, onmouseover, onmousemove, onmouseout, onkeypress, onkeydown, onkeyup

See Chapter 8 for usage.

\<legend>

The legend element is used to define a caption for a fieldset.

Required attributes: None

Optional attributes: None

Core attributes: class, dir, id, lang, style, title

Event attributes: accesskey, onclick, ondblclick, onmousedown, onmousemove, onmouseout, onmouseover, onmouseup, onkeydown, onkeypress, onkeyup

See Chapter 8 for usage.

\<li>

A list item (li) is used to indicate each item to be displayed in a list. The list item element is used in both ordered (ol) and unordered lists (ul).

Required attributes: None

Optional attributes: None

Core attributes: class, dir, id, lang, style, title, xml:lang

Event attributes: onclick, ondblclick, onkeydown, onkeypress, onkeyup, onmousedown, onmousemove, onmouseover, onmouseout, onmouseup

See Chapter 4 for usage.

<link>

The link element is used to define the relationship between two linked documents. It is most often used to link external style sheets to the current document.

Required attributes: None

Optional attributes:

- charset: Sets the character set being used by the document being linked to.

- href: The URL pointing to the document that is being linked to.

- media: Refers to the type of media that the document that is being linked to is meant for. Common values include all, braille, print, projection, screen, and speech.

- rel: Defines the relationship between the document being linked to and the current document. Common values include alternate, appendix, bookmark, chapter, contents, copyright, glossary, help, index, next, prev, section, start, stylesheet, and subsection.

- rev: This is the opposite of rel. It defines the relationship between the current document and the document being linked to. See the rel attribute for possible values.

- type: This attribute specifies the MIME type of the target URL. The most common value is text/css for use with external style sheets, and text/javascript for JavaScript files.

Core attributes: class, dir, id, lang, style, title

Event attributes: onclick, ondblclick, onkeydown, onkeypress, onkeyup, onmousedown, onmousemove, onmouseover, onmouseout, onmouseup

See Chapter 3 for usage.

<map>

The map element specifies a client-side image map with clickable regions.

Required attributes:

- id: Specifies a unique name for the map element

Optional attributes:

- name: Specifies a unique name for the map element

Core attributes: class, dir, id, lang, style, title, xml:lang

Event attributes: onclick, ondblclick, onkeydown, onkeypress, onkeyup, onmousedown, onmousemove, onmouseover, onmouseout, onmouseup

See Chapter 6 for usage.

<meta>

The meta element provides information about the document. This information may be used by search engines that catalog pages on the Internet. You may use the meta element to provide keywords and descriptions for the search engines to use in order to catalog your document. You can also use the meta element to allow for automated refreshes using the http-equiv attribute. The term *meta* refers to metadata, which is a term that is often described as "data about data." The meta element provides data about the data in the document.

Required attributes:

- content: This is the value or data to be associated with a name or http-equiv.

Optional attributes:

- http-equiv: This attribute is used to connect the content attribute value to a specific HTTP response header. You can use it to request the browser to do something or to reference information about the document from an external source.

- name: This attribute is used to assign extra information to a document. The value of this attribute comes from the content attribute. Some common names include author, keywords, description, and summary.

- scheme: This attribute is used to define a format that is used to interpret the value set in the content attribute.

Core attributes: dir, lang, xml:lang

Event attributes: None

See Chapter 3 for usage.

<noscript>

The noscript element is used to specify alternate content if scripting isn't allowed on the client.

Required attributes: None

Optional attributes: None

Core attributes: class, dir, id, lang, style, title, xml:lang

Event attributes: onclick, ondblclick, onkeydown, onkeypress, onkeyup, onmousedown, onmousemove, onmouseover, onmouseout, onmouseup

See Chapter 3 for usage.

<object>

The object element specifies an object to be embedded into the document. Use the param element to specify any values that need to be passed.

Required attributes: None

Optional attributes:

- archive: A space-separated list of URLs that contain any resources for the object.

- classid: Specifies the location of an object's implementation through a URL.

- codebase: Specifies the base path to be used when relative URIs are provided for classid, data, and archive attributes.

- codetype: Specifies the MIME type of the code referred to in the classid attribute.

- data: Specifies a URL that refers to any data for the object.

- declare: Specifies that the object should only be declared and created until needed.

- height: Specifies the height of the object in pixels.

- name: Specifies a unique name for the object, which will be used in JavaScript to access the object. The name attribute is commonly used so that this control can be used in form submissions.

- standby: Specifies the text to display when the object is being loaded.

- type: Specifies the MIME type of data in the data attribute.

- usemap: Specifies a client-side map in the form of a URL that will be used with the object.

- width: Specifies the width of the object.

Core attributes: class, dir, id, lang, style, title, xml:lang

Event attributes: onclick, ondblclick, onkeydown, onkeypress, onkeyup, onmousedown, onmousemove, onmouseover, onmouseout, onmouseup, tabindex

See Chapter 4 for usage.

<ol>

The ol element is used to signify an ordered list. An ordered list must be in the body of the document.

Required attributes: None

Optional attributes: None

Core attributes: class, dir, id, lang, style, title, xml:lang

Event attributes: onclick, ondblclick, onkeydown, onkeypress, onkeyup, onmousedown, onmousemove, onmouseover, onmouseout, onmouseup

See Chapter 4 for usage.

\<optgroup>

The optgroup element is used to define an option group. It allows you to group choices together.

Required attributes:

- label: Specifies the label to be used for the option group

Optional attributes:

- disabled: Specifies the option group as being disabled. The user won't be able to interact with the controls.

Core attributes: class, dir, id, lang, style, title, xml:lang

Event attributes: onclick, ondblclick, onkeydown, onkeypress, onkeyup, onmousedown, onmousemove, onmouseover, onmouseout, onmouseup, tabindex

See Chapter 8 for usage.

\<option>

The option element specifies an option in the drop-down or list control. It is common to have several option elements for each list.

Required attributes: None

Optional attributes:

- disabled: Sets the control as disabled

- label: Allows authors to provide a shorter label for the content of the option element

- selected: Specifies which value is selected by default

- value: Specifies the value for the option that will be sent to the server

Core attributes: class, dir, id, lang, style, title, xml:lang

Event attributes: onclick, ondblclick, onkeydown, onkeypress, onkeyup, onmousedown, onmousemove, onmouseover, onmouseout, onmouseup

See Chapter 8 for usage.

<p>

The p element defines a paragraph within the document.

Required attributes: None

Optional attributes: None

Core attributes: class, dir, id, lang, style, title, xml:lang

Event attributes: onclick, ondblclick, onkeydown, onkeypress, onkeyup, onmousedown, onmousemove, onmouseover, onmouseout, onmouseup

See Chapter 4 for usage.

<param>

The param element allows you to set run-time values for objects that have been inserted into a document.

Required attributes:

- name: Specifies a unique name for the parameter

Optional attributes:

- type: Specifies the MIME type of the resource specified in the value attribute when the valuetype attribute is set to ref

- value: Specifies the actual value associated with the parameter

- valuetype: Specifies the type of the value attribute (data, ref, or object)

Core attributes: id

Event attributes: None

See Chapter 4 for usage.

<pre>

The pre element specifies text as preformatted text and usually preserves spaces and line breaks.

Required attributes: None

Optional attributes: None

Core attributes: class, dir, id, lang, style, title, xml:lang, xml:space

Event attributes: onclick, ondblclick, onkeydown, onkeypress, onkeyup, onmousedown, onmousemove, onmouseover, onmouseout, onmouseup

See Chapter 4 for usage.

<q>

The q element defines a short quotation.

Required attributes: None

Optional attributes:

- cite: If the quote is from an Internet source, a URL will point to where the quote is from.

Core attributes: class, dir, id, lang, style, title, xml:lang

Event attributes: onclick, ondblclick, onkeydown, onkeypress, onkeyup, onmousedown, onmousemove, onmouseover, onmouseout, onmouseup

See Chapter 4 for usage.

<samp>

The samp element is used to specify sample output.

Required attributes: None

Optional attributes: None

Core attributes: class, dir, id, lang, style, title, xml:lang

Event attributes: onclick, ondblclick, onkeydown, onkeypress, onkeyup, onmousedown, onmousemove, onmouseover, onmouseout, onmouseup

See Chapter 4 for usage.

\<script>

The script element plays a key role in making your site more dynamic and feature-rich. It allows you to add scripting languages to your XHTML documents that respond to user actions. Refer to Chapter 10 for the basics of JavaScript.

Required attributes:

- type: This attribute defines the MIME type of the script included. This is typically set as text/javascript when using JavaScript.

Optional attributes:

- charset: Defines the character encoding that is used in the script

- defer: Tells the browser that the script won't generate any document content, so it can continue parsing and drawing the page

- src: Uses a URL to point to a document that contains the JavaScript

Core attributes: xml:space

Event attributes: None

See Chapter 3 for usage.

\<select>

The select element is used to create a drop-down list.

Required attributes: None

Optional attributes:

- disabled: Makes the select element disabled and unresponsive to user interaction

- multiple: Specifies that more than one item can be selected at a time

- name: Specifies the unique name for the select element

- size: Specifies the number of visible items in the drop-down list

Core attributes: class, dir, id, lang, style, tabindex, title, xml:lang

Event attributes: onblur, onchange, onclick, ondblclick, onfocus, onkeydown, onkeypress, onkeyup, onmousedown, onmousemove, onmouseover, onmouseout, onmouseup

See Chapter 8 for usage.

<small>

The small element is used to specify text as being rendered smaller than normal. Using CSS is the preferred method instead of using this element.

Required attributes: None

Optional attributes: None

Core attributes: class, dir, id, lang, style, title

Event attributes: onclick, ondblclick, onkeydown, onkeypress, onkeyup, onmousedown, onmousemove, onmouseover, onmouseout, onmouseup

See Chapter 4 for usage.

<span>

The span element is used to group inline elements within a document.

Required attributes: None

Optional attributes: None

Core attributes: class, dir, id, lang, style, title

Event attributes: onclick, ondblclick, onkeydown, onkeypress, onkeyup, onmousedown, onmousemove, onmouseover, onmouseout, onmouseup

See Chapter 4 for usage.

<strong>

The strong element is used to define text that will stand out when rendered. Typically, the specified text will be bold.

Required attributes: None

Optional attributes: None

Core attributes: class, dir, id, lang, style, title, xml:lang

Event attributes: onclick, ondblclick, onkeydown, onkeypress, onkeyup, onmousedown, onmousemove, onmouseover, onmouseout, onmouseup

See Chapter 4 for usage.

<style>

The sole purpose of the `style` element is for creating internal style sheets for your document. The `style` element provides a placeholder for internal styles that you can use throughout the document.

Required attributes:

- `type`: Defines the style type. It is normally set to `text/css`.

Optional attributes:

- `media`: Defines what media the style should affect. Some of the possible values include `screen`, `tty`, `tv`, `projection`, `handheld`, `print`, `braille`, `aural`, and `all`. Visit `http://www.w3schools.com/css/css_mediatypes.asp` for the specifics on the media types.

Core attributes: `dir`, `lang`, `title`, `xml:space`

Event attributes: None

See Chapter 3 for usage.

<sub>

The `sub` element specifies text that is subscript text. Subscript text is typically rendered in a smaller font below the normal text.

Required attributes: None

Optional attributes: None

Core attributes: `class`, `dir`, `id`, `lang`, `style`, `title`, `xml:lang`

Event attributes: `onclick`, `ondblclick`, `onkeydown`, `onkeypress`, `onkeyup`, `onmousedown`, `onmousemove`, `onmouseover`, `onmouseout`, `onmouseup`

See Chapter 4 for usage.

<sup>

The sup element specifies text that is superscript text. Superscript text is typically rendered in a smaller font raised above the text.

Required attributes: None

Optional attributes: None

Core attributes: class, dir, id, lang, style, title, xml:lang

Event attributes: onclick, ondblclick, onkeydown, onkeypress, onkeyup, onmousedown, onmousemove, onmouseover, onmouseout, onmouseup

See Chapter 4 for usage.

<table>

The table element defines where a table will exist. A table is used to hold tabular data. You can place table headers, rows, cells, and other tables within a table.

Required attributes: None

Optional attributes:

- border: Specifies the width of the border for a table in pixels.

- cellpadding: Specifies the amount of space between the cell walls and the contents in pixels or as a percent.

- cellspacing: Specifies the amount of space between cells in pixels or as a percent.

- frame: Specifies how the outer borders of a table should be displayed. This attribute is used along with the border attribute. Possible values are above, below, border, box, hsides, lhs, rhs, void, and vsides.

- rules: Specifies the divider lines used for horizontal and vertical lines. This attribute is used along with the border attribute. Possible values are all, cols, groups, none, and rows.

- summary: Specifies a summary of what the table is for browsers that provide speech-synthesizing and nonvisual capabilities.

- width: Specifies the width of the table in pixels or as a percent.

Core attributes: class, dir, id, lang, style, title, xml:lang

Event attributes: onclick, ondblclick, onfocus, onkeydown, onkeypress, onkeyup, onmousedown, onmousemove, onmouseout, onmouseover, onmouseup

See Chapter 7 for usage.

\<tbody\>

The tbody element is used to define a table body section. It is contained within a \<table\> tag, and you may have multiple tbody elements. The \<thead\>, \<tbody\>, and \<tfoot\> tags allow you to group rows within a table easily.

Required attributes: None

Optional attributes:

- align: Specifies the alignment of the text within a cell. Possible values are center, char, justify, left, and right.

- char: Specifies which character the text should be aligned on. This requires the use of the align attribute with the value set as char.

- charoff: Specifies in pixels or as a percentage how far the alignment should be adjusted to the first character to align on. This requires the use of the align attribute with the value set as char.

- valign: Specifies the vertical alignment of cell content. Possible values are baseline, bottom, middle, and top.

Core attributes: class, dir, id, lang, style, title, xml:lang

Event attributes: onclick, ondblclick, onkeydown, onkeypress, onkeyup, onmousedown, onmousemove, onmouseover, onmouseout, onmouseup

See Chapter 7 for usage.

<td>

The td element is used to hold each cell within a row in a table.

Required attributes: None

Optional attributes:

- abbr: Specifies a shortened version of the content in a cell in text.

- align: Specifies the alignment of cell content. Possible values are center, char, justify, left, and right.

- axis: Associates a cell with a conceptual category.

- char: Specifies which character the text should be aligned on. This requires the use of the align attribute with the value set as char.

- charoff: Specifies in pixels or as a percentage how far the alignment should be adjusted to the first character to align on. This requires the use of the align attribute with the value set as char.

- colspan: Specifies the number of columns this cell should occupy as a number.

- rowspan: Indicates the number of rows this cell should occupy as a number.

- valign: Specifies the vertical alignment of cell content. Possible values are baseline, bottom, middle, and top.

Core attributes: class, dir, id, lang, style, title, xml:lang

Event attributes: onclick, ondblclick, onkeydown, onkeypress, onkeyup, onmousedown, onmousemove, onmouseover, onmouseout, onmouseup

See Chapter 7 for usage.

<textarea>

The textarea element allows multiple lines of text input. It provides for an unlimited amount of text.

Required attributes:

- cols: A number that specifies the number of columns that are visible in the text area

- rows: A number that specifies the number of rows that are visible in the text area

Optional attributes:

- disabled: Makes the <textarea> control disabled and unresponsive to user interaction

- name: Specifies the unique name for the <textarea> control

- readonly: Sets the <textarea> control so that the user cannot change its content

Core attributes: accesskey, class, dir, id, lang, style, tabindex, title, xml:lang

Event attributes: onblur, onchange, onclick, ondblclick, onfocus, onkeydown, onkeypress, onkeyup, onmousedown, onmousemove, onmouseover, onmouseout, onmouseup, onselect

See Chapter 8 for usage.

<tfoot>

A tfoot element is contained within a table element and specifies a table footer. The <thead>, <tbody>, and <tfoot> tags allow you to group rows within a table easily.

Required attributes: None

Optional attributes:

- align: Specifies the alignment of the text within a cell. Possible values are center, char, justify, left, and right.

- char: Specifies which character the text should be aligned on. This requires the use of the align attribute with the value set as char.

- charoff: Specifies in pixels or as a percentage how far the alignment should be adjusted to the first character to align on. This requires the use of the align attribute with the value set as char.

- valign: Specifies the vertical alignment of cell content. Possible values are baseline, bottom, middle, and top.

Core attributes: class, dir, id, lang, style, title, xml:lang

Event attributes: onclick, ondblclick, onfocus, onkeydown, onkeypress, onkeyup, onmousedown, onmousemove, onmouseout, onmouseover, onmouseup

See Chapter 7 for usage.

<th>

The th element can be used in place of the td element to mark a row as a header. A header row is normally bolded and centered within the cell.

Required attributes: None

Optional attributes:

- abbr: Specifies a shortened version of the content in a cell in text.

- align: Specifies the alignment of cell content. Possible values are center, char, justify, left, and right.

- axis: Associates a cell with a conceptual category.

- char: Specifies which character the text should be aligned on. This requires the use of the align attribute with the value set as char.

- charoff: Specifies in pixels or as a percentage how far the alignment should be adjusted to the first character to align on. This requires the use of the align attribute with the value set as char.

- colspan: Specifies the number of columns this cell should occupy as a number.

- `rowspan`: Indicates the number of rows this cell should occupy as a number.

- `valign`: Specifies the vertical alignment of cell content. Possible values are `baseline`, `bottom`, `middle`, and `top`.

Core attributes: `class`, `dir`, `id`, `lang`, `style`, `title`, `xml:lang`

Event attributes: `onclick`, `ondblclick`, `onfocus`, `onkeydown`, `onkeypress`, `onkeyup`, `onmousedown`, `onmousemove`, `onmouseout`, `onmouseover`, `onmouseup`

See Chapter 7 for usage.

<thead>

The `thead` element is used to specify a table header. It is contained within a `table` element. The `<thead>`, `<tbody>`, and `<tfoot>` tags allow you to group rows within a table easily.

Required attributes: None

Optional attributes:

- `align`: Specifies the alignment of the text within a cell. Possible values are `center`, `char`, `justify`, `left`, and `right`.

- `char`: Specifies which character the text should be aligned on. This requires the use of the `align` attribute with the value set as `char`.

- `charoff`: Specifies in pixels or as a percentage how far the alignment should be adjusted to the first character to align on. This requires the use of the `align` attribute with the value set as `char`.

- `valign`: Specifies the vertical alignment of cell content. Possible values are `baseline`, `bottom`, `middle`, and `top`.

Core attributes: `class`, `dir`, `id`, `lang`, `style`, `title`, `xml:lang`

Event attributes: `onclick`, `ondblclick`, `onfocus`, `onkeydown`, `onkeypress`, `onkeyup`, `onmousedown`, `onmousemove`, `onmouseout`, `onmouseover`, `onmouseup`

See Chapter 7 for usage.

<title>

The title element allows you to provide a title to your document. Browsers typically display this value in the title bar of the browser.

Required attributes: None

Optional attributes: None

Core attributes: dir, id, lang, style, xml:lang

Event attributes: None

See Chapter 3 for usage.

<tr>

The tr element is used to hold a row within a table element.

Required attributes: None

Optional attributes:

- align: Specifies the alignment of the text within a cell. Possible values are center, char, justify, left, and right.

- char: Specifies which character the text should be aligned on. This requires the use of the align attribute with the value set as char.

- charoff: Specifies in pixels or as a percentage how far the alignment should be adjusted to the first character to align on. This requires the use of the align attribute with the value set as char.

- valign: Specifies the text alignment in vertical cells. Possible values are baseline, bottom, middle, and top.

Core attributes: class, dir, id, lang, style, title, xml:lang

Event attributes: onclick, ondblclick, onkeydown, onkeypress, onkeyup, onmousedown, onmousemove, onmouseover, onmouseout, onmouseup

See Chapter 7 for usage.

<tt>

The tt element is used to specify text as teletype or monospaced text. Using CSS is the preferred method instead of using this element.

Required attributes: None

Optional attributes: None

Core attributes: class, dir, id, lang, style, title

Event attributes: onclick, ondblclick, onkeydown, onkeypress, onkeyup, onmousedown, onmousemove, onmouseover, onmouseout, onmouseup

See Chapter 4 for usage.

<ul>

The ul element is used to specify content as an unordered list. An unordered list must be in the body of the document.

Required attributes: None

Optional attributes: None

Core attributes: class, dir, id, lang, style, title, xml:lang

Event attributes: onclick, ondblclick, onkeydown, onkeypress, onkeyup, onmousedown, onmousemove, onmouseover, onmouseout, onmouseup

See Chapter 4 for usage.

<var>

The var element is used to define a variable within text.

Required attributes: None

Optional attributes: None

Core attributes: class, dir, id, lang, style, title, xml:lang

Event attributes: onclick, ondblclick, onkeydown, onkeypress, onkeyup, onmousedown, onmousemove, onmouseover, onmouseout, onmouseup

See Chapter 4 for usage.

■ ■ ■

Color Names and Values

You can apply color to XHTML elements with CSS using either one of a set of descriptive names or a numeric value indicating the intensities of red, green, and blue required for that color. Each color is represented internally by a single 8-bit byte, meaning that you may describe any color by a sequence of six hexadecimal digits. The first two give the intensity of the red component, the middle two denote the strength of the green, and the last two give the intensity of blue in the color. Hence, white is indicated by maximum intensities for each red, green, and blue (RGB) element, or FFFFFF. Conversely, black is indicated by a zero intensity for each element, or 000000.

A brief word on the web-safe color palette is appropriate at this point. This term describes a concept originally devised by Netscape back in 1994 in an attempt to reduce the problem of colors displaying differently when viewed on different systems. This problem occurs mainly when a browser is running on a system that has only a 256-color setup. The web-safe palette (or *Netscape palette*) addresses the issue by restricting the range of available RGB hexadecimal values for colors in the palette to 00, 33, 66, 99, CC, or FF. So, if your web page must be reliably viewable on legacy systems, make sure you use color values that obey this rule. For example, 99FFFF will produce a light blue on any system, and you can be confident that it will quite closely resemble the color seen on your own screen.

CSS only identifies the following 16 colors as being valid: aqua, black, blue, fuchsia, gray, green, lime, maroon, navy, olive, purple, red, silver, teal, white, and yellow. Most browsers support most of the color names listed below. The safest techniques are to use these 16 colors, use the hex value, or use the RGB value.

Colors Sorted by Name

Color Name	Hex Value
aliceblue	F0F8FF
antiquewhite	FAEBD7
aqua	00FFFF
aquamarine	7FFFD4
azure	F0FFFF
beige	F5F5DC
bisque	FFE4C4
black	000000
blanchedalmond	FFEBCD
blue	0000FF
blueviolet	8A2BE2
brown	A52A2A
burlywood	DEB887
cadetblue	5F9EA0
chartreuse	7FFF00
chocolate	D2691E
coral	FF7F50
cornflowerblue	6495ED
cornsilk	FFF8DC
crimson	DC143C
cyan	00FFFF
darkblue	00008B
darkcyan	008B8B
darkgoldenrod	B8860B
darkgray	A9A9A9
darkgreen	006400
darkkhaki	BDB76B
darkmagenta	8B008B
darkolivegreen	556B2F
darkorange	FF8C00
darkorchid	9932CC
darkred	8B0000
darksalmon	E9967A
darkseagreen	8FBC8F
darkslateblue	483D8B

Color Name	Hex Value
darkslategray	2F4F4F
darkturquoise	00CED1
darkviolet	9400D3
deeppink	FF1493
deepskyblue	00BFFF
dimgray	696969
dodgerblue	1E90FF
firebrick	B22222
floralwhite	FFFAF0
forestgreen	228B22
fuchsia	FF00FF
gainsboro	DCDCDC
ghostwhite	F8F8FF
gold	FFD700
goldenrod	DAA520
gray	808080
green	008000
greenyellow	ADFF2F
honeydew	F0FFF0
hotpink	FF69B4
indianred	CD5C5C
indigo	4B0082
ivory	FFFFF0
khaki	F0E68C
lavender	E6E6FA
lavenderblush	FFF0F5
lawngreen	7CFC00
lemonchiffon	FFFACD
lightblue	ADD8E6
lightcoral	F08080
lightcyan	E0FFFF
lightgoldenrodyellow	FAFAD2
lightgreen	90EE90
lightgrey	D3D3D3
lightpink	FFB6C1
lightsalmon	FFA07A
lightseagreen	20B2AA
lightskyblue	87CEFA

Color Name	Hex Value
lightslategray	778899
lightsteelblue	B0C4DE
lightyellow	FFFFE0
lime	00FF00
limegreen	32CD32
linen	FAF0E6
magenta	FF00FF
maroon	800000
mediumaquamarine	66CDAA
mediumblue	0000CD
mediumorchid	BA55D3
mediumpurple	9370DB
mediumseagreen	3CB371
mediumslateblue	7B68EE
mediumspringgreen	00FA9A
mediumturquoise	48D1CC
mediumvioletred	C71585
midnightblue	191970
mintcream	F5FFFA
mistyrose	FFE4E1
moccasin	FFE4B5
navajowhite	FFDEAD
navy	000080
oldlace	FDF5E6
olive	808000
olivedrab	6B8E23
orange	FFA500
orangered	FF4500
orchid	DA70D6
palegoldenrod	EEE8AA
palegreen	98FB98
paleturquoise	AFEEEE
palevioletred	DB7093
papayawhip	FFEFD5
peachpuff	FFDAB9
peru	CD853F
pink	FFC0CB
plum	DDA0DD

Color Name	Hex Value
powderblue	B0E0E6
purple	800080
red	FF0000
rosybrown	BC8F8F
royalblue	4169E1
saddlebrown	8B4513
salmon	FA8072
sandybrown	F4A460
seagreen	2E8B57
seashell	FFF5EE
sienna	A0522D
silver	C0C0C0
skyblue	87CEEB
slateblue	6A5ACD
slategray	708090
snow	FFFAFA
springgreen	00FF7F
steelblue	4682B4
tan	D2B48C
teal	008080
thistle	D8BFD8
tomato	FF6347
turquoise	40E0D0
violet	EE82EE
wheat	F5DEB3
white	FFFFFF
whitesmoke	F5F5F5
yellow	FFFF00
yellowgreen	9ACD32

Colors Sorted by Group

Color Name	Hex Value
Blues	
azure	F0FFFF
aliceblue	F0F8FF
lavender	E6E6FA
lightcyan	E0FFFF
powderblue	B0E0E6
lightsteelblue	B0C4DE
paleturquoise	AFEEEE
lightblue	ADD8E6
blueviolet	8A2BE2
lightskyblue	87CEFA
skyblue	87CEEB
mediumslateblue	7B68EE
slateblue	6A5ACD
cornflowerblue	6495ED
cadetblue	5F9EA0
indigo	4B0082
mediumturquoise	48D1CC
darkslateblue	483D8B
steelblue	4682B4
royalblue	4169E1
turquoise	40E0D0
dodgerblue	1E90FF
midnightblue	191970
aqua	00FFFF
cyan	00FFFF
darkturquoise	00CED1
deepskyblue	00BFFF
darkcyan	008B8B
blue	0000FF
mediumblue	0000CD
darkblue	00008B
navy	000080
Greens	
mintcream	F5FFFA
honeydew	F0FFF0

Color Name	Hex Value
greenyellow	ADFF2F
yellowgreen	9ACD32
palegreen	98FB98
lightgreen	90EE90
darkseagreen	8FBC8F
olive	808000
aquamarine	7FFFD4
chartreuse	7FFF00
lawngreen	7CFC00
olivedrab	6B8E23
mediumaquamarine	66CDAA
darkolivegreen	556B2F
mediumseagreen	3CB371
limegreen	32CD32
seagreen	2E8B57
forestgreen	228B22
lightseagreen	20B2AA
springgreen	00FF7F
lime	00FF00
mediumspringgreen	00FA9A
teal	008080
green	008000
darkgreen	006400
Pinks and Reds	
lavenderblush	FFF0F5
mistyrose	FFE4E1
pink	FFC0CB
lightpink	FFB6C1
orange	FFA500
lightsalmon	FFA07A
darkorange	FF8C00
coral	FF7F50
hotpink	FF69B4
tomato	FF6347
orangered	FF4500
deeppink	FF1493
fuchsia	FF00FF
magenta	FF00FF

Color Name	Hex Value
red	FF0000
salmon	FA8072
lightcoral	F08080
violet	EE82EE
darksalmon	E9967A
plum	DDA0DD
crimson	DC143C
palevioletred	DB7093
orchid	DA70D6
thistle	D8BFD8
indianred	CD5C5C
mediumvioletred	C71585
mediumorchid	BA55D3
firebrick	B22222
darkorchid	9932CC
darkviolet	9400D3
mediumpurple	9370DB
darkmagenta	8B008B
darkred	8B0000
purple	800080
maroon	800000

Yellows

lightgoldenrodyellow	FAFAD2
ivory	FFFFF0
lightyellow	FFFFE0
yellow	FFFF00
floralwhite	FFFAF0
lemonchiffon	FFFACD
cornsilk	FFF8DC
gold	FFD700
khaki	F0E68C
darkkhaki	BDB76B

Beiges and Browns

snow	FFFAFA
seashell	FFF5EE
papayawhite	FFEFD5
blanchedalmond	FFEBCD

Color Name	Hex Value
bisque	FFE4C4
moccasin	FFE4B5
navajowhite	FFDEAD
peachpuff	FFDAB9
oldlace	FDF5E6
linen	FAF0E6
antiquewhite	FAEBD7
beige	F5F5DC
wheat	F5DEB3
sandybrown	F4A460
palegoldenrod	EEE8AA
burlywood	DEB887
goldenrod	DAA520
tan	D2B48C
chocolate	D2691E
peru	CD853F
rosybrown	BC8F8F
darkgoldenrod	B8860B
brown	A52A2A
sienna	A0522D
saddlebrown	8B4513
Whites and Grays	
white	FFFFFF
ghostwhite	F8F8FF
whitesmoke	F5F5F5
gainsboro	DCDCDC
lightgrey	D3D3D3
silver	C0C0C0
darkgray	A9A9A9
gray	808080
lightslategray	778899
slategray	708090
dimgray	696969
darkslategray	2F4F4F
black	000000

Colors Sorted by Depth

Color Name	Hex Value
white	FFFFFF
ivory	FFFFF0
lightyellow	FFFFE0
yellow	FFFF00
snow	FFFAFA
floralwhite	FFFAF0
lemonchiffon	FFFACD
cornsilk	FFF8DC
seashell	FFF5EE
lavenderblush	FFF0F5
papayawhip	FFEFD5
blanchedalmond	FFEBCD
mistyrose	FFE4E1
bisque	FFE4C4
moccasin	FFE4B5
navajowhite	FFDEAD
peachpuff	FFDAB9
gold	FFD700
pink	FFC0CB
lightpink	FFB6C1
orange	FFA500
lightsalmon	FFA07A
darkorange	FF8C00
coral	FF7F50
hotpink	FF69B4
tomato	FF6347
orangered	FF4500
deeppink	FF1493
fuchsia	FF00FF
magenta	FF00FF
red	FF0000
oldlace	FDF5E6
lightgoldenrodyellow	FAFAD2
linen	FAF0E6
antiquewhite	FAEBD7

Color Name	Hex Value
salmon	FA8072
ghostwhite	F8F8FF
mintcream	F5FFFA
whitesmoke	F5F5F5
beige	F5F5DC
wheat	F5DEB3
sandybrown	F4A460
azure	F0FFFF
honeydew	F0FFF0
aliceblue	F0F8FF
khaki	F0E68C
lightcoral	F08080
palegoldenrod	EEE8AA
violet	EE82EE
darksalmon	E9967A
lavender	E6E6FA
lightcyan	E0FFFF
burlywood	DEB887
plum	DDA0DD
gainsboro	DCDCDC
crimson	DC143C
palevioletred	DB7093
goldenrod	DAA520
orchid	DA70D6
thistle	D8BFD8
lightgrey	D3D3D3
tan	D2B48C
chocolate	D2691E
peru	CD853F
indianred	CD5C5C
mediumvioletred	C71585
silver	C0C0C0
darkkhaki	BDB76B
rosybrown	BC8F8F
mediumorchid	BA55D3
darkgoldenrod	B8860B
firebrick	B22222
powderblue	B0E0E6

Color Name	Hex Value
lightsteelblue	B0C4DE
paleturquoise	AFEEEE
greenyellow	ADFF2F
lightblue	ADD8E6
darkgray	A9A9A9
brown	A52A2A
sienna	A0522D
yellowgreen	9ACD32
darkorchid	9932CC
palegreen	98FB98
darkviolet	9400D3
mediumpurple	9370DB
lightgreen	90EE90
darkseagreen	8FBC8F
saddlebrown	8B4513
darkmagenta	8B008B
darkred	8B0000
blueviolet	8A2BE2
lightskyblue	87CEFA
skyblue	87CEEB
gray	808080
olive	808000
purple	800080
maroon	800000
aquamarine	7FFFD4
chartreuse	7FFF00
lawngreen	7CFC00
mediumslateblue	7B68EE
lightslategray	778899
slategray	708090
olivedrab	6B8E23
slateblue	6A5ACD
dimgray	696969
mediumaquamarine	66CDAA
cornflowerblue	6495ED
cadetblue	5F9EA0
darkolivegreen	556B2F
indigo	4B0082

Color Name	Hex Value
mediumturquoise	48D1CC
darkslateblue	483D8B
steelblue	4682B4
royalblue	4169E1
turquoise	40E0D0
mediumseagreen	3CB371
limegreen	32CD32
darkslategray	2F4F4F
seagreen	2E8B57
forestgreen	228B22
lightseagreen	20B2AA
dodgerblue	1E90FF
midnightblue	191970
aqua	00FFFF
cyan	00FFFF
springgreen	00FF7F
lime	00FF00
mediumspringgreen	00FA9A
darkturquoise	00CED1
deepskyblue	00BFFF
darkcyan	008B8B
teal	008080
green	008000
darkgreen	006400
blue	0000FF
mediumblue	0000CD
darkblue	00008B
navy	000080
black	000000

APPENDIX C

■■■

Special Characters

Table C-1 lists the codes that you can employ in order to use special characters in XHTML pages. You use either the decimal code or the equivalent XHTML mnemonic to insert the characters. For example, to insert the registered trademark character, you can use either ® or ®. You can find a cool visual reference at http://www.digitalmediaminute.com/reference/entity/index.php.

Table C-1. *Inserting Special Characters in XHTML Pages*

Character	Decimal Code	XHTML Mnemonic	Description
"	&#34;	&quot;	Quotation mark
&	&#38;	&amp;	Ampersand
<	&#60;	&lt;	Less than
>	&#62;	&gt;	Greater than
			Non-breaking space
¡	&#161;	&iexcl;	Inverted exclamation
¢	&#162;	&cent;	Cent sign
£	&#163;	&pound;	Pound sterling sign
¤	&#164;	&curren;	General currency sign
¥	&#165;	&yen;	Yen sign
¦	&#166;	&brvbar;	Broken vertical bar
§	&#167;	&sect;	Section sign
¨	&#168;	&uml;	Diaeresis/umlaut
©	&#169;	&copy;	Copyright
ª	&#170;	&ordf;	Feminine ordinal
«	&#171;	&laquo;	Left-angle quote
¬	&#172;	&not;	Not sign
	&#173;	&shy;	Soft hyphen

Table C-1. *Inserting Special Characters in XHTML Pages (Continued)*

Character	Decimal Code	XHTML Mnemonic	Description
®	&#174;	&reg;	Registered trademark
¯	&#175;	&macr;	Macron accent
°	&#176;	&deg;	Degree sign
±	&#177;	&plusmn;	Plus or minus
²	&#178;	&sup2;	Superscript two
³	&#179;	&sup3;	Superscript three
´	&#180;	&acute;	Acute accent
µ	&#181;	&micro;	Micro sign
¶	&#182;	&para;	Paragraph sign
·	&#183;	&middot;	Middle dot
¸	&#184;	&cedil;	Cedilla
¹	&#185;	&sup1;	Superscript one
º	&#186;	&ordm;	Masculine ordinal
»	&#187;	&raquo;	Right-angle quote
¼	&#188;	&frac14;	Fraction one-quarter
½	&#189;	&frac12;	Fraction one-half
¾	&#190;	&frac34;	Fraction three-quarters
¿	&#191;	&iquest;	Inverted question mark
À	&#192;	&Agrave;	Capital A, grave accent
Á	&#193;	&Aacute;	Capital A, acute accent
Â	&#194;	&Acirc;	Capital A, circumflex
Ã	&#195;	&Atilde;	Capital A, tilde
Ä	&#196;	&Auml;	Capital A, diaeresis/umlaut
Å	&#197;	&Aring;	Capital A, ring
Æ	&#198;	&AElig;	Capital AE, ligature
Ç	&#199;	&Ccedil;	Capital C, cedilla
È	&#200;	&Egrave;	Capital E, grave accent
É	&#201;	&Eacute;	Capital E, acute accent
Ê	&#202;	&Ecirc;	Capital E, circumflex
Ë	&#203;	&Euml;	Capital E, diaeresis/umlaut
Ì	&#204;	&Igrave;	Capital I, grave accent
Í	&#205;	&Iacute;	Capital I, acute accent

Table C-1. *Inserting Special Characters in XHTML Pages (Continued)*

Character	Decimal Code	XHTML Mnemonic	Description
Î	&#206;	&Icirc;	Capital I, circumflex
Ï	&#207;	&Iuml;	Capital I, diaeresis/umlaut
Ð	&#208;	&ETH;	Capital Eth, Icelandic
Ñ	&#209;	&Ntilde;	Capital N, tilde
Ò	&#210;	&Ograve;	Capital O, grave accent
Ó	&#211;	&Oacute;	Capital O, acute accent
Ô	&#212;	&Ocirc;	Capital O, circumflex
Õ	&#213;	&Otilde;	Capital O, tilde
Ö	&#214;	&Ouml;	Capital O, diaeresis/umlaut
×	&#215;	&times;	Multiplication sign
Ø	&#216;	&Oslash;	Capital O, slash
Ù	&#217;	&Ugrave;	Capital U, grave accent
Ú	&#218;	&Uacute;	Capital U, acute accent
Û	&#219;	&Ucirc;	Capital U, circumflex
Ü	&#220;	&Uuml;	Capital U, diaeresis/umlaut
Ý	&#221;	&Yacute;	Capital Y, acute accent
Þ	&#222;	&THORN;	Capital Thorn, Icelandic
ß	&#223;	&szlig;	German sz
à	&#224;	&agrave;	Small a, grave accent
á	&#225;	&aacute;	Small a, acute accent
â	&#226;	&acirc;	Small a, circumflex
ã	&#227;	&atilde;	Small a, tilde
ä	&#228;	&auml;	Small a, diaeresis/umlaut
å	&#229;	&aring;	Small a, ring
æ	&#230;	&aelig;	Small ae, ligature
ç	&#231;	&ccedil;	Small c, cedilla
è	&#232;	&egrave;	Small e, grave accent
é	&#233;	&eacute;	Small e, acute accent
ê	&#234;	&ecirc;	Small e, circumflex
ë	&#235;	&euml;	Small e, diaeresis/umlaut
ì	&#236;	&igrave;	Small i, grave accent
í	&#237;	&iacute;	Small i, acute accent

Table C-1. *Inserting Special Characters in XHTML Pages (Continued)*

Character	Decimal Code	XHTML Mnemonic	Description
î	&#238;	&icirc;	Small i, circumflex
ï	&#239;	&iuml;	Small i, diaeresis/umlaut
ð	&#240;	&eth;	Small eth, Icelandic
ñ	&#241;	&ntilde;	Small n, tilde
ò	&#242;	&ograve;	Small o, grave accent
ó	&#243;	&oacute;	Small o, acute accent
ô	&#244;	&ocirc;	Small o, circumflex
õ	&#245;	&otilde;	Small o, tilde
ö	&#246;	&ouml;	Small o, diaeresis/umlaut
÷	&#247;	&divide;	Division sign
ø	&#248;	&oslash;	Small o, slash
ù	&#249;	&ugrave;	Small u, grave accent
ú	&#250;	&uacute;	Small u, acute accent
û	&#251;	&ucirc;	Small u, circumflex
ü	&#252;	&uuml;	Small u, diaeresis/umlaut
ý	&#253;	&yacute;	Small y, acute accent
þ	&#254;	&thorn;	Small thorn, Icelandic
ÿ	&#255;	&yuml;	Small y, diaeresis/umlaut

The HTML 4 specification (which XHTML 1.0 is based on) defines additional character references beyond the decimal code range of 0-255, primarily for Greek letters and other useful symbols for technical documents. Table C-2 shows some of the codes you can use to create these characters. You can find the full list at http://www.w3.org/TR/html401/ sgml/entities.html.

Table C-2. *Inserting Greek Letters and Technical Symbols in XHTML Pages*

Character	Decimal Code	XHTML Mnemonic	Description
Œ	Œ	Œ	Capital OE, ligature
œ	œ	œ	Small oe, ligature
A	Α	Α	Capital Alpha, Greek
W	Ω	Ω	Capital Omega, Greek
a	α	α	Small alpha, Greek
w	ω	ω	Small omega, Greek
€	€	€	Euro currency sign
::	∝	∝	Proportional to
∞	∞	∞	Infinity symbol
@	≅	≅	Approximately equal to

APPENDIX D

■ ■ ■

CSS Browser Support

To help you avoid browser-support problems and troubleshoot your style sheets, we've compiled this simple chart of the majority of common CSS properties, leaving out properties that don't work properly in any modern browser. The browsers listed make up the vast majority in use as of this writing.

In reading the chart, note the following:

- F represents Mozilla Firefox (Linux/Mac OS X/Microsoft Windows, version 2.0). You can use the Firefox column to represent Netscape version 8.0, since it uses the same rendering engine as Firefox.

- 6 represents Internet Explorer version 6 (Windows).

- 7 represents Internet Explorer version 7 (Windows).

- S represents Safari (OS X, version 2).

- Y means the browser supports the property.

- N means the browser doesn't support the property.

Note that we've split the properties into groups based on usage and placed the groups into alphabetical order.

Background

Property	Description	F	6	7	S
background	Shorthand property that sets all the the background properties	Y	Y	Y	Y
background-attachment	Defines whether the background image scrolls with the element when the document is scrolled	Y	Y	Y*	Y
background-color	Sets a solid color for the background of the element	Y	Y	Y	Y
background-image	Sets an image as the background of the element	Y	Y	Y	Y
background-position	Sets the position of the background's image	Y	Y	Y	Y
background-repeat	Defines the pattern for the background image	Y	Y	Y	Y

background-attachment:fixed is supported on all elements in Internet Explorer 7, but only the body element is supported in Internet Explorer 6.

Border

Property	Description	F	6	7	S
border	Shorthand property that defines the width, color, and style of a border	Y	Y	Y	Y
border-bottom	Shorthand property that defines the width, color, and style of the bottom border	Y	Y	Y	Y
border-bottom-color	Sets the color of the bottom border	Y	Y	Y	Y
border-bottom-style	Sets the style of the bottom border	Y	Y	Y	Y
border-bottom-width	Sets the width of the bottom border	Y	Y	Y	Y

Property	Description	F	6	7	S
border-color	Shorthand property that sets the color of the top, bottom, left, and right borders	Y	Y	Y	Y
border-left	Shorthand property that defines the width, color, and style of the left border	Y	Y	Y	Y
border-left-color	Sets the color of the left border	Y	Y	Y	Y
border-left-style	Sets the style of the left border	Y	Y	Y	Y
border-left-width	Sets the width of the left border	Y	Y	Y	Y
border-right	Shorthand property that defines the width, color, and style of the right border	Y	Y	Y	Y
border-right-color	Sets the color of the right border	Y	Y	Y	Y
border-right-style	Sets the style of the right border	Y	Y	Y	Y
border-right-width	Sets the width of the right border	Y	Y	Y	Y
border-style	Shorthand property that sets the styles for each side individually	Y	Y	Y	Y
border-top	Shorthand property that defines the width, color, and style of the top border	Y	Y	Y	Y
border-top-color	Sets the color of the top border	Y	Y	Y	Y
border-top-style	Sets the style of the top border	Y	Y	Y	Y
border-top-width	Shorthand property that defines the width, color, and style of the top border	Y	Y	Y	Y
border-width	Shorthand property that sets the width of each side individually	Y	Y	Y	Y

Classification

Property	Description	F	6	7	S
clear	Keeps an element from floating on one or both sides of an element	Y	Y	Y	Y
cursor	Sets the cursor's shape	Y	Y	Y	Y
display	Sets how and if an element should be displayed	Y	Y	Y	Y
float	Set which side of an element other elements are permitted to float on	Y	Y	Y	Y
visibility	Hides an element but leaves it in the flow	Y	Y	Y	Y

Dimension

Property	Description	F	6	7	S
height	Defines the height of an element's content area	Y	Y	Y	Y
max-height	Sets a maximum on the height of the element	Y	N	Y	Y
max-width	Sets a maximum on the width of the element	Y	N	Y	Y
min-height	Sets a minimum on the height of the element	Y	N	Y	Y
min-width	Sets a minimum on the width of the element	Y	N	Y	Y
width	Sets the width of an element's content area	Y	Y	Y	Y

Font

Property	Description	F	6	7	S
font	Shorthand property that sets multiple properties of an element	Y	Y	Y	Y
font-family	Sets the font family to be used in the display of an element's text	Y	Y	Y	Y
font-size	Sets the size of the font to be used in the display of an element's text	Y	Y	Y	Y
font-style	Sets an italic, oblique, or normal font face	Y	Y	Y	Y
font-variant	Sets text in small caps	Y	Y	Y	Y
font-weight	Sets or removes bold formatting of text	Y	Y	Y	Y

List

Property	Description	F	6	7	S
list-style	Shorthand property that sets all the properties for a list	Y	Y	Y	Y
list-style-image	Sets a graphic to use instead of the bullet in an unordered list	Y	Y	Y	Y
list-style-position	Sets the position of a list's marker	Y	Y	Y	Y
list-style-type	Sets the marker to be used	Y	Y	Y	Y

Margin

Property	Description	F	6	7	S
margin	Shorthand property that sets the width of the element	Y	Y	Y	Y
margin-bottom	Sets the amount of space between the bottom and its parent element	Y	Y	Y	Y
margin-left	Sets the amount of space between the left and its parent element	Y	Y	Y	Y
margin-right	Sets the amount of space between the right and its parent element	Y	Y	Y	Y
margin-top	Sets the amount of space between the top and its parent element	Y	Y	Y	Y

Outline

Property	Description	F	6	7	S
outline	Shorthand property that sets all the outline properties	Y	N	N	N
outline-color	Sets the color of the outline of an element	Y	N	N	N
outline-style	Sets the style of the outline for an element	Y	N	N	N
outline-width	Sets the width of the outline for an element	Y	N	N	N

Padding

Property	Description	F	6	7	S
padding	Shorthand property that sets the padding of the element	Y	Y	Y	Y
padding-bottom	Sets the distance between the bottom of an element's content area and its border	Y	Y	Y	Y

Property	Description	F	6	7	S
padding-left	Sets the distance between the left of an element's content area and its border	Y	Y	Y	Y
padding-right	Sets the distance between the right of an element's content area and its border	Y	Y	Y	Y
padding-top	Sets the distance between the top of an element's content area and its border	Y	Y	Y	Y

Positioning

Property	Description	F	6	7	S
bottom	Sets the distance an element should be from its parent element's bottom	Y	Y	Y	Y
clip	Determines if only a portion of an element should be displayed	Y	Y	Y	Y
left	Sets the distance an element should be from its parent element's left edge	Y	Y	Y	Y
overflow	Determines what to do when content doesn't fit in the element's content area	Y	Y	Y	Y
position	Sets how an element should be positioned with respect to flow	Y	Y*	Y	Y
right	Sets the distance an element should be from its parent element's right edge	Y	Y	Y	Y
top	Sets the distance an element should be from its parent element's top	Y	Y	Y	Y
vertical-align	Sets the alignment of elements vertically	Y	Y	Y	Y
z-index	Sets the depth of an element with respect to other elements	Y	Y	Y	Y

*position:absolute is buggy in Internet Explorer 6; position:fixed doesn't work in Internet Explorer 6.

Pseudo Classes

Property	Description	F	6	7	S
:active	Sets a style to an activated element	Y	Y	Y	Y
:focus	Sets a style to an element when it has focus	Y	N	N	N
:hover	Sets a style to an element when the mouse hovers over it	Y	Y*	Y	Y
:link	Sets a style to an unvisited link	Y	Y	Y	Y
:visited	Sets a style to a visited link	Y	Y	Y	Y
:first-child	Sets a style to an element that is the first child of another element	Y	N	Y	Y
:lang	Sets the language to use in an element	Y	N	N	Y

* hover is only supported for anchors in Internet Explorer 6.

Pseudo Elements

Property	Description	F	6	7	S
:first-letter	Sets a style on the first letter of text	Y	N	N	N
:first-line	Seta s style to the first line of text	Y	Y	Y	Y
:before	Adds content before an element	Y	N	Y	Y
:after	Adds content after an element	Y	N	Y	Y

Table

Property	Description	F	6	7	S
border-collapse	Sets the border model of a table	Y	Y	Y	Y
border-spacing	Sets the amount of space between borders in a table	Y	N	N	Y
caption-side	Sets the position of a caption for a table	Y	N	N	Y
empty-cells	Determines whether cells with no visible content should have borders	Y	N	N	Y
table-layout	Sets the algorithm that should be used to determine the widths of cells	Y	Y	Y	Y

Text

Property	Description	F	6	7	S
color	Sets the foreground color of an element	Y	Y	Y	Y
direction	Sets the direction of the text	Y	Y	Y	Y
letter-spacing	Sets the amount of white space between the characters	Y	Y	Y	Y
line-height	Sets the amount of space between lines of text	Y	Y	Y	Y
text-align	Sets the alignment of the text	Y	Y	Y	Y
text-decoration	Sets the text decoration within the element	Y	Y	Y	Y
text-indent	Sets the amount of space the first line of a paragraph should be indented	Y	Y	Y	Y
text-shadow	Sets one or more shadow effects to be applied to the text content	N	N	N	Y
text-transform	Sets the case of letters in an element	Y	Y	Y	Y
white-space	Determines how white space within an element is handled during layout	Y	Y	Y	Y
word-spacing	Sets the distance between words	Y	Y	Y	Y

Index

Find it faster at http://superindex.apress.com